LAND-USE AND PREHISTORY IN SOUTH-EAST SPAIN

Geography is a wide-ranging field of knowledge, embracing all aspects of the relations between people and environments. This series makes available work of the highest quality by scholars who are, or have been, associated with the various university and polytechnic departments of geography in the London area.

One of geography's most salient characteristics is its close relationships with virtually all the sciences, arts and humanities. Drawing strength from other fields of knowledge, it also adds to their insights. This series highlights these linkages. Besides being a vehicle for advances within geography itself, the series is designed to excite the attention of the wider community of scholars and students. To this end, each volume is chosen, assessed and edited by a committee drawn from all the London colleges and the whole range of the discipline, human and physical.

LAND-USE AND PREHISTORY IN SOUTH-EAST SPAIN

Antonio Gilman
California State University, Northridge

and

John B. Thornes
University of Bristol

with
Stephen Wise

London
GEORGE ALLEN & UNWIN
Boston   Sydney

George Allen & Unwin (Publishers) Ltd,
40 Museum Street, London WC1A 1LU, UK

George Allen & Unwin (Publishers) Ltd,
Park Lane, Hemel Hempstead, Herts HP2 4TE, UK

Allen & Unwin Inc.,
Fifty Cross Street, Winchester, Mass. 01890, USA

George Allen & Unwin Australia Pty Ltd,
8 Napier Street, North Sydney, NSW 2060, Australia

First published in 1985

ISSN 0261-0485

British Library Cataloguing in Publication Data

Gilman, Antonio
    Land use and prehistory in South-east Spain. –
(The London research series in geography, ISSN 0261-0485; 8)
1. Man, Prehistoric – Spain, Southern
2. Site catchment analysis (Archaeology) – Spain, Southern
3. Spain, Southern – Antiquities
I. Thornes, John B.   II. Wise, Stephen   III. Series
936'.6   GN836.S6
ISBN 0-04-913022-6

Library of Congress Cataloging in Publication Data

Gilman, Antonio.
    Land use and prehistory in south-east Spain.
(The London research series in geography, ISSN 0261-0485; 8)
Bibliography: p.
Includes index.
1. Economics, Prehistoric – Spain. 2 Copper age – Spain.
3. Bronze age – Spain. 4. Land settlement patterns, Prehistoric – Spain.
5. Land use – Spain – Social aspects. 6. Spain – Antiquities.
I. Thornes, John B.   II. Wise, Stephen.
III. Title.   IV. Series.
GN835.G55   1984   936.6   84-9363
ISBN 0-04-913022-6 (alk. paper)

Set in 10 on 12 point Bembo by Computape (Pickering) Limited
and printed in Great Britain by Mackays of Chatham.

Preface

This work seeks to improve understanding of the prehistory of south-east Spain by establishing a systematic geographic context within which to evaluate the archaeological record. South-east Spain includes the most arid region of Europe, and that arid sector, today largely poverty-stricken, has yielded some of the continent's richest Copper and Bronze Age remains. Traditionally this paradox has been explained by supposing that south-east Spain was a focus of influences from the already civilised Eastern Mediterranean, but this view has been rendered untenable by the new, lengthened chronology established for Europe by radiocarbon dating. By studying the location of ancient settlements with respect to agricultural resources and by integrating this information with excavated data from those sites, we can develop evidence that points to an alternative to the *ex Oriente lux* account of the processes governing the Copper and Bronze Age florescence of south-east Spain. Site catchment analysis, the method we have adopted, involves deduction of the economic orientation of the inhabitants of an ancient settlement from the distribution of resources in the settlement's vicinity. Two assumptions are essential to this approach. The first, that sites were located so as to minimise the cost of access to resources, is unproblematical in the cultural context of prehistoric Iberia. The second, that the distributions of ancient and modern resource spaces correspond systematically to one another, requires control over the major factors governing landscape change over the millennia since the sites were occupied. These factors are vegetational degradation, erosion and agricultural modernisation. Given appropriate methodological controls and thanks to the large number of well known later prehistoric settlements available within our region of study, we can use site catchment analysis to show that the Copper and Bronze Age florescence was based on the development of an intensive, hydraulic agriculture. This intensification of production permitted surpluses to be concentrated in the hands of an élite, whose wealth is recovered in the archaeological record.

A. GILMAN

J. B. THORNES

Acknowledgements

In a joint enterprise such as the research presented here, it is important to assign responsibility for the various aspects of the work. Antonio Gilman conducted the prehistoric and land-use investigations. John B. Thornes designed and directed the geomorphological investigations, with the collaboration of Stephen M. Wise, who carried out the field mapping and implemented the data processing.

Robert Provin and David Fuller, staff cartographers in the Department of Geography, California State University, Northridge (CSUN), prepared the land-use maps. B. J. Duffy, J. Pugh and J. Wyatt of the London School of Economics drawing office prepared the water diversion potential maps.

The land-use investigations were initiated in the summer of 1977 with the support of a National Endowment for the Humanities Summer Stipend to Gilman, and were continued in the summer of 1978 with the assistance of grants from the Sociedad de Estudios y Publicaciones and the California State University Foundation, Northridge. Full project funding for fieldwork and analysis in 1979–80 was made possible by a National Endowment for the Humanities Matching Grant, by a Tinker Foundation Post-Doctoral Fellowship to Gilman, and by Grants from the Fundación Juan March, the Fundación Universitaria Española, the Sociedad de Estudios y Publicaciones, the Northridge Archaeological Research Center (CSUN) and the Institute for Social and Behavioral Sciences (CSUN). Analysis of the results of the fieldwork was greatly facilitated by the extension of a second Fellowship year to Gilman by the Tinker Foundation. We acknowledge our profound gratitude to all of these organisations and to their officers, of whom Katharine Abramovitz, Andrés Amorós, Emilio Gómez Orbaneja, Andrés González, William Knowles, Kenneth Maxwell, Katherine Miller and Pedro Sainz Rodríguez were of particular assistance. Domonic Vallese, Financial Officer of the United States Embassy, Madrid, most kindly helped to arrange the transatlantic matching of grants. C. C. Lamberg-Karlovsky, Director of the Peabody Museum, Harvard University, generously sponsored Gilman as a Tinker Post-Doctoral Fellow and made it possible for him to spend 1980–81 as a Visiting Scholar in Cambridge, Massachusetts.

We wish to extend thanks also to those officials of various agencies who facilitated our work in Spain. Manuel Fernández-Miranda, Subdirector de Bellas Artes of the Ministerio de Cultura, kindly granted us official permission for our work. Jorge Porras Martín, head of the División de Aguas Subterráneas in the Instituto Geológico y Minero de España, permitted us to consult his organisation's Inventario de Puntos de Agua. In this consultation we received the help of José Luis Guzmán del Pino, Manuel Ruiz-Taglé, Melchor Senent and

Manuel del Valle Cardenete of the IGME offices in Málaga, Almería, Murcia and Granada, respectively. Angela Cuenca (Director, Archivo Histórico Provincial, Almería), María Pilar Núñez Alonso (Director, Archivo de la Real Chancillería, Granada) and María Luisa Pérez Mas (Director, Archivo Histórico Provincial, Murcia) permitted us to consult volumes of the *Catastro de la Ensenada* in their care.

In addition, we wish to thank Cristina Echavarría, Laura Joines and Donald Thompson for volunteering their assistance during various phases of our fieldwork.

Gregory Truex, Department of Anthropology (CSUN), provided statistical advice and implemented the analysis of variance of land uses. It is impossible to give adequate thanks to a colleague whose support, in this as in other things, makes the struggle worth while.

In addition, we wish to express our gratitude for help and advice of various kinds to Nicolás Cabrillana, Francisco Carbonell Cadenas de Llano, Javier Carrasco Rus, Robert Chapman, Carlos Dabezies, Timothy Earle, Manuel García Sánchez, Josefina Gómez Mendoza, Richard Harrison, Robert Howard, Francisco Jiménez Garrido, Manuel Laza Palacios, Keith Morton, Angel Pérez Casas, José Manuel Ramírez Arjona, Ginés Ridao, Luis Sacristán, Judith Sáenz de Tejada, Ruth Tringham, Ralph Vicero, Bernard Wailes and Juan Zozaya.

No survey project of the kind undertaken here would have been possible without the co-operation of the many people in the Spanish countryside who with unfailing politeness answered our questions and tolerated our trespassing. To them all we express our thanks.

Finally, we wish to thank our wives, not just for the many acts of direct assistance in the research, but for putting up with our absences and our presences.

J.B.T, A.G.

Contents

List of tables

1 *Introduction*

The work reported on here had its inception during a train ride which one of us (A. Gilman) took from Granada to Valencia some 10 years ago. The line runs through the area that was the heartland of the Los Millares and El Argar Cultures, which together constitute the culmination of the richest later pre-historic sequence in the Iberian Peninsula and one of the richest in Europe. It was surprising for a student reasonably well acquainted with the archaeological literature on these cultures to find that he was riding through an apparent desert (the 'Níjar Desert' of Meigs (1966)). Indeed, that one of Europe's most remarkable cultural successions occurred in that continent's most arid region was a paradox that prehistorians had left practically unmentioned. Here, then, was a promising subject for future investigation.

The failure to consider the distinctive geographical setting in which the early villagers of south-east Spain succeeded in making their living for millennia is symptomatic of the general neglect of the economic aspects of prehistory by archaeologists of the Iberian Peninsula. This neglect is the result of the theoreti-cal approach that has prevailed since the inception of research a century ago until the present. With only a few exceptions, the most important task of pre-historians has been to reconstruct a history of the highest achievements of the human spirit as these are manifested in the material record of artifacts and architecture. This essentially art-historical approach sees cultural changes over time as simple shifts in ideas, mostly brought about by influences from abroad. Archaeologists have disagreed about the sources of particular cultural features and about the specific mechanisms by which these may have been introduced. Some have even maintained that certain Iberian developments were indigenous in character. But until very recently there has been general agreement that the proper objects of archaeological study were stylistically distinctive artifacts and buildings and that the economic and geographical aspects of prehistory were inherently uninteresting: the study of subsistence practices and of man–land relations could only reveal mundane common denominators of little relevance to the human history that mattered. Even the excavator who recently dis-covered an irrigation ditch of Copper Age date reports this find as an example of yet another trait diffused into Iberia from the civilised centre of the Orient (Schüle 1967).

The later prehistoric record in south-east Spain is remarkable in that a considerable number of settlement sites are attested for each successive period. (A list of the sites that we have studied, a reasonably comprehensive sample of the better-known localities, is given in Table 1.1 and their location is indicated in Figure 1.1.) Research has tended to concentrate on the burials found in or near these villages, since the graves yield stylistically distinctive materials more

Table 1.1 Localities studied.

Site name	Period*	Reference	Location
La Almoloya	B	Cuadrado Díaz (1946)	Pliego, Murcia
Cerro de la Virgen	C, B	Schüle & Pellicer (1966), Schüle (1980)	Orce, Granada
Cueva de Ambrosio	N	Jiménez Navarro (1962)	Vélez Blanco, Almería
Cerro de las Canteras	C	Motos (1918)	Vélez Blanco, Almería
Campico de Lébor	C	Val Caturla (1948)	Totana, Murcia
La Bastida	B	Martínez Santa Olalla et al. (1947)	Totana, Murcia
La Ceñuela	B	Zamora Camellada (1976)	Mazarrón, Murcia
Cueva de los Murciélagos (Zuheros)	N	Vicent Zaragoza & Muñoz Amilibia (1973)	Zuheros, Córdoba
Torre Cardela	C	Molina Fajardo & Capel Martínez (1975)	Torre Cardela, Granada
Cueva de la Carigüela	N	Pellicer Catalán (1964b), Almagro Basch et al. (1970)	Piñar, Granada
Cerro de los Castellones (Laborcillas)	C	Mendoza et al. (1975)	Laborcillas, Granada
Cerro del Culantrillo	B	García Sánchez (1963)	Gorafe, Granada
El Malagón	C	Arribas et al. (1977)	Cúllar-Baza, Granada
El Picacho	B	Hernández Hernández & Dug Godoy (1975)	Oria, Almería
Cabez Negro de Pastrana	B	Aubet et al. (1979)	Lorca, Murcia
Zapata	B	Siret & Siret (1887)	Lorca, Murcia
Parazuelos	C	Siret & Siret (1887)	Lorca, Murcia
Ifre	B	Siret & Siret (1887)	Mazarrón, Murcia
Los Castillejos (Montefrío)	N, C	Arribas & Molina (1977, 1979)	Montefrío, Granada
Cuesta del Negro	B	Molina González & Pareja López (1975)	Purullena, Granada
Cerro del Gallo	B	Torre Peña & Aguayo de Hoyos (1976)	Fonelas, Granada
Campos, Tres Cabezos	C, N?	Siret & Siret (1887)	Cuevas, Almería
Fuente Álamo	B	Siret & Siret (1887) Schubart & Arteaga (1978, 1980)	Cuevas, Almería
El Oficio	B	Siret & Siret (1887)	Cuevas, Almería
Cerro de la Encina	B	Arribas et al. (1974)	Monachil, Granada
Lugarico Viejo	B	Siret & Siret (1887)	Antas, Almería
Fuente Bermeja	B	Siret & Siret (1887)	Antas, Almería
El Argar, El Gárcel, La Gerundia	B, N?, C	Siret & Siret (1887)	Antas, Almería
Gatas	B	Siret & Siret (1887)	Turre, Almería
Cueva de la Mujer, Cueva del Agua	N	MacPherson (1870)	Alhama, Granada
Los Millares	C	Almagro Basch & Arribas (1963)	Santa Fe de Mondújar, Almería
Terrera Ventura	N?, C	Gusi Jener (1975)	Tabernas, Almería
Cerro de Enmedio	B	Molina et al. (1980)	Pechina, Almería
El Barranquete, El Tarajal	C	Almagro Gorbea (1973, 1976)	Níjar, Almería
Cueva de Nerja	N	Pellicer Catalán (1963)	Nerja, Málaga

* B = Bronze Age; C = Copper Age; N = Neolithic.

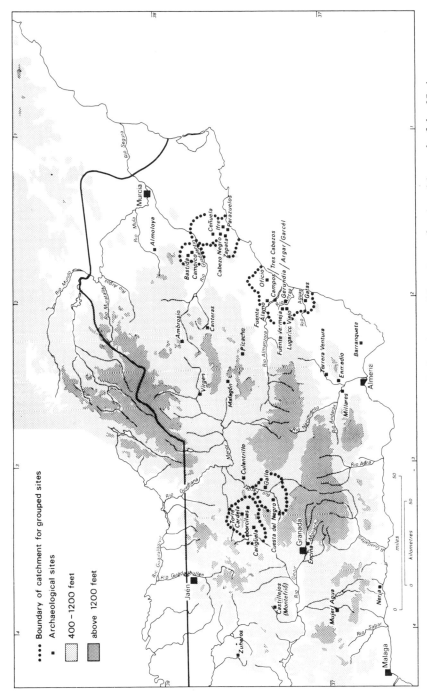

Figure 1.1 General map of south-east Spain with elevations and locations of major cities and of the 35 sites.

frequently than the settlement refuse. Even the excavations conducted at the end of the last and the first half of the present century made clear, however, that the inhabitants of the villages made their living by mixed farming: they cultivated wheat, barley and various legumes; they tended sheep, goats, cattle, pigs and horses. These earlier results have been confirmed (and, to a certain degree, elaborated) at the increasing number of settlements excavated over the past 20 years. The available evidence will be reviewed elsewhere, but the agricultural character of the long-term, often fortified, sites of prehistoric south-east Spain is quite certain.

To obtain a list of the animals and plants under domestication in later prehistoric times has been enough for those workers whose interests have centred on the higher aspects of the cultures of the Iberian Peninsula. For those who see man–land relations as a crucial nexus for understanding historical change, the state of knowledge emerging from traditional research is hardly adequate, however. It is necessary to know not just that agriculture was practised, but how it was practised. From the introduction of farming about 7000 years ago to the end of the Argaric, 3200 years ago, changes occurred in the mix of plants and animals, wild and domestic, that were exploited, in the purposes for which they were exploited, and in the methods by which the exploitation took place. Given the considerable variation in climate within the region, considerable spatial contrasts in agricultural practice must also have occurred within any given time period. Today, dry farming is highly precarious in the arid coastal areas of south-east Spain (Vilá Valentí 1961a). Unless very substantial changes in climate have occurred since later prehistoric times (we shall review the evidence against this elsewhere), it is a reasonable hypothesis that the prehistoric farmers of the arid zone irrigated their crops (Gilman 1976, Chapman 1975, 1978). This intensive agricultural regime presumably would develop first in the more arid regions, but, given the general advantages of irrigation under Mediterranean climatic conditions, it may be expected that hydraulic agriculture would spread to less arid regions over time. Thus, we can hypothesise a pattern of changing regional contrasts in agricultural regimes over the course of later prehistoric time. Documentation of the detailed relations between men and the domesticated (and wild) plant and animal species they exploited in the Neolithic, Copper and Bronze Ages awaits appropriately designed excavations at considerable numbers of sites. The many known settlements of those periods permit, however, the direct testing of hypotheses concerning the relations between men and the land from which they drew their sustenance.

Geographical approaches in prehistoric archaeology go back at least to Fox (1923), but the systematic study of sites in their landscapes has received great impetus since the development of site catchment analysis by the Early History of Agriculture Project (Vita-Finzi & Higgs 1970, Higgs & Vita-Finzi 1972, Jarman 1972, Jarman et al. 1972). The underlying principle of this approach, derived from von Thünen (1826) by way of Chisholm (1962), is that, since costs of production increase with the distance over which production is carried out, settlements will be located close to the resources that are most important to their inhabitants. Thus, examination of the relative proximity of resources near settlement sites will be instructive in considering the activities carried out from those sites. In this study, as in others, site catchment analysis is intended to systematise the gathering of information about the distribution of resources contained within site exploitation territories, the area taken to be regularly used from a site.

The practice of site catchment analysis varies from study to study, but generally speaking it proceeds by three steps. First, one defines the area that is taken to have been exploited on a regular basis from the site under study. The size of this area, the site territory, has often been determined by comparison with the exploitation territory of similar, ethnographically documented, societies. Secondly, one describes the distribution of resources within the site territory. In most studies these resource spaces are defined in terms of modern land use, vegetation or soil types (or some combination of these). Thirdly, one uses the distribution of resource spaces within the site territory to infer the economic orientation of the settlement site's inhabitants. This has been done either directly by assigning practicable values to each of the defined resource categories and then assuming that the most abundant or productive spaces near the site constituted the focus of its inhabitants' activities or indirectly by interpreting the variability in resource distribution near numbers of sites in terms of differences in other known characteristics of those sites (e.g. their size, the artifact inventory recovered from them, etc.). Thus, in this study we take the maximum territory likely to have been exploited from a site to be within 2 h walk of it and we subdivide that area into rings of 12, 30 and 60 min walking time. We define resource spaces in terms of potential for agricultural land use by examining modern and historically documented exploitation patterns and estimating water diversion and erosion potential for each territory. In our analysis we evaluate differences in the distribution of resources within the 35 territories described and differences in the overall proportion of resources between site territories in the light of other evidence from the sites themselves and from their settings in order to arrive at an overall assessment of changes in farming over the period that the sites span.

Within the general sequence of procedures just outlined, the practice of site catchment analysis over the past decade has been as varied as the settings in which it has been used. We defer a detailed review and critique of the spectrum of field and analytic methods used by others to our detailed exposition of the methods we have used in this study. Two general criticisms of site catchment analysis should be met at the start, however. The first concerns the validity of its least-cost assumptions, the second the relevance of the measures it uses to estimate economic potential. Both address real deficiencies in the way site catchment analysis has been used in the past.

A Thünian least-cost model such as site catchment analysis is, necessarily, an ideal one. The distribution of agricultural resources near a settlement site serves as an indication of the subsistence practices of its ancient inhabitants to the extent that it can be assumed that its inhabitants depend on local resources for their food and located their dwellings so as to minimise their effort in the acquisition of food. The developers of site catchment analysis tended to assume that these ideal conditions are real ones:

> We have made the modest assumption that a human group will in the long run make use of those resources within its territory that are economic for it to exploit and that are within reach of the available technology. . . . A site placed in a territory largely composed of grazing country will have been inhabited by human groups intent on the exploitation of grazing animals. Similarly, provided a suitable technology is available, agriculture will have been a prime concern in territories largely suitable for arable cultivation. (Vita-Finzi & Higgs 1970, p. 2)

Matters are not so simple and this easy endorsement of a primitive *Homo economicus* has been rightly criticised (cf. Hodder & Orton 1976, pp. 233–5). In any given instance non-economic factors and economic factors beyond the local arena may be important determinants of settlement location. The degree of fit of a particular setting to the ideal conditions of a Thünian model should be demonstrated. In prehistoric south-east Spain, the available archaeological evidence indicates a reasonably close fit, especially during the earlier (Neolithic and Copper Age) phases of the sequence. Settlements are small and the materials from them are overwhelmingly of local provenance. Nothing in what we can infer about the political economy of the times suggests that their inhabitants were constrained to locate their dwellings far from the land that gave them sustenance.

Rather than dismiss the fact that human groups very often do not maximise resource exploitation, one should use site catchment analysis to assess deviations from economically rational behaviour. The degree to which settlements are located to meet priorities other than the reduction of transportation costs in subsistence production can be judged by comparing observed locations to those expected from Thünian considerations. In south-east Spain it is apparent that many Bronze Age settlements are located in extreme defensive locations. The degree to which warfare imposed constraints on the daily life of the times can, accordingly, be assessed by comparing the resource distribution within Bronze Age site territories with that of their Neolithic and Copper Age predecessors, in which site location was not governed by social considerations to the same degree. If one studies an adequately large number of site territories, site catchment analysis is sufficiently robust in its least-cost assumptions to permit one to evaluate deviations from economic rationality (instead of dismissing them as 'random noise' (Higgs & Jarman 1975, p. 3)).

Site catchment analysis takes the distribution of resource spaces found near an

ancient site today to be indicative of the distribution of resource spaces near that
site when it was inhabited. One must establish, therefore, the nature of the
changes that have occurred since ancient times in the environment of the site
under study. Reconstructing the ancient landscape near a specific site is no easy
task, however, so that most catchment analyses have used whatever (usually
scanty) palaeoenvironmental evidence may be available and hoped for the best.
As Flannery (1976, pp. 94–5) puts matters:

> ... A consistently raised objection to site catchment analysis is that of
> changing environments. How justifiable is it to reason, from a land use
> map of the 1970s, back to the environment of 10 000 or even 1000 years
> ago? Might not the proportions of the various zones have been very
> different? As we see it, this is a question that will always be with us, not
> merely in site catchment analysis but in all phases of archaeology. One has
> two choices: He can throw up his hands in defeat or he can reconstruct the
> prehistoric environment to the best of his ability and plunge ahead.

In the 3200 years since the close of the period dealt with here, the landscape of
south-east Spain has suffered vegetational degradation (Freitag 1971) and
erosion (Thornes 1976), so that it would be unwise to plunge ahead. Instead, we
have attempted to establish the magnitude of the changes in various aspects of
the landscapes under study.

The conclusions drawn from site catchment analysis (like those obtained
from any body of archaeological evidence) depend not so much on the intrinsic
content of data sets as on the contrasts between them. The inevitable inaccura-
cies in the detailed mapping of resource zones within the site territories are
tolerable to the extent that these do not affect the contrasts in the proportions of
the various zones between the central and peripheral areas of particular territories and between the different territories as wholes. We wish to argue, for
example, that the higher proportion of irrigable land near certain sites indicates
that their inhabitants exploited this potential land use, and we make this
judgment using the present landscape as our guide. Now the specific area of
irrigable land in the vicinity of the site may have changed in the 3500 (or 6000)
years since the site was occupied due to changes in water availability or in
landforms or in both. But this will not affect our conclusions unless the changes
have operated at different rates near the site and farther away from it, or unless
the changes have operated at different rates at different site territories taken as
wholes. Accordingly, it is essential to assess those aspects of landscape change
that are likely to have operated at different rates within and between site
territories. Three factors are of particular concern in south-east Spain:

(a) *Vegetational degradation.* The natural vegetation of all south-east Spain has
    been reduced to relict stands by deforestation resulting from sheep and goat
    grazing, charcoal burning and the extension of cultivation. While this

degradation is widespread throughout our study area, it has not been equally and uniformly distributed throughout all the site territories. The detailed reconstructions of potential vegetation provided for the arid coastal zone by Freitag (1971) and for Granada province by Rivas Goday and Rivas Martínez (1971) constitute a detailed guide with which to control the differential effects of deforestation.

(b) *Erosion.* Extensive badlands, reduced soil cover and consequent down-stream alluviation all indicate intensive past erosion in south-east Spain (Thornes 1976). Erosion is governed by factors such as vegetation cover, effective precipitation, topography, the degree of drainage network development and the strength of the material to be eroded. All of these conditions are differentially distributed within and between the site territories. Where erosion takes place, it will, of course, reduce the extent of arable land, just as it will increase it where the eroded materials are redeposited down stream. Since erosion distorts the systematic relation between ancient and modern land-use potential, a significant portion of our work has been directed towards estimating the magnitude of the erosion that may have taken place on the various lithologies within our site territories.

(c) *Agricultural modernisation.* In recent years the shift from subsistence-oriented to market-oriented farming and the attendant introduction of sophisticated agricultural technologies have begun to transform the landscape of south-east Spain. This tendency is particularly acute in the arid coastal zone, where traditional farming was comparatively unproductive and where warm winters permit vegetables to be grown for urban European markets so that the necessary investment for deep wells can return a profit. This recent wave of modernisation extends irrigation to new lands, but at the same time leads to the abandonment of some traditionally irrigated areas, where the lowering of the water table by new wells has dried springs or where the amounts of water available are either too small or too irregular to support operations at a profitable scale. In addition, the general depopulation of the countryside over the past 25 years has led to the widespread abandonment of marginal dry-farmed lands.

These various trends operate at different intensities in various areas of the south-east and would tend to bias any simple reconstruction of ancient land uses on the basis of modern ones. In order to control the distorting effects of recent changes in agricultural technology on our assessment of palaeotechnic land-use potential, we have developed two lines of investigation. First, we have reviewed the pre-modern land uses described in the *Catastro de la Ensenada* of 1751–57. This detailed tax survey of all municipalities in south-east Spain dates to a period when farming was mostly subsistence-oriented and entirely traditional in technology. Secondly, we have estimated the amount of water flowing in streams during the winter growing season. These estimates are based on the size of the stream catchment basins and on available discharge and rainfall records over a 30–40 year period and are, therefore, not affected by recently developed groundwater use. Furthermore, they give the amounts of water most easily available for irrigation under palaeotechnic conditions. (The applicability of these estimates to prehistoric times depends on the assumption, which we believe to be justified, that climate changes over the past 6000 years have not been large enough to affect in any great measure the contrasts between site territories (cf. Delano Smith 1979, pp. 312–14).)

The prehistoric sequence in south-east Spain is characterised by a substantial number of extant settlements from each successive period, Neolithic, Copper Age and Bronze Age. By developing the lines of evidence outlined above, we are able to describe the distribution of resources within the territories of these sites accurately enough to make reliable comparisons between them. This meets the essential requirement for a successful programme of site catchment analysis. As has recently been noted:

> When applied to a single site the technique is simply a useful descriptive device. It is only when the catchment characteristics of a series of sites are examined statistically in search of one or more repetitive patterns that the technique serves to define systems of land use. (Isaac 1981, p. 141)

Based on the land-use descriptions for the areas near a comprehensive sample of better-known settlement sites in contrasting environmental settings and from different time periods, we are able to document the changing agricultural base on which one of the most striking cultural sequences in later prehistoric Europe evolved. At the same time, we are able to provide a new context in which to assess the known documents from those cultures. Up to now archaeologists of Iberia have focused their attention almost exclusively on that segment of variability in the archaeological record that covaries with the dimensions of time and space. They have interpreted similarities between site collections of different ages as the result of 'traditions' and similarities between site collections from different areas as the result of 'influences'. This present study provides an economic dimension which we hope will revitalise research on the existing documents by making accessible to analysis hitherto untapped aspects of archaeological variability.

2 Background and problem

The environmental setting

South-east Spain has a Mediterranean climate with a typical summer drought and winter rain pattern, the winter rains being caused predominantly by a westerly air flow bringing cyclonic depressions from the Atlantic. In the east the rainy season has two peaks (September–November and April–May) while in the west there is only one (December–March). This seasonal distribution of rainfall is combined with high summer temperatures and high potential evapotranspiration rates (four to five times the annual rainfall), as well as strong interannual variations in the amount of precipitation arising from shifts in the zonality of the circumpolar westerlies. However, the main climatic contrasts within the region arise largely from the distribution of relief, which induces sharp differences over short distances.

The extensive mountain uplands, formed during the Alpine orogeny, reach nearly 4000 m in the Sierra Nevada and generally attain between 1500 and 2500 m elsewhere. A series of major ridges, the Sierra Nevada, Sierra de los Filabres, Sierra de la Sagra and others, are largely comprised of metamorphosed rocks, notably schists and slates or limestones and shales. These mountains were extensively eroded during the Tertiary, and the eroded materials were re-deposited in the extensive intermontane basins to form conglomerates, breccias and sandstones, many of which are only weakly consolidated. These intermontane basins were also flooded by the sea or provided endorrheic basins where playa lakes developed and now contain saline or freshwater calcareous deposits, such as gypsiferous marls and chalks. Most of these intermontane basin deposits were subsequently folded or tilted during the late stages of the Tertiary, after which extensive pedimentation around the edges of the basins occurred.

The contrast of upland and lowland, mountain and basin, has two important climatic effects. First, the mountains tend to cut off the rain-bearing winds from the west and south-west. This produces a strong rain shadow effect and enhances the dryness of the Mediterranean summer. Secondly, the mountains themselves cause significant orographic precipitation, which may come as snow during the winter. The lowland coastal areas are the most arid regions of Europe. From Adra to Alicante, areas below 500 m receive on average less than 400 mm of precipitation annually, and this falls to about 200 mm along the immediate coast. Rainfall is, furthermore, highly variable, the wettest years being five times wetter than the driest (Camilleri Lapeyre 1969). Rain also falls on relatively few days (on average less than 20 rainy days a year at Almería city (Neumann 1960)), for relatively short durations, and often occurs in torrential spasms accompanied by flash floods, sometimes of catastrophic proportions

(Thornes 1974, 1976). Since winter temperatures are high in the low-lying coastal zone, with a January mean of 12°C at Almería city for example, nine to eleven months of the year can be considered arid (Geiger 1973). Summer rains are predominantly convective, normally last less than an hour, and may be quite intense. The interior basins have similar summer rainfall regimes, though temperatures tend to be higher and potential evapotranspiration rates correspondingly greater. In winter, by contrast, the temperatures average about 5°C, dropping below freezing at night, so that evapotranspiration rates are lower. As one climbs out of the basins, rainfall amounts rise rapidly, temperatures fall and available moisture increases. For example, from Benalúa in the Guadix basin to Torre Cardela on the edge of it, precipitation doubles and potential evaporation halves in a distance of 24 km.

Regionally, as one moves west and north out of the rain shadow of the Betic mountain system, rainfall increases and becomes less variable. Still concentrated in the winter season, rainfall ranges from 400 to 600 mm, rising to 1500 mm in the high mountains. Perennial streams replace ephemeral ones, and springs show less seasonal variation in their flows. The differences in climate within the south-east are stable and long-term ones arising from the orographic pattern. Only very major changes in atmospheric circulation would reduce the contrasts between the arid regions of Murcia and Almería and what Lautensach (1964) has called *Hochandalusien*.

These contrasts in relief and climate must have given rise under natural conditions to contrasts in vegetation and soils. The natural vegetation of all south-east Spain has been reduced to relict stands by deforestation through expansion of cultivation, sheep and goat grazing, charcoal burning and so on. In arid portions of the south-east, vegetation is steppe-like (Sermet 1967, pp. 122–4): low plains covered by alfa grass and thorny shrubs are overlooked by mountains bearing a degraded garrigue vegetation in which Mediterranean aromatics such as rosemary predominate (cf. Völk 1973). In moister sections extensive dry farming makes the landscape less bleak, but no closer to its original state. Given the lack of resilience of Mediterranean woodlands, the process of degradation would have begun with the initiation of intensive exploitation in Copper–Bronze Age times, but the present degree of alteration is apparently a product of the recent historical epoch (Arabic and post-Reconquest) (Freitag 1971, pp. 170–1). On the basis of analysis of relict stands of vegetation and comparative studies of plant communities in climatically similar, but less degraded, settings elsewhere, Freitag (1971) and Rivas Goday and Rivas Martínez (1971) have been able to reconstruct the natural vegetation zones (the potential climax communities of the arid south-east and of Granada province, respectively).

In areas along the immediate coast that receive less than 250 mm annual rainfall (with very warm temperatures year-round), the climax vegetation is a thorny scrub with species such as ephedra (*Ephedra fragilis*), esparto grass (*Stipa tenacissima*) and box thorn (*Lycium intricatum*) (Freitag 1971, pp. 261–70). Areas receiving 250 to 400 mm annual rainfall (that is to say, inland areas to an elevation of about 500 m) are characterised by a chaparral formation with species such as Aleppo pine (*Pinus halapensis*), the kermes oak (*Quercus coccifera*), oleaster (*Olea oleaster*), mastic tree (*Pistacia lentiscus*), palmetto (*Chamaerops humilis*) and buckthorn (*Rhamnus*) (Freitag 1971, pp. 239–61). A similar formation would cover the Guadix–Baza basin in the interior (Rivas Goday & Rivas Martínez 1971), which, although quite high (800–1000 m), receives rainfall as low as 300 mm annually. At higher elevations (above 500 m, where rainfall is generally above 400 mm), the climax vegetation is a typical Eu-Mediterranean sclerophyllous forest with holm oak (*encina*) (*Quercus ilex rotundifolia*) as the dominant species (Freitag 1971, pp. 228–39). In this zone year-round streams would have a gallery forest of poplar and elm in their vicinity (Rivas Goday & Rivas Martínez 1971, pp. 55–6). High mountain areas would, of course, carry deciduous forest, alpine and other cold-tolerant plant communities. The combination of rapidly varying relief, lithology and vegetation makes site catchment analysis of prehistoric sites in south-east Spain both a potentially productive and an operationally complex research strategy.

The nature of the present-day landscape is relevant to the prehistoric past to the extent that climatic and other conditions have remained unchanged since the early times in question. Palaeoclimatological evidence is scanty in south-east Spain and, as elsewhere, must be treated with extreme caution. Much palaeo-climatology is based on fragmentary evidence and doubtful premises. Even with pollen analysis there is doubt as to how much change can be attributed to climate and how much to other ecological controls. The only pollen spectrum in the study area is from the 70 m core at Padul (Florschütz *et al.* 1971). The top 2 m of the profile are radiocarbon dated to between 4800 ± 90 bc (GrN 2187) and 3030 ± 60 bc (GrN 2185).[1] The analysis indicates the presence of *encinar* in the vicinity of the peat bog, with a decline in tree (especially oak) pollen after 4410 ± 85 bc (GrN 1949). It appears, then, that Eu-Mediterranean sclerophyl-lous woodlands became established in 'Atlantic' times, subsequent deforestation being attributable to human intervention. Several pollen diagrams from other areas of eastern Spain – Ereta del Pedregal, Valencia (Menéndez Amor & Flors-chütz 1961a); Torreblanca, Castellón (Menéndez Amor & Florschütz 1961b); Olot, Gerona (Menéndez Amor 1964); Verdelpino, Cuenca (López García 1977) – are consistent with this interpretation. This hypothetical vegetational history also tends to be confirmed in other regions of the Mediterranean: see, for example, the studies by Renault-Miskovsky (1976) for southern France; by Beug (1967) for Dalmatia; by Frank (1969) for central Italy; by Wijmstra (1969) and Turner and Greig (1975) for Greece; and by van Zeist *et al.* (1975) for Asia Minor.

Other lines of evidence are even more tenuous. Thus, the fauna from the Copper Age site of Terrera Ventura includes substantial amounts of game (red deer bones are 17% by weight of the identifiable fragments (Driesch & Morales 1977)); this suggests that Freitag's chaparral climax community, which hypo-thetically would cover most of the site's territory, actually existed during the

Copper Age. Likewise, the xerorendsina palaeosols which have been identified at the Copper Age site of Los Millares (Kubiena, in Almagro Basch & Arribas 1963, p. 261) suggest that soil formation in prehistoric times took place under conditions similar to those of the present. Cuenca Payá and Walker (1974, 1976, 1977) and Walker and Cuenca Payá (1977) have suggested that in northern Murcia and southern Alicante provinces (immediately to the north-east of our study area) conditions between 7000 and 3000 BC were drier than those of the present. This is based on radiocarbon determinations from samples collected below 'aeolian sands' in a river terrace deposit at Elda and above 'aeolian sands' in the Abrigo Grande rock shelter near Cieza. The textural similarity of materials in different depositional contexts 60 km distant from one another constitutes slender evidence for a difference in climate (cf. Thornes & Brunsden 1977, pp. 126–7). Climatic interpretations of the recent alluviation along river courses in the south-east – the Younger Fill of Vita-Finzi (1969) – are as problematical here as they are elsewhere in the Mediterranean (Davidson 1980, p. 149) and for the same reasons. Geomorphological response of river valleys supplying different materials under different slope, geological and soil conditions over different areas must invariably be more complex than this attractive but simple thesis suggests. Part of the difficulty in assessing Holocene climatic changes in south-east Spain (or elsewhere in the Mediterranean) is, of course, that the effects of human action on the landscape may have been so large as to mask the effects of changes in the amount and seasonal distribution of precipitation and temperature. Still, Lamb (1971) has shown that it is possible for meteorological models to account for changes in climate in temperate Europe after 5000 BC without positing great changes in Mediterranean regions. It seems reasonable, therefore, to follow the preponderance of the scanty available evidence and to proceed on the assumption that major differences in climate within and between site territories in south-east Spain were similar in kind to the contrasts in those areas today.

The premise that climate has remained approximately stable over the past 6000 years in south-east Spain is important for three reasons.

First, it enables us to use the available reconstructions of potential vegetation in the region today as reconstructions of the actual vegetation in the region in Neolithic to Bronze Age times, when human interference with climax communities was only just beginning.

Secondly, the conclusion of approximate climatic constancy has as its corollary that the early agriculturalists of prehistoric south-east Spain would have encountered many of the same environmental constraints on their operations as are present for farmers in the region now. For, although soils may have degraded independently of climate (see Ch. 4), there can be no doubt that the availability of water remains the fundamental limitation to what can be achieved by farmers in the lowland areas. In *Hochandalusien*, where (with the exception of the Guadix–Baza basin) rainfall is above 450 mm annually, the full range of grains and legumes of Near Eastern origin can be dry-farmed. The principal constraints on Mediterranean agriculture are those imposed by cold at higher elevations (farming stops at about 1600 m in the Sierra Nevada). In the arid coastal areas the principal constraints are, of course, those imposed by lack of rainfall. As Whyte (1963) points out, the lower threshold for dry farming in Mediterranean areas is 250 mm rainfall annually, and in most years this amount is not reached in the arid coastal zone. In Rioja in the lower Ándarax region (current rainfall mean, 215 mm yr^{-1} (Sáenz Lorite 1977, p. 385)), the respondents to the 1752 *Catastro de la Ensenada* questionnaire described their dry-farmed (*secano*) land as follows: 'They are thought to be useless in this locality, due to the great lack of rain which prevails, on account of which their owners leave them deserted and unsown.' According to Navarro (1968, p. 36), barley yields of 5 : 1 on *secano* would be expected no more frequently than one year in 10 in the most arid areas. Llobet (1958), Vilá Valentí (1961a), Klein-penning (1965) and Geiger (1972, 1973) describe the means by which the problems presented by a dry climate have traditionally been solved in south-east Spain:

(1)   Every possible source of irrigation is exploited. This is reflected, for example, in the level of detail with which the Instituto Geológico y Minero de España (IGME) has compiled its *Inventario de Puntos de Agua*. In Granada province, of the 195 springs recorded by IGME in the areas covered by our site territories, only two have flows of less than 0.11 s^{-1}. In Almería province 41 of the 111 springs recorded within our site territories fall below that level.

(2)   Farming on *secano* is opportunistic: when the rainy season begins promisingly, planting takes place (cf. Navarro 1968). The effect is that of a long fallow cycle. Responses to the Ensenada questionnaire often report long planting intervals: at Níjar (326 mm yr^{-1} (Sáenz Lorite 1977, p. 381)), four to five years; at Tabernas (250 mm yr^{-1}), four to ten years. As Vilá Valentí (1961a) notes, 'in the southeast a year with a good to medium grain harvest is followed, in general, by three to five years with a deficient or completely failed harvest.'

(3)   Where possible, *secano* is improved by the construction of check dams (*boqueras*) across dry washes (*ramblas*) so as to permit floodwater farming of adjacent fields during the occasional flows (Vilá Valentí 1961b).

(4)   Terracing of dry-farmed fields is widespread. This not only prevents erosion, but also retains moisture from surface runoff during the relatively few rainy days each winter.

(5)   Finally, *secano* tends to be put to relatively drought-resistant crops. Barley is planted more frequently than wheat because the former's shorter growing season takes better advantage of relatively few waterings. Arbori-culture (traditionally of olives, more recently of almonds) is also important because tree crop yields are less variable than grain yields (25% from crop to crop vs 60% for barley, according to Geiger (1973, p. 202)).

In short, a variety of capital investments in the land are the means by which the effects of aridity are mitigated. It is our central contention that this 'strong humanisation of the landscape', to use Ferre Bueno's (1977, p. 185) apt expression, began to take place in later prehistoric times.

Thirdly, the conclusion that climate has been fairly stable in south-east Spain facilitates our attempts to reconstruct the probable degree of geomorphological change that has occurred and the extent to which such changes would have substantially altered the pattern of cultivable and irrigable land distribution. We have attacked the question of erosion and redeposition in three ways. First, we have avoided certain special cases. By excluding from the sample to be studied low-lying sites in coastal areas – for example, the important Copper Age settlement of Almizaraque, Cuevas, Almería (Siret 1948, Almagro Basch 1965) – we have eliminated the necessity of assessing recent deltaic accretions (cf. Bovis 1974) and other changes in coastline, tectonic and/or eustatic. Then, by analysing in detail the immediate settings of archaeological sites in marl badlands, we have been able to assess the magnitude of change in the worst cases of potential erosion. Finally, we have estimated the depth of soil loss on the various lithologies present within our study area by means of a physically realistic model. This integrates field measures of the character of the parent materials on which erosion takes place (infiltrability, bulk density, etc.) and of the topography in the site territories with published information on rainfall intensities, potential evapotranspiration and actual runoff. The relevance of these latter inputs is enhanced by the conclusion of climatic stability.

Past archaeological research

Study of the south-east's prehistory goes back to the 1860s (Góngora y Martínez 1868, MacPherson 1870), but the foundation of our knowledge of the region's prehistory was laid by Henri and Louis Siret's (1887) monumental *Les Premiers Ages du Metal dans le Sud-Est de l'Espagne*, a work that even now provides our only information on a substantial proportion of the region's settlement sites (11 of the 35 localities in our sample). The Sirets organised information gathered from both settlement and burial sites into the typological-evolutionary system – Neolithic, Copper Age ('*Age de Transition*'), Bronze Age – which still forms the backbone of the sequence today. Louis Siret's extensive later researches, carried out until his death in 1934, were only reported as notes and comments on the original synthesis (Siret 1893, 1906, 1907, 1913, 1948, Gossé 1941), except for the megalithic burial monuments incorporated into Leisner's (1943) corpus of southern Iberian megaliths. Apart from Siret, work on the south-east's prehistory done before the Spanish Civil War was scattered (Motos 1918, Cabré Aguiló 1922, Cuadrado Ruiz 1930, Mergelina 1942, 1946). In the decade following the Civil War most published excavations were small in scale (Cuadrado Díaz 1945–46, Jiménez Navarro 1962). Julio Martínez Santa Olalla and his associates conducted extensive operations at the Argaric settlement of La Bastida and other nearby sites in the late 1940s (Martínez Santa Olalla *et al.* 1947), but their work on the key Copper Age site of Terrera Ventura remains unpublished (Topp & Arribas 1965). (For references to and locations of sites included in our sample see Table 1.1 and Figure 1.1). Accordingly, in spite of the lack of stratigraphic precision with which the Siret collections were excavated and the unfortunate vicissitudes they have undergone in the decades since being unearthed (Almagro Basch & Arribas 1963, pp. 20–3), this enormous initial gathering of information was, as late as 1960, the basis of a major synthesis of the Almería sequence (Blance 1971).

The greatly increased field research of the past 25 years has been almost exclusively oriented towards necessary and traditional culture-historical tasks: refining the Sirets' basic sequence by stratigraphic excavations within settlements, giving the sequence a radiocarbon-based absolute dimension, and elucidating cultural variation within the south-east. The initial impetus given by the renewed excavation of Los Millares in the mid-1950s by Almagro Basch and Arribas has been followed by the Deutsches Archäologisches Institut's excavations at Cerro de la Virgen and Fuente Álamo, by the University of Granada excavations at Los Castillejos (Montefrío), Cerro de la Encina, Cuesta del Negro and other sites, as well as by other projects (especially the excavations at Cueva de la Carigüela, El Barranquete/El Tarajal, Cueva de los Murciélagos (Zuheros) and Terrera Ventura). Information relevant to non-culture-historical concerns, such as subsistence practices, has, of course, been obtained from many of the more recent excavations, but study of plant and animal remains has not been integrated into overall research strategies.

The archaeological sequence

The culture-historical sequence that has emerged from a century of research remains rudimentary. The present divisions of the period from the Neolithic to the Bronze Age is only a little more refined than that presented by the Sirets in 1887. The reason for this is the paucity of reliable sequences and of closed finds (assemblages). The materials recovered from the settlements are in the main aggregates. Thus, attempts to seriate the settlements (e.g. Bosch Gimpera 1969) rest on insecure foundations (cf. Rowe 1962). Likewise, the artifact lots recovered from megalithic tombs by and large consist of aggregates. Thus, when Blance (1971, pp. 31–4) attempts to group various artifact types according to their degree of concurrence in earlier Almerian burial monuments, the type clusters are difficult to interpret chronologically, quite apart from the statistical difficulties noted by Walker (1977, p. 361). The main improvements in our knowledge since the Sirets' time are that radiocarbon dates from the south-east and elsewhere around the western Mediterranean give us the general chronological dimensions of the sequence and that work in the last 15 years has permitted

Table 2.1 Summary of major features of the later prehistoric sequence in south-east Spain.

	Neolithic	Copper Age	Bronze Age
date	5000 to (?)3500 BC	(?)3500 to 2000 BC	2000 to 1200 BC
culture	Cultura de las Cuevas	Los Millares Culture	El Argar Culture
settlement type	caves	open-air settlements with round houses; some sites fortified	open-air settlements with rectangular houses; extreme defensive locations
burial type	unknown	collective burials in megalithic tombs (or caves) located outside settlements; grave goods: ritual objects such as phalange idols, figurines	individual burials in cists or jars underneath house floors; grave goods: personal finery of the dead (weapons, ornaments)
ceramic diagnostics	incised, impressed, *almagra* wares	mostly plain, rarely painted or incised; Beakers at some later sites	plain wares, carinated vessel forms, chalices
lithic diagnostics	nondescript lithic industry	bifacially flaked points, large blades	nondescript lithic industry
metal diagnostics		tanged daggers and points	riveted daggers, halberds, silver ornaments

a more accurate definition of the sequence in *Hochandalusien*. Table 2.1 presents a greatly simplified summary of the archaeological sequence from Neolithic to Bronze Age in south-east Spain taken as a whole. This oversimplification is qualified, amplified and documented in the sections that follow.

Epipalaeolithic As Fortea Pérez's (1973) review of Holocene pre-Neolithic industries from Mediterranean Spain shows, few sites in the south-east can be assigned to this period (cf. Chapman 1975, pp. 70–6). Of the scattering of sites mentioned, but scarcely described, by Louis Siret, only one – Cueva de la Palica (Antas, Almería), re-excavated by Fortea Pérez (1970) – provides reliable data. The only other Epipalaeolithic site with an industry large enough to be compared meaningfully to other samples is Hoyo de la Mina (Málaga) (Such 1920). These artifact series form part of the microlaminar (non-geometric) facies of the Spanish Epipalaeolithic, whose main analogues abroad are the Romanel-lian or 'Epigravettian' industries of Mediterranean France and Italy. The assemblage from the basal 'Epipalaeolithic' levels of Cueva de Nerja (Boessneck & Driesch 1980) have not been described.

Neolithic   In the moist areas of south-east Spain, Neolithic sites belong to the 'Cultura de las Cuevas' (cave culture), so named by Bosch Gimpera (1920) after the type of locality in which the materials are found. This complex is the eastern Andalusian facies of the Earlier Neolithic Impressed Ware group found everywhere around the western Mediterranean (Guilane 1976) and has recently been reviewed in detail by Navarrete Enciso (1976) (see also Pérez de Barradas 1961, Tarradell 1964, Arribas 1972). Sites of this group are characterised by a ceramic industry with comb-impressed, incised, cordon-decorated and/or red-slipped (*almagra*) wares, by decorative elements such as stone bracelets and by a rather nondescript lithic industry of slightly retouched flakes and bladelets. Pellicer Catalán's (1964b) excavations at the deeply stratified Cueva de la Carigüela indicate that earlier phases of the Neolithic have higher frequencies of comb-impressed sherds and later phases more incised and *almagra* sherds (see the analysis of Navarrete Enciso (1976, pp. 85–258)). At Murciélagos (Zuheros) three Neolithic layers (III, IV and V in order of increasing depth) have yielded 11 radiocarbon determinations (Hopf & Muñoz 1974) – III: 3980 ± 130 bc (CSIC 59); IV: 4240 ± 130 bc twice (CSIC 53, 54), 4220 ± 130 bc (CSIC 55), 4150 ± 130 bc (CSIC 58), 4200 ± 45 bc (GrN 6169), 4075 ± 45 bc (GrN 6639); V: 4010 ± 130 bc (CSIC 56), 4030 ± 130 bc (CSIC 57), 4300 ± 35 bc (GrN 6638), 4345 ± 45 bc (GrN 6926). Since the ceramic assemblage at Murciélagos (Zuheros) consists mainly of *almagra* and incised elements, correlative to the later Neolithic phases at Carigüela, it seems reasonable to suppose that the Cultura de las Cuevas, like other facies of the Impressed Ware complex, may begin in the late sixth–early fifth millennium BC. A *terminus ante quem* for the end of the Neolithic in *Hochandalusien* is given by a radiocarbon determination on grain from a pit inserted into the topmost layer with incised pottery at Cueva de Nerja: 3115 ± 40 bc (GrN 5526) (Hopf & Pellicer Catalán 1970). Other sites of the Cultura de las Cuevas in our sample (Cueva de la Mujer/del Agua, Los Castillejos (Montefrío), Cueva de Ambrosio) also belong to the later phase of the Neolithic.

In the arid portions of the south-east there are few sites that can be attributed to the Earlier Neolithic (cf. Mercader 1970): five incised and impressed sherds are known from Cueva del Castillico (Cóbdar, Almería) (Navarrette Enciso 1976 I, pp. 395–7); Siret and Siret (1887, plate 2) report a large impressed ware vessel from Cueva de los Tollos (Mazarrón, Murcia). These essentially stray finds constitute the entirety of the inventory. The existence of a plain ware Later Neolithic, the 'Almería Culture', has often been proposed, however (most recently by Savory (1968, pp. 79–81, 90–6)). The distinction between a Neolithic Almería Culture and a later Copper Age 'Los Millares Culture' is primarily based on the Sirets' (1887) initial, and the Leisners' (1943) more systematic, typological analysis of megalithic burial monuments and their associated artifact inventories. Tombs of the earlier, Neolithic phase consist either of round, passageless, dry-stone-walled structures (*Rundgräber*) or of megalithic cists and passage graves. Burials are mostly collective and are accompanied by grave goods which include stone axes, geometric microliths (an archaic feature of presumably Mesolithic 'ancestry': cf. Walker 1977), bifacially flaked projectile points, undecorated pottery, shell bracelets and flat anthropomorphic figurines; the inventories of tombs assigned to this phase do not include metal implements. On a somewhat speculative basis, as Arribas (1967, p. 90) correctly points out, settlements have also been attributed to the Later Neolithic Almerían: El Gárcel because of its geometric lithic industry (Siret & Siret 1887, pp. 1–6, plate 1, Gossé 1941); Tres Cabezos because of the presence of generically Neolithic items, such as stone axes, and the absence of distinctive Copper Age type fossils (Siret & Siret 1887, pp. 21–8, plate 3); Terrera Ventura because of the similarity of a figurine from the site to a Danubian II counterpart in Hungary (Topp 1959, p. 121). No mortuary or settlement site attributed to the 'Almería Culture' has provided a radiocarbon sample with a clear provenance, however. The interesting early date from Terrera Ventura, 3420 ± 350 (HAR 155) (Walker & Cuenca Payá 1977, p. 317), was collected from the section of an earlier excavation. It may well be that the arid south-east was occupied in the fourth millennium BC by people who as yet knew nothing of metallurgy, lived in open-air villages and buried their dead in simple megalithic tombs. Although the Sirets reported copper slag from El Gárcel, the bulk of the collection is not of Copper Age character. While the recent excavations at Terrera Ventura indicate that the occupation there was mainly during the third millennium BC, the few *almagra* sherds at the base of the deposits indicate perhaps an earlier occupation (Gusi Jener 1975, p. 313). In Portugal, simple megaliths similar to those assigned to the 'Almería Culture' have produced early thermoluminescence dates in the fifth millennium BC (Whittle & Arnaud 1975). In the absence of securely provenanced dating samples and modern excavations at a number of mortuary and settlement sites, however, it is difficult to assign localities to the putative pre-Copper Age phase in the arid south-east.

Copper Age In the coastal zone the Los Millares Culture (the 'Bronce I' of Spanish prehistorians) is best known at its type site, the settlement and megalithic cemetery of Los Millares. This phase, in contrast to its hypothetical predecessor, is principally characterised by the development of metallurgy and the elaboration of the collective burial ritual. The tombs are large passage graves with corbelled vaults (*tholoi*) and contain both utilitarian and ritual items: stone axes; a varied bifacially worked lithic industry; cast copper axes, chisels, knives, points, saws and tanged daggers; pottery, some painted, some incised (*Symbolkeramik*), occasionally Beaker, mostly plain; idiosyncratic ritual items, such as phalange idols; and a variety of exotic raw materials (such as callais, amber, ivory and ostrich eggshell). Sometimes the burials are placed in caves, as at Los Blanquizares de Lébor (Totana, Murcia) (Cuadrado Ruiz 1930, Arribas 1953).

According to Leisner and Leisner (1943, pp. 566–72), the considerable variability in tomb form and content may partly be explained by change over time.

They subdivide the megaliths at Los Millares (the largest series at one locality) into two groups: one has more complex architectural features, such as side chambers giving onto the passage and main chamber of the tomb, and Beaker pottery, which dates to the end of the third millennium BC (Harrison 1977); the other has less elaborate tomb layouts and no Beakers, and is presumably earlier. The available radiocarbon dates do not tend to support this scheme, however, and further criticisms of the Leisners' analysis are outlined by Chapman (1975, pp. 204–10). The Los Millares XIX tomb, which has side chambers, but no Beakers or other chronologically distinctive grave goods, has a ^{14}C determination on charcoal of 2430 ± 120 bc (KN 72) (Almagro Gorbea 1970, p. 18). At the El Barranquete megalithic cemetery, Tomb 7, without side chambers or Beakers, has ^{14}C determinations on a wood beam of 2330 ± 130 bc (CSIC 81) and 2350 ± 130 bc (CSIC 82) (Almagro Gorbea 1973, p. 245). Thus, the typologically earlier tomb has the later date. Given the difficulties of a chronological approach to the variability of the Los Millares cemetery materials, Chapman (1981a) has suggested that differences in the aggregate wealth of grave goods may reflect the ranked social prestige of the groups using the collective tombs.

The Copper Age settlements of the arid south-east are dated by the presence in small quantities of some of the distinctive type fossils (such as decorated ceramics or metal items) found in greater concentration in funerary lots. Several of the settlements are placed close to groups of megaliths: besides Los Millares, there is Campico de Lébor (Los Blanquizares' settlement), El Tarajal (El Barranquete's settlement) and Almizaraque (next to the 'Las Encantadas' *tholoi*) (Almagro Gorbea 1965). Many of the sites are deeply stratified: 1.5 m of deposits at Campos (Siret & Siret 1887, plate 9) and Los Millares (Almagro Basch & Arribas 1963, p. 39), 2.5 m at Terrera Ventura (Gusi Jener 1976, p. 204), 3 m at El Tarajal (Almagro Gorbea 1977, p. 313). Round hut structures are reported at the last three of the above (Almagro Basch & Arribas 1963, p. 41; Gusi Jener 1975, p. 313; Almagro Gorbea 1977, p. 312). At least two of the sites (Los Millares and Campos) are fortified. We can, however, say little about the character of changes in the occupational assemblages over time, either because the excavations were not conducted stratigraphically (Campos) or because they have been very limited in extent (Los Millares, El Tarajal) or because they remain substantially unpublished (Terrera Ventura). Three sites have produced radiocarbon dates on materials associated with Copper Age artifact series.[2] The Gusi Jener excavations at Terrera Ventura (not as yet published in full) have produced dates of 2450 ± 90 bc (I 6934), 2315 ± 90 bc (I 6935), 2290 ± 60 bc (CSIC 264), 2250 ± 60 bc (CSIC 265) and 2160 ± 60 bc (CSIC 267) (Chapman 1975, p. 306; Almagro Gorbea & Fernández-Miranda 1978, p. 174). Excavations at El Tarajal (also not yet published in full) have produced a dozen radiocarbon dates (CSIC 218–255, 277–230) with an average of 2088 bc (Chapman 1975, Almagro Gorbea & Fernández-Miranda 1978). Finally, at Los Millares a determination of 2345 ± 85 bc (H 204/207) (Almagro

Gorbea 1970, p. 18) on a wood beam under the rubble of the collapsed fortification wall gives a *terminus ante quem* for the wall's use.

Thus, once the appropriate calibrations are taken into account, the Los Millares Culture must have been well under way by the beginning of the 3rd millennium BC. The Beakers found in late Millaran contexts – they are close to the surface at Terrera Ventura (Gusi Jener 1975, p. 313) – put the end of the Copper Age at the close of the 3rd millennium BC.

Until recently, the Copper Age in the moist sector of south-east Spain was known from a few early excavations in settlements (Los Castillejos (Montefrío), Cerro de las Canteras) and from megalithic cemeteries such as the Gor-Gorafe, Fonelas, Laborcillas and Montefrío groups, all of which are in Granada province (Leisner & Leisner 1943, pp. 84–173; Mergelina 1942; García Sánchez & Spahni 1959). Copper Age collective burials are also found in caves, both natural – for example, Cueva de los Murciélagos (Albuñol, Granada) (Góngora y Martínez 1868), Cerro del Castellón (Campotéjar, Granada) (Molina Fajardo 1979) – and artificial – for example, Cerro del Greal (Iznalloz, Granada) (Pellicer Catalán 1957–58). The megaliths are smaller and simpler in design than the Millaran *tholoi* and have poorer artifact inventories (little metal, no ivory, etc.), but share the same ritual, both in terms of artifacts (phalange idols, anthropomorphic figurines) and practice.[3] Together with the Nerja date mentioned above (p. 18), the recent ^{14}C determination on one of the esparto sandals found with the dead at Murciélagos (Albuñol) – 3450 ± 80 bc (CSIC 246) (Alfaro Giner 1980) – suggests that the beginning of the Copper Age is certainly as early in the moist as in the arid sector. The frequent presence of Argaric remains in the burials (more than in the arid zone megaliths) suggests that the collective burial ritual was carried on well into the 2nd millennium BC in *Hochandalusien*.

Recent excavations have added greatly to our knowledge of Copper Age settlements in the moist sector of the south-east. The University of Granada excavations at Los Castillejos (Montefrío) have uncovered over 5 m of deposits from Cultura de las Cuevas levels through late Copper Age (Arribas and Molina 1977, p. 393). A 4 m deep Copper Age sequence is also present at Cerro de los Castellones (Laborcillas) (Mendoza *et al.* 1975, p. 317). Cerro de la Virgen, with 4.4 m of deposits (Schüle & Pellicer 1966, p. 6) is the only Copper Age settlement in our sample to be occupied into the Bronze Age. The two basal, Copper Age layers (I,II) show continuity in the bulk of their assemblages, with Beakers and related elements (V-perforated buttons, archers' wrist guards) appearing with considerable frequency in level II. The frequency of Beakers at sites such as Cerro de la Virgen and Torre Cardela and their rarity at other sites, such as Los Castillejos (Montefrío) (Arribas & Molina 1977, p. 321) and Los Castellones (Laborcillas) (Mendoza *et al.* 1975, p. 321) further demonstrate the intrusiveness of Beakers in south-east Spain (cf. Harrison 1977). At Cerro de la Virgen (Kalb 1969) and El Malagón (Arribas *et al.* 1977) the Copper Age huts, like those from sites in the arid zone, are round. Fortifications are present at Cerro de la Virgen (Schüle 1980), Cerro de los Castellones (Laborcillas)

(Aguayo de Hoyos 1977) and perhaps at other sites. At El Malagón two radio-carbon determinations – 2570 ± 220 bc (UGRA 11) and 2120 ± 150 bc (UGRA 12) – indicate occupation during the earlier 3rd millennium BC (González Gómez *et al.* 1982). Las Angosturas (Gor, Granada), a Copper Age site excavated after the fieldwork phase of our project, has yielded ^{14}C determinations of 1910 ± 140 bc (UGRA 80), 2200 ± 170 bc (UGRA 81) and 2260 ± 140 bc (UGRA 82) (González Gómez *et al.* 1982). The Beaker deposits at Cerro de la Virgen have yielded a consistent series of radiocarbon determinations (Almagro Gorbea 1972, p. 232): 1940 ± 40 bc (GrN 5593), 1970 ± 35 bc (GrN 5596), 1970 ± 60 bc (GrN 5597), 1885 ± 35 bc (GrN 5598) and 1850 ± 35 bc (GrN 5764). The next-to-uppermost layer at Los Castillejos (Montefrío) has a ^{14}C determination of 1890 ± 35 bc (Arribas & Molina 1979, p. 136). Thus, the close of the Copper Age occurs at the end of the 3rd millennium BC.

Bronze Age   The El Argar Culture (the 'Bronce II' of Spanish prehistorians) follows upon the Copper Age in all of south-east Spain. The classic sites of the Sirets (El Argar, Fuente Álamo, El Oficio, Ifre and so on, all in the arid zone) have now been augmented by recent excavations in Granada (Cerro de la Encina, Cuesta del Negro, Cerro de la Virgen) and in upland Almería province (El Picacho), so that a reasonably complete picture of the cultural assemblage is now available throughout the area of its distribution. The change from Copper to Bronze Age is strongly marked in both burial and settlement patterns, as well as in artifact styles. Instead of being collective in megalithic tombs, burials are now single or double and placed under floors within settlements. Argaric materials continue to be placed in megaliths, however, especially in *Hochandalusien*. Instead of the Millaran ritualia, the burials contain the personal equipment of the dead: ornaments (diadems, bracelets, rings of copper, bronze or silver); beads, sometimes of exotic materials such as ivory; copper and bronze weapons (rivet-ed daggers, swords, points, halberds); ceramic vessels (such as the characteristic chalices); among other items. The relative wealth of the burials has not been studied in detail, but it is clear that extreme contrasts exist in the quality and quantity of the grave goods. That many of the wealthy burials are of women suggests that the superordinate status reflected by them was ascribed rather than achieved. No published burials at any of the upland sites, however, approach the degree of wealth concentration exhibited at some of the coastal lowland sites, such as El Argar Grave 9 (Siret & Siret 1887, plates 55 & 56) or Fuente Álamo Grave 1 (Siret & Siret 1887, plate 66).

   The nature of the settlements also changes from Millaran to Argaric. Instead of the typically round houses of the Copper Age, structures are now rectangular. Some Argaric settlements (the type site of El Argar, for example) continue to be placed on promontories and dissected terraces above river courses, but many others are now located in extreme defensive positions high above the surround-ing countryside. Most Argaric sites are first-time occupations (Cerro de la Virgen is the exception). The construction of acropoles, together with the weaponry in the graves, suggests that militarism was more important in the social landscape of Argaric times than in that of earlier periods.

The chronology of the Argaric, as established by Blance (1964), 1971), is based on a seriation and comparative analysis of the affinities of the grave assemblages published by the Sirets in 1887. (Some of the unpublished Siret materials are presented by Ruiz-Gálvez (1977), but an up-to-date corpus is as yet unavailable.) Blance concluded that burials in earth trenches and stone cists, with items such as halberds and V-perforated buttons, are earlier (Argar 'A') than burials in large jars, with items such as four-riveted or narrow-bladed daggers and silver diadems (Argar 'B'). Schubart (1975) has argued that the Argar 'A'/'B' distinction is also observable in changes in ceramic vessel form (but see Lull Santiago (1982) on the statistical weaknesses of Blance's and Schubart's analyses). The affinities of some of the Argar 'A' materials with the Central European Early Bronze Age and of the Argar 'B' lots with the Aegean Late Bronze Age (cf. Schubart 1973) led Blance to place the development of the culture between *ca.* 1700 and 1200 BC. The validity of these dates, based as they are on scanty long-distance resemblances, is open to question, as Coles and Harding (1979, pp. 222–3) have correctly pointed out. Furthermore, the application of a seriation based on funerary contexts to settlement deposits has proven to be problematic. At Cerro de la Virgen an Argar 'A' associated sample from the third phase of the site's occupation has given a radiocarbon determination of 1785 ± 55 bc (GrN 5594) (the 1915 ± GrN 5995 date for the superjacent Argar 'B' is rejected as anomalous) (Almagro Gorbea 1972, p. 232). At Cuesta del Negro, however, an Argar 'O' associated ^{14}C sample has given a date almost as early: 1675 ± 35 bc (GrN 7286) (Arribas 1976, p. 155). The lowermost level at Cerro de la Encina, also characterised as Argar 'B', has produced a series of early dates: 1675 ± 40 bc (GrN 6634) (Arribas 1976, p. 155), 1670 ± 130 bc (UGRA 15) and 1600 ± 140 bc (UGRA 16) (González Gómez *et al.* 1982). (The 1340 ± 140 bc – UGRA 14 – determination from the same horizon is regarded as 'probably too young' (González Gómez *et al.* 1982).) The settlement of El Picacho has given ^{14}C determinations of 1500 ± 120 bc (CSIC 156) and 1440 ± 120 bc (CSIC 157) (Hernández Hernández & Dug Godoy 1975, p. 114) and is, thus, attributed to Argar 'B', but the hollow-footed chalices found at the site would be *early* Argaric in the recently re-excavated, deeply stratified site of Fuente Álamo (Schubart & Arteaga 1980, p. 50). Stratigraphic excavations of Argaric sites are few and recent and, while Torre Peña (1978) has correlated the sequences from sites in Granada province, comparison of the Argaric sequences in the uplands and the coastal zone is not yet possible. Wood of unstated associations at El Argar itself has provided a radiocarbon determination of 1720 ± 70 bc (CSIC 248) (Almagro Gorbea & Fernández-Miranda 1978, p. 173). From La Cenuela there are dates of 2100 ± 70 bc (CSIC 140) and 1640 ± 70 bc (CSIC 141) reported (Almagro Gorbea & Fernández-Miranda 1978, p. 171). Thus it is apparent that the beginning of the Argaric must be brought into the later 3rd millennium BC and that a satisfactory internal chronology is yet to be worked out. Blance's end date of 1200 BC seems, however, to be approximately correct, given the radiocarbon dates of 1120 ± 35 bc (GrN 7284) and 1185 ± 35 bc (GrN 7285) for the post-Argaric 'Bronce Final' level at Cuesta del Negro (Arribas 1976, p. 155).

Subsistence

Given our lack of solid information about the Neolithic in the arid sector of south-east Spain, very little can be said about the subsistence economy with which it is associated: at El Gárcel, beans, wheat, rye and olive stones are reported (Gossé 1941, p. 81; Arribas 1968, p. 43). It is apparent, however, that the Neolithic occupants of moist areas were agriculturalists. At Cueva de Nerja, fauna from the Neolithic layers consists predominantly of domesticated species: sheep–goats, cattle and pigs (in order of decreasing frequency) form a total of 88% of the bones (by weight) in the Early Neolithic layers, and 83% in the Late Neolithic; by contrast, in the Epipalaeolithic layers below the emphasis is on a variety of wild species, both terrestrial and marine (Boessneck & Driesch 1980, pp. 21–2). The Neolithic basal layer at Castillejos (Montefrío) also contains an animal bone assemblage in which domesticates predominate: sheep–goats are 53% of the series by weight and cattle 29% (Uerpmann, in Arribas and Molina 1979, p. 156). At Murciélagos (Zuheros), where sheep–goats, pigs and cattle are also reported (Vicent Zaragoza & Muñoz Amilibia 1973, p. 98), abundant quantities of emmer wheat, bread wheat and barley were recovered (Hopf & Muñoz 1974).

For the arid south-east, information on Copper Age subsistence patterns is restricted to the analysis of fauna from the Gusi Jener excavations at Terrera Ventura (Driesch & Morales 1977), to Driesch's (1973a) report on the animal bones from the El Barranquete tombs and to scattered references in the older literature, summarised by Arribas (1968). It is apparent that the inhabitants of the settlements cultivated barley, flax[4] and legumes (fava beans, lentils). The domesticated animals reported are horse, cattle, sheep, goats and pigs. The proportions of these species (together with red deer, another economically significant resource) at Terrera Ventura are given in Table 2.2. The high proportion of cattle in the El Barranquete series (83 of the 165 fragments of economically significant species are *Bos*) no doubt reflects as much on the ritual as on the subsistence practices of the Millarans.

In the moist sectors of the south-east, recent excavations leave us better informed about Copper Age subsistence. The grain in the Nerja silo (which provided the radiocarbon date cited on p. 18) was composed of barley (80%) and wheat (*Triticum* sp., 20%), as well as 12 olive stones of smaller than modern size (Hopf & Pellicer Catalán 1970). There are faunal analyses available for Copper Age series from Castillejos (Montefrío), Laborcillas and Cerro de la Virgen. The proportions of the economically significant species (with references) are given in Table 2.2. Interpretation of the differences in faunal composition at the various sites is complicated by the variability in sample size and the lack of control over functional provenance. To take the differences at face value would be to assume that the areas on the sites which happened to be excavated were used in the same way during the time of their occupation and were subjected to the same depositional processes. We shall defer detailed assessment of the faunal evidence to our analysis of the sites' territories in Chapter 5, but at this point one salient pattern must be stressed. Although the sites have been variably sampled and although they are located, as we shall see, in quite varied settings, the overall proportions of the several species are surprisingly similar. With exceptions whose implications will be considered later (the high proportion of pigs in Virgen I and of horses in Virgen II, the low proportion of sheep at Castillejos (Montefrío)), the inhabitants of these sites practised an animal economy in which cattle and sheep–goats were central and in which pigs and red deer played important secondary roles. The available evidence indicates that the Copper Age inhabitants of both arid and moist sectors of south-east Spain were cultivating the same plants and animals and that they were ranking them, so to speak, in similar fashion. Given the variability of the environment, they would not, of course, have been able to achieve their common goals by identical means throughout the region. The irrigation ditch reported by Schüle (1967) from Cerro de la Virgen is one archaeologically concrete example of the means by which the differences in environment were overcome (see also Gilman (1976) and Chapman (1978) for discussions of the hitherto available evidence for hydraulic agriculture).

Occasional palaeobotanical finds from both older and more recent excavations make it clear that the inhabitants of Bronze Age settlements cultivated wheat, barley and a variety of legumes, as well as flax (linen textiles wrapped around bronzes have been preserved by copper salts). Lugarico Viejo and El Argar (Siret & Siret 1887, plates 16 & 24) have produced a representative selection of finds confirmed at other localities as well. The olive stones and carob pod from the latter site suggest the possibility of tree crop cultivation. Faunal analyses are available for the Argaric occupations at Cerro de la Virgen, Cerro de la Encina and Cuesta del Negro. The overall proportions of economically significant species are given (with references) in Table 2.2. The main changes in animal husbandry with respect to the preceding Copper Age are the following: First, horses are now very important. (The very high percentage at Cerro de la Encina, however, is partly the result of the extraordinary concentration of horse bones within the bastion structure which has been the main focus of the excavation (Lauk 1976, p. 94, Figs 26 & 27). This is an example, as yet not satisfactorily explained, of the within-site functional–taphonomic differentiation mentioned above.) Secondly, cattle increase in proportion to sheep. Thirdly, there is a general decline in the proportion of pigs in the assemblages. At Cerro de la Virgen, Driesch (1973b) sees this as the result of the progressive conversion of riverside gallery forest to irrigated fields. Thus, the main trends in

Table 2.2 Proportions* of economically significant species at Copper and Bronze Age sites in south-east Spain.

	Terrera Ventura: Levels II–IV			Montefrío: Levels I–IV			Laborcillas: Copper/Bronze			Encina: Levels I–II		
	A	B	C	A	B	C	A	B	C	A	B	C
horse (Equus caballus)	4	200	0.6	5	195†	5.4	0	0	0.0	2023	64964	61.0
cattle (Bos taurus + B. primigenius)	388	9898	30.5	32	1385	38.3	169	5210	42.3	1067	17550	16.5
sheep-goats (Ovis aries, Capra hircus + C. pyrenaica)	1451	10915	33.7	135	558	15.4	680	3876†	38.9	2758	13656	12.8
pigs (Sus scrofa + S. domesticus)	610	5730	17.7	83	720	20.0	155	1168	11.7	1221	8799	8.3
red deer (Cervus ephalus)	253	5680	17.5	43	749	20.8	10	700	7.0	115	1529	1.4

Table 2.2 (continued)

| | Cerro de la Virgen: | | | | | | | | | Cuesta del Negro: Levels I–IV | | |
| | Phase I | | | Phase II | | | Phase III | | | | | |
	A	B	C	A	B	C	A	B	C	A	B	C
horse	14	960	1.9	1061	41015	15.9	519	25000	27.6	50	2542	4.1
cattle	616	16590	32.4	3341	93265	35.0	1125	34200	37.8	1678	41159	66.2
sheep–goats	2716	13990	27.3	12348	67125	25.9	3176	18975	21.0	1800	9878	15.9
pigs	1797	18500	36.1	3890	46700	18.0	874	8870	9.8	697	7379	11.9
red deer	60	1218†	2.4	557	11307†	4.3	160	3248†	3.6	66	1211	2.0

★ Proportions shown are: A = number of fragments; B = weight of bones (g); C = percentage (by weight).
† Weights were not given for *Equus* at Montefrío, for *Capra pyrenaica* at Laborcillas or for *Cervus* at Cerro de la Virgen. Weights were estimated by the grams/bone at the other sites.
References: Driesch (1972), Driesch and Kokabi (1977), Driesch and Morales (1977), Lauk (1976), Uerpmann in Arribas and Molina (1979).

animal husbandry from Neolithic to Bronze Age as indicated by the overall proportions of species reflect an increasing emphasis over time on larger animals useful not only for their meat but also for their traction power.

The suggestion that cattle and horses were kept as beasts of burden is strongly supported by the age distribution of these animals in Argaric deposits. At Cerro de la Encina, 23 of the 29 minimum number of individual horses whose jaws permitted the progress of tooth eruption to be assessed were four or more years old (Lauk 1976, p. 16). The same measure of age distribution indicates that seven of 11 cattle at Virgen III and 18 of 21 cattle at Cuesta del Negro were over $2\frac{1}{2}$ years old (*ibid.*, p. 31). If animals were being kept for their meat, it would be most rational to cull the herd of all except breeding stock before the animals became adults. This is the pattern documented for sheep–goats (Cerro de la Encina, 29 of 76 over two years old; Cuesta del Negro, 37 of 63 (*ibid.*, p. 44)) and pigs (Cerro de la Encina, seven of 31 over two years old; Cuesta del Negro, 10 of 27 (*ibid.*, p. 57)). Thus, the animal husbandry reflected in animal bones from Bronze Age sites is best interpreted as part of an intensive subsistence agriculture.

Theoretical perspectives

Diffusionism   Until recently most prehistorians of Europe have characterised the essential processes of later European prehistory as 'the irradiation of European barbarism by Oriental civilization' (Childe 1958a, p. 70). Oriental power and knowledge (transmitted by emissaries described, according to the archaeologist and the case, as colonists, prospectors, traders, missionaries or simply 'influences') would have transformed prehistoric Europe, much as European power and knowledge has transformed the world under capitalism.

Prehistorians of Iberia have maintained a particularly strong attachment to diffusionism. Virtually every important cultural change between 5000 and 1000 BC has been viewed as the product of outside influences, mainly from the eastern Mediterranean. The Impressed Ware Neolithic is the result of maritime influences from an eastern Mediterranean source, possibly Syria (Childe 1957, p. 266; cf. Maluquer de Motes 1975, p. 33). The Almerian is a *cultura iberosahariana* (Martínez Santa Olalla 1946), ultimately derived from Palestine (Savory 1968, pp. 82, 90). The Millaran is brought by Aegean colonists (Blance 1961; Almagro Basch & Arribas 1963, pp. 203–45; Maluquer de Motes 1975, pp. 48–9). The Argaric is produced by Central European ('Beaker reflux': Blance 1964) and/or Anatolian (Evans 1956, Schubert 1973) influences. There may have been disagreements about the sources of the new cultural practices and about the mechanisms by which they were introduced, but, as Chapman (1975, pp. 1–38) has pointed out, from Siret (1913) to Savory (1968) there has been general agreement that a diffusionary explanation was a sufficient one.

This outlook has tended to limit our knowledge of the prehistory of south-east Spain. With recent exceptions, evidence on subsistence has been gathered sporadically, if at all, because it has not been important to the questions asked. To demonstrate the existence of various influences, connections, migrations and so on, knowledge of the ways of life of the prehistoric inhabitants of the south-east was unnecessary. What was needed were stylistically distinctive artifacts, and of these archaeologists found quantities.

Acceptance of the diffusionist outlook has not, of course, been universal. Some prehistorians (such as Bosch Gimpera 1932, 1944) have given all possible weight to the demonstrable typological continuities between earlier and later cultural assemblages. In recent years, furthermore, the concrete factual basis of diffusionist claims has received sharp empirical blows, especially from C. Renfrew (1967, 1973). First, one can show that trait complexes found together in Spain and held to be derived from the east do not form assemblages in their supposed homelands. Secondly, radiocarbon dates show that many allegedly Oriental features are found as early in Spain as, and sometimes earlier than, in the eastern Mediterranean. Finally, the diffusionist claims are based on rather general typological parallels between eastern and western materials: not a single undoubted object of east Mediterranean manufacture has been found in the Iberian Peninsula before 1000 BC (Childe 1958b, pp. 116–18).

These empirical considerations create problems for diffusionism, but they do not of themselves involve an alternative explanation of the cultural changes. Accordingly, as Kuhn (1970) would predict, workers have continued to reject mere facts and to maintain the *ex Oriente lux* line. As Almagro Gorbea (1973, p. 198) puts it:

> We believe . . . that a mere few C-14 dates, from at most five sites, do not constitute adequate grounds on which to presume to change the origin of the entire megalithic culture of the west . . .

Rethinking the evidence in terms of a general theoretical alternative, namely social evolution, has already begun in the independently developed and somewhat differently focused studies of Chapman (1977, 1978, 1981a, b) and Gilman (1976, 1981).

An evolutionary perspective From one point of view the Neolithic through Bronze Age sequence of south-east Spain is a history of foreign invasions and influences. From another point of view, however, the sequence, even in its present rudimentary state, is a history of autochthonous social evolution. Over time one can observe the following trends:

(1) Increasing craft specialisation is indicated by the development of metallurgy. The metal analyses of Junghans *et al.* (1960, 1968–74) describe the composition of numerous artifacts from Millaran and Argaric sites. During

the Millaran, artifacts were made of pure and arsenical copper; in the Argaric, arsenical copper was supplemented by tin bronze (Harrison 1974). Full control of casting in two-part moulds is also an Argaric achievement. Silver metallurgy has been claimed for the Millaran (Bosch Gimpera & Luxán 1935), but this seems doubtful since silver ornaments only came into use (and then in abundance) in the Argaric. The increasing control over metallurgy in the full Bronze Age is accompanied by a decline in the refinement of the lithic technology from the fine pressure-flaked industry of the Millaran to the typologically nondescript industry of the Argaric.

(2) Increasing class divisions within communities are indicated by changes in burial patterns (general sources are Leisner and Leisner (1943) and Blance (1971)). In the 'Almerian' (assuming for the moment that such a phase exists), the dead are interred collectively in round, passageless, dry-stone-walled *Rundgräber* or in megalithic cists and passages graves. Their grave goods consist of simple ritual and utilitarian items. In the Millaran the collective burial ritual is more elaborate. The larger, corbelled-vaulted passage graves continue to include burial furniture consisting mainly of ritual and utilitarian items, but these are sometimes fashioned of exotic and expensive raw materials (such as ivory or metal). The distribution of grave goods is quite unequal between tombs. The differential wealth and spatial arrangement of the various tombs at the Los Millares cemetery suggest to Chapman (1981a) the emergence of a 'ranked' society, in the sense of Fried (1967). (If a later Neolithic 'Almerian' should prove not to exist and the simpler megaliths of the arid south-east are to be assimilated into the Millaran Copper Age, this will only accentuate the progress of social differentiation in the south-east, since the contrasts between the Cultura de las Cuevas and the Millaran will be even more stark and the degree of wealth differentiation within the Millaran even more dramatic.) In the Argaric, burials are single or double and placed under floors within settlements. The grave goods consist of the personal equipment of the dead: jewellery, weapons, fine pottery. The extreme wealth of the burials indicates 'a clear social differentiation' (Muñoz 1969; cf. Childe 1957, p. 284; Maluquer de Motes 1975, p. 70). As C. Renfrew (1973) has suggested, the very passage from collective burial rituals (as in the 'Almerian' and Millaran) to 'individualising' rites (as in the Argaric) suggests the development of social stratification.

(3) Increasing militarism is indicated by the development of settlement fortifi-cations and high-status weaponry. The walls at Los Millares are the earliest dated settlement fortification. This beginning foreshadows the great devel-opment of defences in the Argaric, when many settlements are first-time occupations located on high summits (cf. Arribas 1959). The actual increase in warfare indicated by these acropoles is acccompanied by its social recognition, as indicated by the importance of weapons among Argaric grave goods.

These trends comprise, in fact, the major substantial changes in the archaeological record in the arid south-east over time. They are indicative of a change
from a simpler, more egalitarian to a more complex, more stratified social
organisation. Furthermore, the trends towards increasing inequalities are more
marked in the arid portions of the south-east than in the environmentally more
favourable areas, where, as we have seen, the trends develop later and with
lesser intensity. Copper Age megaliths in *Hochandalusien* are smaller; the grave
goods are poorer both in the megaliths and in the individual burials which are
gradually introduced in the Bronze Age. The diffusionist approach explains this
contrast straightforwardly: the interior was in less contact with the civilising
currents from the Mediterranean. If the diffusionist outlook is to be displaced,
this contrast in the pattern of development must be explained in terms of the
internal dynamics of an evolving cultural system. That is to say, the changes in
social structure that are reflected in the archaeological record of south-east
Spanish societies from 4000 to 1000 BC must be related in a plausible causal
framework to the development of economic systems in the region.

In this task a major impediment is the paucity of information available on
economic matters. According to classic archaeological principles (cf. Hawkes
1954), one is supposed to be able to reconstruct the economy of an extinct
society better than its social organisation or its ideology. For the Millaran and
Argaric, however, we are better informed about how the dead were buried than
about how the living survived. We must, therefore, reverse the usual series of
questions and ask what economic constraints could have propelled the social
changes manifest in the archaeological record.

To attempt an evolutionary explanation of the origins of complex societies has
been an important goal of anthropological archaeology for the past 20 years (see,
for example, the recent review by Wenke (1981)), and it is not possible in any
brief space to do justice to the variety of arguments that have been presented and
of the cases to which these arguments have been applied (see Gilman (1981) for a
review of the theories applied to the European case). Our task here is simplified
by the relatively limited development of social complexity in south-east Spain.
All of the manifestations we have noted are reflections of two underlying
phenomena: the progressive emergence of an elite wealthier than the mass of the
population and the perfection of a craft – metallurgy – whose technical difficulty
suggests an elaboration of the division of labour. We must consider, then, what
aspects of the economy propelled the development of metallurgy and permitted
a surplus to come into the hands of an elite increasingly over time and more so in
the arid than in the moist sectors of the south-east.

Problems

Metallurgy Virtually the only factor that has been considered influential in
shaping the cultural development of south-east Spain has been the availability of

metal ores. From the Sirets to the present, authorities have taken metal to be what lured foreigners to this area of the peninsula more than to others. Childe (1957, p. 274) argued, for example, that 'the urbanisation of the Almerian economy ... is presumably a reflection, however indirect, of oriental cities' demand for metal'. The Leisners (1943) juxtapose the distribution of megaliths and present-day copper mines. García Sánchez (1963) relates the distribution of Argaric sites to known copper sources and hypothetical trade routes.

The argument that metalworking played a critical role in the cultural flores-cence of the south-east is usually bound up with hypothetical foreign pros-pectors and merchants. One could easily allow local factors more play, however. Metalworking tends to be a specialist craft. To the extent that metal artifacts increase overall production, 'the individual householder ... must henceforth produce a surplus beyond his needs to support specialists who produce not food, but indigestible ores, ingots, and axes' (Childe 1954, p. 87). Metal is produced for exchange between households, not as a good to be used within the household. Thus, to follow Sahlins (1972), metalworking would be incompatible with the household independence characteristic of the 'Domestic Mode of Production'. Insofar as households depend upon metal implements for their livelihood, they depend upon the controllers of the network of commodity exchange which supplies them. This idea is developed for south-east Spain by Lull Santiago (1983). One might further suppose that having metal weapons would help a ruling class maintain its military sway over its neighbours (Childe 1954, p. 158). By arguing along these lines, one could put metallurgy at the base of the south-east's social evolution without any need for foreigners.

Even in modified form, however, arguments for the fundamental importance of metallurgy in the Millaran–Argaric culture process face difficulties. Some of these are empirical. One cannot accept on present evidence that the metal implements actually manufactured in the south-east helped increase overall production to any great extent. As Arribas (1968, p. 49) tells us, 'we know of no agricultural tools made of metal from the Bronze Age'. Indeed, most metal is found in burials. Such a context suggests that metal had a social rather than a practical value. Adams (1966) has shown how specialisation in the basic, subsistence sector of the economy can promote social stratification. It is not clear, however, that craft specialisation in the production of primarily 'sociotechnic' (cf. Binford 1962) items would have a comparable effect on social organisation. At the same time, history shows repeatedly that purely technolo-gical advantages tend to be ephemeral: the mere possession of copper weapons would not in and of itself have been enough to give the elite a decisive monopoly of force. In south-east Spain, as elsewhere around the western Mediterranean (see, for example, Barker (1981, pp. 186–8) on the Copper Age of central Italy), there are good contextual and theoretical reasons for believing that a metallurgi-cal industry came into being for social more than for practical reasons.

Be that as it may, the recently published 1 : 200 000 sheets of the *Mapa Metalogenético de España* by the IGME permit us to test some of the spatial consequences of theories which put metalworking at the root of Millaran–Argaric florescence. These comprehensive maps of metal sources at reasonably large scales enable us to tell whether Copper and Bronze Age settlements were placed so as to maximise their access to ore bodies, as claimed by some authorities (see Ch. 6).

Subsistence intensification   Apart from the development of metallurgy, the other aspect of the archaeological record from later prehistoric south-east Spain to show progressive techno-environmental development is the subsistence sector. Over the millennia which concern us, there is scanty but unmistakable evidence that agriculture was intensified. First, there is an increase in the importance of cattle and horses, animals exploited not just for their meat, but also for their traction power. To maintain these beasts as adults requires a substantial investment for a partially deferred return. If, as elsewhere in Europe in Copper and Bronze Age times, this change in animal husbandry is accompanied by the introduction of the plough (Sherratt 1981), even more extensive investment in the land is implied (Gilman 1981). Secondly, it is possible that tree crops such as olives and carobs were introduced (cf. Gilman 1976). Arboriculture provides stable sources of food whose production does not conflict with that of annuals, but the long growth of trees to maturity makes them also significant investments. Thirdly, there is evidence direct (the ditch at Cerro de la Virgen) and indirect (the existence of permanent agricultural settlements in areas receiving less than 250 mm median annual rainfall; the cultivation of flax in the arid sector), for irrigation. Once again, the dams, ditches, and terraced fields required for hydraulic agriculture represent a heavy investment by the farmer in future production. An intensified subsistence sector accompanies the development of social inequalities, not just in south-east Spain of course, but in all instances of emergent stratification.

While the association between intensification of subsistence and the development of social stratification is of *prima facie* evolutionary significance, the precise nature of the relationship involved remains a matter of considerable debate (cf. Gilman 1981). In south-east Spain, however, the most immediate problem is not the theoretical approach best suited to linking the two (a matter to which we shall return), but the practical one of upgrading the scanty evidence for agricultural change. We are fortunate in having comparatively good evidence for animal husbandry. An adequate palaeobotanical basis on which to evaluate changes in cultivation in the south-east from Neolithic through to Bronze Age continues to await an appropriately designed programme of excavations at several sites of different periods and settings. It is not to be expected, however, that much more evidence for the existence of prehistoric irrigation systems will be provided by the spade. The few pieces of concrete data which are now available – scraps of linen from Argaric sites in the coastal zone, the irrigation ditch at Cerro de la Virgen – are more than welcome, but the long history of irrigation in the south-east virtually guarantees that most traces of early canals and such will have been destroyed. In Spain prehistoric cultivation did not exceed modern agriculture in extent, and we may be assured that newer irrigation systems obliterate older ones. The best approach to investigating prehistoric irrigation in south-east Spain is, therefore, to examine systematically the positioning of settlement sites with respect to present land and water resources. In other words, site catchment analysis is the best strategy by which we can obtain further evidence of the importance of irrigation to the dynamics of culture change in later prehistoric south-east Spain.

Notes

1   Radiocarbon dates are reported, following archaeological usage, on uncalibrated radiocarbon years ad/bc. Ages in calendar years are quoted in years AD/BC.

2   Dates on samples taken from the standing sections of earlier excavations at Almizaraque (Schubart 1965; Almagro Gorbea 1972, p. 236; Almagro Gorbea & Fernández-Miranda 1978, p. 172) and Terrera Ventura (Walker & Cuenca Payá 1977, p. 317) and from the surface at Parazuelos (Walker & Cuenca Payá 1977, p. 317) need only be mentioned because they are in reasonable agreement with more reliably associated determinations. The Almizaraque dates are 1860 ± 60 bc (KN 73) and 1910 ± 60 bc (CSIC 269). The Terrera Ventura and Parazuelos dates are 2080 ± 80 bc (HAR 298) and 2400 ± 80 bc (HAR 521).

3   At Murciélagos (Albuñol), for example, Góngora y Martínez (1868) reported that the dead were arranged radially with their heads at the periphery of the circle. A similar arrangement is reported by Pellicer Catalán (1957–58) at Cerro del Greal. The arrangement of skeletal remains around the peripheries of the main chambers at El Barranquete Tombs 4 and 7 (Almagro Gorbea 1973, plates XI & XXIII) may reflect a similar concept.

4   As Chapman (1978, p. 282) points out, the cultivation of flax in the coastal zone of south-east Spain can only have been carried out if the crop was watered, since it requires 450 mm or more of rainfall for dry-farmed cultivation (J. M. Renfrew 1973, p. 124).

3 Land-use investigations

Methods of site catchment analysis

Any site catchment analysis necessarily involves four steps. First, one must select the sites to be studied. Secondly, one must delimit the exploitation territory of those sites. That is to say, one must estimate the size of the area regularly exploited from the sites. Thirdly, one must establish a relevant categorisation of resources within the site exploitation territories. Fourthly and finally, one must describe the distribution of resources within the territories. Given the set of problems described in the previous chapter, our procedures were specifically as follows.

Selection of sites to be studied   Site catchment analysis takes as its essential premise that, as Roper (1979, p. 122) puts it, humans are refuging animals who maintain home bases from which they carry out various activities according to least–cost principles. It obviously follows from this that the archaeological sites used for a catchment analysis must be settlements. The location of mortuary or other special activity sites cannot be related systematically to the proportions of the resource spaces in their vicinity. The dead may be presumed to have been buried near where they lived and worked, but the degree of proximity cannot be estimated precisely. (See Francis and Clark (1980) for an example of the difficulties in obtaining coherent results from a catchment analysis of localities of undetermined function.) Accordingly, the localities that we studied (Table 1.1) were chosen because evidence from them indicates that they were used as habitations. That is to say, they possess structures, hearths, abundant pottery, querns, loom weights, broken-up animal bones and/or other such domestic debris. (The evidence for settlement function will be reviewed on a site-by-site basis in Chapter 5.) Although the fact that caves constitute ready-made dwellings arguably may affect the least–cost considerations governing their use, we have included them in our sample if their habitation areas were of substantial size and if the evidence from them indicates that they were lived in (and were not primarily used as repositories for the dead). Open-air sites of earlier Neolithic age have not been identified within our study area, but they are known from other parts of Spain (e.g. Soler García 1961). Given, then, that the construction of dwellings was within the technological capabilities of the later prehistoric inhabitants of south-east Spain, the added work of building a house would, over the lifetime of its use, have been small in comparison with the daily work of making a living from a cave which was inconveniently situated with respect to important resource spaces.

The problems defined in the previous chapter require us to include within our sample sites in both the arid and moist sectors of the south-east and sites from each of the successive phases of the cultural succession. The use of sites whose characteristics are reasonably well known not only resolves the question of site function, it also ensures that all sites can be dated with some reliability.[1] The sites that we have studied constitute a comprehensive sample of the better-known Neolithic through Bronze Age settlements throughout south-east Spain.

The use of a sample consisting exclusively of sites whose age and function have been determined by previous excavations carries definite advantages. It provides necessary controls without which any analysis would be meaningless. It affords, furthermore, the maximum possibility of strengthening the results of the analysis by confronting it with the evidence already available for the prehistory of south-east Spain. At the same time, the use of known sites carries the disadvantage of incorporating within our sampling strategy whatever biases have governed the discovery of sites in the past. This, of course, is an unavoidable aspect of any archaeological research that incorporates older data. A prehistorian working now can either reject the evidence already gathered (the bulk of what will ever be available to him) in the interests of methodological purity or he can do the best he can in integrating available and new evidence with full conscience of the problems that this may present. We prefer the latter course.

Determination of site territory size   Under ideal conditions (sometimes claimed to have been attained) archaeologists would know the location and degree of contemporaneity of all settlements within a given region. In that limiting case the site exploitation territories could be estimated by Thiessen polygons. In our study area no such claims can be made. Even in the Vera basin (which, being the locale of Louis Siret's home base of Herrerías, has been thoroughly canvassed), documentation is incomplete and the contemporaneity of sites can only be estimated to the nearest millennium. Sites must be considered in their individual relation to the environment. In order to cope with this problem, the developers of site catchment analysis in the Early History of Agriculture Project (Vita-Finzi & Higgs 1970, Higgs & Vita-Finzi 1972, Jarman 1972, Jarman *et al.* 1972) estimated the size of site territories by ethnographic analogy. Following Lee's (1969) study of the Kung San, the site exploitation territories of hunter–gatherers were set at 2 h walking distance (or 10 km) from the home base; following Chisholm's (1962) examples from rural Europe, those of agriculturalists were set at 1 h walking distance (5 km). The economy of the inhabitants of a site was then estimated from the global proportions of the various resource spaces within its territory. As Roper (1979, p. 124) notes, this approach has received 'uncritical acceptance' and 'mechanical use'.

The pioneering work of the Early History of Agriculture Project in regard to site catchment approaches has received cogent criticism (Dennell 1980). The ethnographic data on which the size of site territories was estimated are an inadequate base for so sweeping an empirical generalisation. The categorisation of hunter–gatherers as 'mobile' occupants of large territories and of agriculturalists as 'sedentary' occupants of smaller territories does little justice to the variability of each and to the gradations between them. The solution to these problems does not lie in developing a wider or more appropriate set of analogues so as to establish a more secure set of generalisations. Flannery (1976, p. 93) indicated the appropriate course when he noted that it is not the global proportion of resource spaces within site territories that are meaningful, but rather the changes in those proportions as one moves closer or further from the site. (Of the members of the Early History of Agriculture Project, only Webley (1972) appreciated this point.) Unless we have excavated evidence that makes site catchment analysis unnecessary (cf. Flannery 1976, pp. 103–17), we can never know what the actual territory exploited from a site was. What we can do is assess the preferences of the occupants by contrasting the proportions of resources closer to and further from the site. This flexible approach has two advantages: it does not prejudge by analogy the character of the prehistoric economy under study, and it makes direct use of the cost–distance logic underlying the approach as a whole. Accordingly, we have studied the area within a 2 h walk of all of our sites and have delimited 12, 30 and 60 min time contours within the 2 h territory. The 2 h territory gives an overall picture of the environment of a site; the internal subdivisions enable one to assess the preferences of the site's inhabitants.

In the site catchment analyses conducted to date, site territories have very often been defined by circles of fixed (1, 5 or 10 km) radii. 'Possibly one reason for the predominance of [this] technique is the fact that circles are more readily employed when data are taken from available maps rather than collected from actual walks taken in the field' (Roper 1979, p. 124). The problem with this simplification is that it conflicts with the least-cost premises of the overall approach. Hilly areas, which are more time consuming to walk through, tend to be overrepresented within site territories. In his brief treatment of field procedures for site catchment analysis, Higgs (1975, pp. 223–4) recommended that site territories be measured and mapped by walking a series of straight-line transects out from the site. As Dennell (1980, p. 11) has noted, this recommendation is impracticable:

> The crossing of drainage ditches and irrigation canals by wading or on improvised rafts, the jumping over electric fences, or the walking through 7' high maize are probably indelibly etched in the memories of many who have tried to maintain a straight line. . . . I have yet to learn how to walk at a steady pace across irrigated maize, cotton, and melon fields, through vineyards, or across freshly plowed alluvium.

Difficulties of this sort were manifest from the very beginning of our fieldwork at Cueva de los Murciélagos (Zuheros) in July 1977. During our walks (which after the first day stuck to more or less beaten tracks), stops were made every 12 min to locate the position on the 1 : 50 000 maps, to take notes on land uses, etc. At the conclusion of the 1977 season it was possible, therefore, to establish a systematic relation between the distance covered and the contours traversed in the more reliable of the 12 min segments (those in which bearings were clear, footing secure, etc.). Making the assumption (borne out by our experience) that uphill and downhill travel time is the same, we took the distance covered in reliable segments against the number of 20 m contours and streams traversed in those segments, rounded off and spaced regularly the average distance for each number of contours, and arrived at the following estimates:

Number of streams and 20 m contours crossed	Metres travelled in 12 min
8	400
7	500
6	600
5	700
4	775
3	850
2	950
1	1050
0	1100

This is only a rough approximation to the more formal method proposed by Ericson and Goldstein (1980), but it is quite close to Naismith's hill–walking formula (1 h per three map miles and 1 h per 2000 ft (Dennell 1980, p. 13)) and predicts distances covered in 2 h to within 100 m. Although transects were walked for all sites in order to obtain a more detailed appreciation of the landscapes under study and to reach areas inaccessible by car, the time distance zones of our analysis were defined by applying the above formula with calipers to the 1 : 50 000 maps.

Categorisation of resource spaces   Site catchment analysis seeks to determine the economic orientation, and especially the subsistence practices, of the ancient inhabitants of archaeological sites from the site's location with respect to present resources. To establish a relevant typology of present–day resources is, there-fore, an essential step. Various workers have categorised resources in terms of types of modern land uses, more (Barker 1975a) or less (Vita-Finzi & Higgs 1970) elaborately subdivided, and/or soil (Webley 1972, Jarman & Webley 1975, Barker 1975b) and vegetation types (King 1974, Zarky 1976). In south-east Spain detailed soil maps are not available (and would, in any event, only record relicts, at best, of the soil cover of prehistoric times). Vegetation, furthermore, is today a function of land use. Modern land uses must, therefore, be our guide to ancient ones.

In all areas of Mediterranean climate, the use of the land falls into three fundamental categories: uncultivated woodland (in Spain, '*monte*'), dry arable land (in Spain, '*labor*' or '*secano*') and irrigated land (in Spain, '*huerta*' or '*regadío*'). All subdivisions of these categories classify historically contingent uses of the land. Whether *secano* is put to cereals or planted with tree crops is the result of market opportunities, the capital available for landowners to invest, and so on. Whether *monte* retains its climax vegetation, has been degraded to scrub ('*matorral*'), or has been reforested depends on landownership and the uses contingent to it. Whether *regadío* is put to cereals or gardened intensively again depends in large part on land tenure patterns. Thus, a fine-grained categorisation of land uses is not apt to be particularly relevant to.the determination of the resource options of the inhabitants of ancient sites. (Barker (1975a) distinguishes between 'dry arable–cereals' and 'dry arable–interculture' when mapping the site territories in central Italy, but lumps these subdivisions into 'arable/potentially arable–light soils' for purposes of his analysis.)

Even the basic categories are, of course, to some degree contingent upon recent exploitation patterns. A landowner may allow some land that could be *secano* to remain *monte*; irrigable land will not be irrigated unless someone makes it so. As we have defined the categories, however, these difficulties are held to a minimum. Our first basic distinction, between arable and non-arable land, is based on potential, not actual, use. Non-arable land consists of steep slopes, stream beds, dunes and other land whose cultivation is inherently unlikely. Our work on the erosion potential of lithologies within the site territories enables us to reinforce this distinction by estimating the amount of soil loss in areas not now cultivable. Our second basic distinction, between irrigated and dry-farmed land, is based on actual land uses, but the advantage of irrigating in south-east Spain is so great that the actual extent of *regadío* approximates the potential. Indeed, the problem we face is not that land that might be irrigated is not, but that land that is now irrigated could not be irrigated using a traditional technology. To control this source of error by use of historical sources on land use and by estimating the winter flows of streams within the site territories has been a major focus of our research.[2] With exceptions, which we shall discuss on a site-by-site basis in Chapter 5, the basic categories of *monte* (non-arable), *secano* (dry arable) and *regadío* (irrigable) may be considered reasonable approximations of potential land use.

In addition to these basic classes we have recognised two further land-use categories whose presence and absence undoubtedly are the result of contingent factors, but whose nature and differential distribution within the south-east suggest their potential significance. The first of these is floodwater farming ('*riego de boquera*' or '*riego de aguas turbias*'). This intrinsically primitive hydraulic technique is, as Vilá Valentí (1961b) notes, practised mainly in the arid sector of south-east Spain. (Only one site territory in *Hochandalusien* – El Malagón – has them.) Earth dams (*boqueras*) are built across *rambla* beds so as to divert the occasional flows onto suites of terraces beside the stream. The silt-laden waters (the '*aguas turbias*') not only irrigate the crops but replenish the soil. *Ramblas* will have a series of *boqueras* to capture flows that overrun upstream check dams. (For descriptions of the operation of these systems in various settings, in addition to Vilá Valentí (1961b) and Morales Gil (1970), see Hack (1942), Despois (1961) and Kirkby and Kirkby (1973).) Even within the arid sector, not all land that could be watered by *boqueras* is,[3] but, because of its inherent simplicity, its antiquity (cf. Gil Olcina 1971, pp. 116–17) and its evident relevance as a response to aridity, *boquera* fed land was noted where it occurred.

The second land-use category that we have recognised, in spite of the fact that its presence is partly governed by historical contingencies, is terraced land. Terracing serves to extend arable land to slopes otherwise too steep for cultivation and its presence, thus, depends on factors such as local population density and land hunger. When placed along drainage lines, terracing also serves to prevent erosion and retain moisture. Terracing is present throughout south-east Spain, but is more frequent in the arid sector because of its value for moisture retention. Since the presence of terracing today partly responds to the fundamental environmental constraints that inform the problems set forth in the previous chapter, we have described it where it occurs.

It should be noted that the land-use categorisation we have used – *monte*, *secano*, terracing, *boquera* and *regadío*, in order of progressive intensity – constitutes a scale of increasing capital investment in the land. This makes it possible for our site catchment analysis to address the question of the significance of intensified farming for the development of social inequalities.

Description of resource spaces   The starting point for a site catchment analysis is a set of maps describing the distribution of relevant resources near the ancient settlements under study. If soil, vegetation or land-use maps of the right kind have been prepared by other agencies, the archaeologist may find the maps (or the basis for them) ready-made. Within our study area only two sheets of the 1 : 50 000 scale *Mapa de Cultivos y Aprovechamientos* have been published by the Ministerio de Agricultura (1974, 1975), so that a major goal of our fieldwork was to prepare land-use maps using the categories outlined above. The base maps that we used were the 1 : 50 000 scale sheets of the *Mapa Militar de España*, prepared by the Servicio Geográfico del Ejército, and of the *Mapa Nacional de España*, prepared by the Instituto Geográfico y Catastral. These maps have indications of land use, but the reliability and uniformity of the land-use descriptions is very variable from sheet to sheet and even within sheets. The essential guide for mapping land uses was, therefore, the air photographic cover of Spain conducted for the Spanish army in 1956–57 and available through the SGE. The air photographs are 1 : 30 000 scale stereo pairs and cover all our site territories, and 1 : 15 000 scale enlargements of every other photograph were used in the field. Fieldwork (three to five days per site territory) consisted of vehicle and foot surveys to permit accurate interpretation of the air photographs over the entirety of the *ca.* 9000 to 24 000 ha in each territory. For the most part, of course, the topographic maps and the air photographs could be simply interpreted, so that field survey was intended to clear up whatever problems of interpretation might remain (not all dark patches are irrigated land) and to obtain information not ascertainable from maps or photographs (such as the sources from which irrigated patches were fed) by on-the-spot observation and by asking questions of local farmers. This work was assisted by the information on spring locations in the *Inventario de Puntos de Agua* prepared by the Instituto Geológico y Minero de España. Final mapping, which integrated the information in field notebooks, photographs and field-annotated maps with the information obtained from historical sources and the estimates of water diversion and erosion potential, was done on the stereo pairs and then transferred (by eye) to the 1:50 000 topographic maps. The areas of the various land-use categories within each isochrone in each site territory were measured using a Numonics Electronic Graphics Calculator.

Historical dimensions: the Catastro de la Ensenada

Any site catchment analysis, and especially one describing resources in terms of categories as mutable as land-use types, must attempt to control the major factors that have caused the landscape to change since prehistoric times. 'Otherwise a study of Neolithic land use could easily degenerate into an exercise in plotting the distribution of modern crops on Medieval soils' (Dennell 1980, p. 14). The magnitude of recent changes in agricultural practices in south-east Spain is evident, but, while it is relatively easy for a fieldworker to see what is modern, it is harder for him by inspection to know what the modern has replaced, to tell what might have been there under palaeotechnic conditions. Historical sources on land-use practices offer us, therefore, a valuable way of evaluating the nature of agricultural change within our site territories.

In recent times, particularly within the last 25 years, modern agricultural technology has begun to transform the landscape of south-east Spain. These changes have particularly affected irrigation agriculture, an area of central concern in our research. Deep motor-pumped wells now tap (and significantly deplete) aquifers throughout much of south-east Spain. One result is that irrigation in the most arid areas is much more extensive and intensive than it was in the past, when the sources of water were gravity fed or (in a few areas) lifted by animal power harnessed to *norias*. In the Campo de Níjar, for example, a number of deep wells sunk since the 1950s support sand-mulched vegetable patches in areas formerly devoted to grazing and occasional dry farming (Sáenz Lorite 1977, pp. 254–64). The 1037% increase in the surface devoted to the new technology between 1964 and 1977 (*ibid.*, p. 255) has greatly altered the landscape (and, in passing, has destroyed the settlement site of El Tarajal (Almagro Gorbea 1977)). Similar developments are widely seen in the Totana and Mazarrón areas of Murcia and in the Vera, Tabernas and lower Ándarax areas of Almería (cf. Geiger 1973, pp. 204–5). The introduction of deep motor-pumped wells not only increases the area devoted to irrigation but also depletes the aquifers that feed natural springs, with a consequent reduction in the area irrigated by traditional, gravity-fed methods. The situation near the site of Fuente Álamo is typical: the marl interfluves south of the site are now covered by tomato patches irrigated by water pumped up from deep wells; the site's eponymous spring, which once was the principal source of potable water for the town of Cuevas, 4 km to the south (Siret & Siret 1887, p. 200), no longer produces enough water to feed the 3 ha of irrigated terraces in its immediate vicinity. A new wave of capital intensification, responding to the profit opportunities of selling winter vegetables on the European market, is transforming the agricultural landscape of the arid coastal belt of south-east Spain.

Recent changes are also apparent in the nature and extent of dry farming in the 35 site territories under study. The most striking of these, of course, is the abandonment of cleared land and its partial reversion to rough pasture. The more marginal lands exploited during the high point of rural population density in the later 19th and earlier 20th centuries are falling out of use, so that abandoned farmhouses dot the landscape throughout our study area from Zuheros to Mazarrón. At the same time, in some areas land clearance continues even now: thus, in the El Malagón site territory in November 1979 there were fields of no more than a few months age newly cleared from oak woodland. While, generally speaking, it is probable that in most areas land hunger was sufficient in recent times to ensure that most cultivable land was, in fact, cleared, it is apparent that one cannot simply and straightforwardly take the 1977–80 distribution of dry-farmed land vs rough pasture or woodland to be a measure of arable potential. With dry farming as with irrigation, land use is technologically and socially mediated. Over the past century the landscape has changed as a result of two interrelated processes: the introduction of modern technology and the shift from the subsistence-oriented farming of a society with a tributary mode of production (Wolf 1981) to the market-oriented farming of a capitalist society.

The effects on land use of some recent changes in agricultural technology, such as the expansion of sand-mulched irrigation in the Campo de Níjar, can be determined by examination of the air photographs of 1956–57. The degree of change brought about by the transformation of the social relations of agricultural production over the course of the 19th and 20th centuries can only be assessed by consultation of historical sources antedating modernisation (for a review of the available sources, see Réparaz (1964)). The fundamental basis for study of the rural geography of 18th-century Spain is the *Catastro de la Ensenada* of 1749–57 (Matilla Tascón 1947). The Marquis of la Ensenada, chief minister to Ferdinand VI, hoped to replace the patchwork system of tolls and duties by which the Spanish monarchy raised revenues with a single tax on property ('*la única contribución*'). His first (and only[4]) step was to order a comprehensive survey of property holdings in every village and town in the then Kingdom of Castile (including all six modern provinces in our study area). For each locality the *Catastro* has two parts: a *Respuesta General* (one volume) and a *Relación Particular* (often several volumes). The former is a general questionnaire, which gives a summary account of the sources of wealth within the municipality (the types of land; the area devoted to each; the variety, plantings and yields of annual crops; the variety and distribution of tree crops; crop prices; the types of and income from domestic animals; the mines, mills and commercial establishments; etc.) and of the duties levied upon them. The latter is a detailed census and tax register in which every property holder, secular or religious, local resident or absentee, declares the type, size, location, and quality (productivity) of each of his holdings within the reporting locality. While the *Catastro de la Ensenada* is hardly exempt from the difficulties attendant on questionnaire-derived data, it is an invaluable source for our purposes for two reasons. First, it antedates agricultural modernisation in the south-east. In the mid-18th century the *ancien régime* was in full force. Farmers were subsistence oriented and employed a technology that was, in its major features, archaic in character. Secondly, it is a systematic source of evidence that collects formally comparable data for the entirety of our study region and, thus, permits comparison between site territories. Thus, we can assess the changes in land use that have occurred over the past two centuries within each site territory and contrast these changes between them.

The *Respuestas Generales* are preserved complete in the Archivo General of Simancas. The responses to the first 20 questions (the ones directed to agricultural production) have been studied for all 85 localities whose jurisdictional territories overlap substantially with the 35 site territories under study. (See the Appendix for a list of the Ensenada localities studied.) The *Relaciones Particulares* are housed in the historical archives of the modern provinces in which the various places they describe are situated. They constitute a much more massive body of data than the *Respuestas*, so that only a sample of them could be studied. This selection was made on the basis of preservation and overlap with the site territories. Of the localities for which complete, legible registers are preserved only eight fairly small ones whose extent falls substantially within site territories were selected for further analysis: Pliego (Murcia); Santa Fe de Mondújar and Turre (Almería); and Benalua de Guadix, Gobernador, Laborcillas, Moreda and Purullena (Granada). These offer the opportunity not only to examine certain localities in greater detail, but also to test the internal consistency of the Ensenada survey.

Comparison of the *Respuestas* and the *Relaciones* indicates a high degree of mutual consistency and this may be taken as a good index of accuracy (cf. Gómez Mendoza 1977, p. 102). There obviously would be a tendency to under-report one's wealth to tax assessors, but this systematic bias would be minimised in the case of agricultural property by the unconcealable nature of the assets. Olive groves, terraced fields, and so on are available for anyone to see and their ownership is public knowledge. In the event, the severe penalties for false testimony and the proferred rewards for denunciations that accompanied the execution of the survey seem effectively to have ensured accuracy. In all but one of the eight cases examined in detail (Turre), the estimates of the amounts of the various types of land given in response to Question 10 of the *Respuestas* are very close to the results obtained by adding up the areas of each plot as enumerated in the individual declarations of the *Relaciones*.

The *Relaciones Particulares* themselves are coherent, internally consistent registers of property. For each plot listed under a particular landowner one is told its type, quality, size, general location by district, and specific location as defined by the names of neighbours in the four cardinal directions. Thus, Fulano will be listed as having a plot of such-and-such type, quality, and size; in such-and-such district; neighboured by Zutano to the east, Mengano to the west, and so on. To the extent that the data are complete and consistent it should be possible to reconstruct a map for a given district by juxtaposing the abutting plots of propertyholders within that district (cf. Kendall 1971). Ferrer Rodríguez (1975) has done just this in her complete reconstruction of the property map for Alhama de Granada. This is not an isolated instance of exceptional accuracy within the *Catastro* as a whole. We have been able to reconstruct abuttal maps from the *Relaciones* we examined as well.

While the Ensenada survey's reporting of the amounts of various types of land use within each locality is reasonably reliable, it is not so easy to translate these into standard measures. The general questionnaire attempted to resolve the diversity of local land measures by asking that these be defined in terms of '*varas castellanas*' (a 'yard' of 0.8359 m). Only 37 of the 85 *Respuestas* answer this question for *regadío* and of these only 26 also have a reported measure for *secano*. The unevenness (characteristic of the *ancien régime*) of 18th century land measurements means that for many site territories we shall have to compare present and past land uses qualitatively.

Various questions in the *Respuestas Generales* seek information on agricultural productivity: the major crops were to be enumerated, the plantings and yields per unit area specified, the fallowing and rotational cycles described, and so on. Together with the information obtained on crop prices, these data would permit the state to establish the income landowners would derive from the properties that they would declare in the *Relaciones Particulares*. The *Respuestas*' information on farming practices contribute to a comparative understanding of the agricultural landscape of 18th century south-east Spain, but cannot be taken entirely at face value. Yield ratios, for example, are unrealistically low. In the Granada region as a whole average maximum wheat yields in the 1750s were reported to be about $600 \, \text{kg ha}^{-1}$, as opposed to about $2200 \, \text{kg ha}^{-1}$ now (Ocaña Ocaña 1974, pp. 455, 458). A similar disparity is seen in the 7 : 1 ratio reported as the *maximum* wheat yield on *secano* in the Montefrío (Granada) *Respuesta* and the 13 : 1 *average* yield prevalent for wheat now (Onieva Mariegos 1977, p. 368). Partly this is to be explained by the primitive quality of the agriculture of the 18th century (the limited use of crop rotations, the limited manuring, etc.). Partly it reflects the tendency towards underproduction characteristic of any farming system in which absentee landownership is important (cf. Heitland 1921, pp. 153–4). Largely, however, the low yields reported in the Ensenada survey reflect the fact that, as Ferrer Rodríguez (1975, pp. 195–8) points out, yields were the critical figure for estimating income from agriculture and so would have been understated by the unanimous collusion of all witnesses. In general, of course, one cannot expect a high standard of accuracy in response to such requests for statistical information. As the *Respuesta* for Alicún (Almería) states (in avoiding the question on plantings), 'each owner sows what he can or deems appropriate'. One must recognise that, on matters of yields, plantings and other variables of interest, the testimony in the *Respuestas* must be interpreted as it was intended, as plausible rather than accurate.

The interest of the *Catastro de la Ensenada* as a control for our study depends on two facts: that 18th-century farming was subsistence oriented and that it used an archaic technology. The *Respuestas Generales* for the 85 localities overlapping with our site territories describe an agricultural regime which indeed is palaeo-technic and devoted to '*una economía de autosubsistencia*' (Sáenz Lorite 1977, p. 148). The local orientation of farm production is most clearly revealed in the great similarity of crops reported from all the environmentally quite diverse localities: all of them produced wheat, 91.8% of them barley, 73.3% of them wine, 67.4% olive oil – the staples of Mediterranean polyculture. This contrasts with the substantial regional specialisation of modern market-oriented production. Today grain farming in the arid sector of the south-east is practically entirely devoted to barley: in the absence of the necessity to grow wheat for their own bread, farmers can afford to concentrate on the more drought-resistant species. Of the 16 crops cited in the *Respuestas* of more than seven localities, only three minor ones were regionally specialised in the 18th century: spelt and vetch (in the moist uplands north and west of Granada) and saltwort (in the arid coastal region). The ubiquitous vineyards of the 18th-century south-east were destroyed by the phylloxera epidemic and only restocked where production was oriented to a wide market: in the Granada *vega*, for example, the *ca.* 1500 ha of vineyard cultivated in the 1750s are now reduced by two-thirds (Ocaña Ocaña 1974, pp. 218–21) and this drop is less than in the region as a whole. Of our site territories the only ones in which vines have not practically disappeared are Cueva de los Murciélagos (Zuheros) – on the edge of the Moriles/Montilla wine district – and Los Millares in the Ohanes table grape area: this shows the extent to which pre-phylloxera viticulture was oriented towards local consumption. Even the main cash crops of the 18th-century south-east depended on the region's isolation: flax, hemp and silk were only commercially viable if cotton, jute and oriental silk were absent from the market.

The archaic production technologies employed in the 18th-century south-east can be most directly inferred from the long fallowing intervals indicated by the *Respuestas*. On *regadío*, crops were obtained in successive years in many areas, but where water was scarce, soil poor, or salinisation a problem, fallowing intervals of as much as four years are reported (in the lower Ándarax localities). Only seven places, all in the moist uplands north-west of Granada, had *any* continuously cropped *secano*. For dry farming, fallowing of one to three years was common and in some areas even longer intervals are recorded (from 10 to 40 years in the lower Ándarax area). The long fallowing periods were partly the result of fertilising limited to animal manure. The *Respuesta* from Cúllar-Baza, for example, specifies that the difference between the annually cropped *regadío* near the town and the more distant *año-y-vez* plots was that the first were manured. Long fallowing was also due to the lack of systematic crop rotation in many areas. Nitrogen-fixing legumes are listed among the crops of only 49 of the 85 *Respuestas*. Only a fraction of these would have planted legumes as part of a regular rotation: only 10 and five places report such rotations on *regadío* and *secano* respectively in specific terms (the five reporting a *secano* rotation are among the seven localities having some annually cropped *secano*). Elsewhere time alone was relied upon to replenish soil nutrients. The upshot of primitive cropping is low yields and these are well attested in the Ensenada *Respuestas*.

It is clear, then, that basic improvements in farming of a type earlier than those associated with mechanisation and chemical fertilising had only begun to be introduced in the south-east in the 1750s. Indeed, the conservatism of the agricultural regime described in the Ensenada *Respuestas* is striking. Maize and kidney beans are the only New World cultigens mentioned. Of the crops associated with the 'Arab agricultural revolution' (Watson 1974), only sugar cane is mentioned as important, and only in one site territory (Nerja) at that. Qanats are also an Arab introduction (Troll 1965), but were not important water sources in the study area. Norias, also of limited importance, may also have been introduced in Islamic times (although water wheels were certainly known to the Romans (White 1970, p. 157)). Apart from these peripheral novelties, 18th-century farming in our study area was much like that of Roman times (White 1970). Indeed, the principal crops (wheat, barley, rye, millet, broad beans, flax, olives, grapes) are all represented by palaeobotanical remains from prehistoric sites in the region.

The contrasts between archaic and modern land uses within our study area will be treated on a site-by-site basis in Chapter 5. One general point is worth stressing now, however. We have seen in the previous chapter that the available excavated evidence suggests that in Copper and Bronze Age times (in the 18th century BC, as it were) much the same animals and plants were exploited by farming communities throughout south-east Spain. In the 18th century AD much the same uniformity prevails. As we have seen, the same crops were exploited throughout the region. Not only that, as Table 3.1 shows, the Totana, Vera and Almería groups of localities (with annual rainfall in the 200–300 mm range), the Guadix and Cúllar-Baza (north-east Granada and northern Almería provinces) groups (with annual rainfall in the 300–400 mm range) and the remaining groups (with annual rainfall above 400 mm) all have yield ratios in the same range. It should not be surprising that the archaic production technology of the 1750s should buffer the effects of the environment more effectively than modern agricultural methods: in a subsistence economy what is most necessary is to attain a minimum level of production. What is interesting is that the adjustment to local conditions needed to achieve that minimum level entailed an adjustment not of the goals of the inhabitants of the arid sector, but in the means to achieve those goals. In the arid sector the desired subsistence pattern was achieved by transforming the landscape by capital investments more extensively than in moist areas. With a more concentrated reliance on irrigation systems, with the construction of *boqueras* and of moisture-retaining terraces, production on the best lands in the arid south-east could match that of moister areas. Our central contention, of course, is that this transformation of a natural landscape into a cultural one, a transformation that is the result of these investments and was fully developed in the 18th century AD, had its beginnings in later prehistoric times.

Notes

1 Many site catchment analyses take as their starting point a systematic survey of a region in order to obtain as complete a sample as possible of all the prehistoric settlements that ever existed within it. Even if the areas to be covered within south-east Spain were limited to the point of making such an approach feasible, a survey-based strategy would face a major technical obstacle: the rarity of temporally diagnostic artifacts in surface collections. As the review of the culture-historical sequence in the previous chapter indicated, decorated ceramics are infrequently and unevenly represented in Copper and Bronze Age collections. Thus, the main type fossils are either metal and other intrinsically valuable items or ritual objects, both artifact categories that are rare in general, very rare in habitation deposits and correspondingly unlikely to be found in surface collections from settlement sites. In the absence of abundantly represented diagnostic types to indicate the age of a site by inspection, test excavations would be required to place the site in the cultural sequence. The financial cost and administrative difficulties of a site survey approach are prohibitive.

2 The area that is irrigated at a particular locality depends, of course, not just on the amount of water and suitable land available, but on the intensity of watering demanded by the crops under cultivation. As the information on 18th-century cropping patterns in the *Catastro de la Ensenada* makes clear, however, the principal crop planted on *regadío* was wheat, which demands relatively little water. Thus, traditional irrigation in Spain is relatively extensive. Except in extremely moist areas, where irrigation is intended for summer crops, the extent of *regadío* within our site territories is not limited by a preference for water-demanding crops.

3 Several factors seem to govern the absence of *boqueras* where they might otherwise be expected. One is the availability of a sufficient supply of irrigation water from more reliable sources. Another is the nature of the lithologies in the *rambla's* catchment. *Boqueras* are mainly found where the primary runoff occurs on schists or conglomerates, but not where it occurs on marls. The quality of the water in the occasional flows off marls may be inferior. Another reason for the absence of *boquera* systems along suitable *ramblas* is, of course, recent rural depopulation. The elderly couple who in August 1977 showed one of us the operation of their *boquera* system along the Rambla de los Rincones, north of Tabernas, will not have successors, and only a few winter flows will suffice to obliterate their disused dams and terraces.

4 Ensenada was dismissed before the survey he had ordered was completed and his tax proposal was, needless to say, scuttled.

L?L

4 Geomorphological investigations

In order to assess the problem of the development of intensive agriculture (and especially irrigation) in later prehistoric south-east Spain by means of site catchment analysis, we must estimate insofar as possible the degree to which the distribution of land (and more particularly soil) has changed within the territories of the sites under study since these were occupied. There are at least two different aspects to the question, each requiring a rather different approach.

First, one may ask if there has been significant loss of soil over the available land area. This is a matter of conventional soil erosion, that is to say, the stripping of the regolith cover from the underlying rock without significant changes in the overall availability of land. We have tackled this problem directly by attempting to estimate the comparative magnitude of soil losses on the various lithologies within our site territories under current climatic conditions. We have assumed that climatic parameters have not changed significantly over the 3–7 millennia since the sites under study were occupied and that the most important variables controlling erosional variability are the nature of the regolith cover and of the slopes within the site territories. The assumption of no significant climatic change is not made lightly. There is no period in Earth's history in which climate was not undergoing some fluctuations and the dry margins are clearly highly susceptible to the effects of such changes. Our view (e.g. Starkel & Thornes 1981) is that fluviatile responses to climatic change are still so poorly understood, even under present regimes, that attempts to assert past climates from localised sedimentary sequences are still too primitive and conflicting to provide a more secure base than the one we have adopted here. Even under the contemporary regimes, it is quite possible to have heavy sedimentation and significant channel incision in adjacent river valleys as a result of changes in intrinsic thresholds at the two sites. It is hard to imagine what trend a future palaeohydrologist would infer from contemporary fluvial activity!

Secondly, one may ask if gully erosion has changed the area available for cultivation. The extension of drainage networks makes land unusable both by increasing channel density and slope and by draining the land more effectively (thereby reducing its water-holding capacity). Our strategy has been to examine selected site territories in which gullying is very extensive for evidence of changes in the channel network pattern and to bring into play theoretical and empirical evidence concerning the development of such networks, so as to account for the evident lack of change in pattern that they exhibit. Soil erosion and gully erosion are not independent of one another, as geomorphologists well know (Schumm 1974), so that, although our interest in each is somewhat separate, we should expect the conditions pertaining to one to satisfy the conditions required by the other.

Finally, in this chapter we attempt to evaluate how much water was available for palaeotechnic irrigation in the various site territories. This is based on an estimation of present-day winter runoff and on the relationship between stream flows and catchment areas established by empirical equations.

Soil erosion

Our attempts to define soil erosion must operate within certain clearly defined limits. The first is that the approach adopted must be satisfied by relatively simple climatic information. Knowledge of recent climatic fluctuations is improving, but for the greater part of the timespan that concerns us we can do little more than hazard the informed guess that annual precipitation totals and the distribution of extreme events would have exhibited the same contrasts over our study area in the past as they do now. Secondly, although we know that land use (especially as it affects vegetation cover) is important in controlling erosion, we do not know (since it is what we seek to discover) what land uses were in later prehistoric times. Even if we did know more about these issues, the third constraint – the spatial scale on which we are operating – would restrict analysis of the effect of vegetation on erosion to a quite general level. Finally, we have to realise that the art of modelling soil erosion processes is itself still only imperfectly developed, especially for semi-arid environments (see, for example, Renard 1980). Consequently we have oriented our approach towards a dynamic model based on physically realistic assumptions concerning underlying causes, a model in which the processes are driven by a set of inputs to operate on a pre-existing set of conditions to produce variations in the response character-istics. Alternative strategies are reviewed in Thornes and Gilman (1983).

A great many dynamic models, varying widely in their degree of complexity, are available in the literature (Kirkby & Morgan 1980). The essential breakpoint in this spectrum is whether the hillslope flows themselves are to be routed (i.e. whether there is to be concern for the character and timing of flows of water and sediment across individually defined hill slopes) or whether the process is to be generalised to a larger area and timescale. We have opted for the second, 'lumped' approach and operate at a scale of a square kilometre or more. We have not been able to assess mass movement effects quantitatively, although it is obviously important within some site territories (see discussion on pp. 64–74). We have also neglected rainsplash because, although it is obviously important in preparing material for transport, the simple models in which the rainsplash effect would be controlled by easily available information (such as rainfall intensities or slope gradients) seem inadequate. Accordingly, at the expense of some inevitable oversimplification, we assume that the capacity and competence of flowing water to remove material is the critical factor in determining overall soil loss.

These considerations have led us to the well known 'Musgrave-type' formula for estimating soil loss:

$$Y = kq^m s^n \tag{4.1}$$

where Y is the sediment yield, q is the overland flow responsible for the yield and s is the tangent of the slope angle over which the flow takes place. The parameter k is a coefficient that, among other things, depends on the character of the material entrained in the flow. The exponents m and n are empirically determined. A widespread literature together with theoretical considerations (see the review by Morgan (1980)) lead to values of 2.0 for m and 1.66 for n. Further discussion of the suitability of this approach for semi-arid environments is contained in Thornes (1976). The coefficient k in the Musgrave equation should incorporate the effects of lithological constraints on the availability of materials for erosion. The ratio of mean particle size to the sorting of sizes in the material to be transported would be a logical way to establish the value of k, since this would express the relative availability of different materials for entrainment by overland flow. Some of the background to this problem is discussed in Thornes (1980) and Kirkby (1980a). For the moment we can do no better than to set k to a constant of 0.02 (following Kirkby (1980b)) and to discuss the characteristics of the regolith and the factors controlling them on a qualitative basis.

Controlled field measurements, theory and qualitative observations indicate that on unrilled slopes there is a rapid increase (over a few metres) of sediment load carried by overland flow to a capacity that remains relatively constant regardless of slope length. The Musgrave equation applied to ungullied slopes therefore takes the form:

$$Y = kp^2 s^{1.66} \tag{4.2}$$

where p is the rainfall excess (i.e. the amount of rainfall in excess of infiltration). For gullied slopes, overland flow is made a function of the area over which discharge is concentrated. For planar slopes this is a direct function of slope length and the Musgrave formula becomes:

$$Y = k(pL)^2 s^{1.66} \tag{4.3}$$

where L is slope length. Two sets of properties influence the above model. The hydrological properties of the materials that make up the slopes determine the excess water production (p). The topographic properties of the slopes determine their lengths and angles. These two sets of properties are now discussed.

We wish to consider both the average annual rate of soil loss and that due to extreme events. For the first, precipitation excess is modelled using the approach of Kirkby (1977), in which annual overland flow (q_{ann}) is given by:

$$q_{ann} = R^{-r_c/r_0} \tag{4.4}$$

where R is the mean annual rainfall, r_c the estimated amount lost to storage and r_0 the mean rainfall per rainy day. The assumption of a simple negative exponential distribution of events is entirely reasonable for this part of Spain (Thornes 1976, Scoging 1976). For bare (i.e. unvegetated) slopes, r_c is estimated by the procedures outlined a little later. For vegetated slopes, the amount lost to storage is obtained from:

$$r_c = 100(E_a/E_p)^{0.5} \tag{4.5}$$

where E_a is the actual evapotranspiration and E_p the potential evapotranspiration. As the actual annual evapotranspiration and the potential become equal (i.e. as vegetation becomes more dense), storage approaches 100. Both equations 4.4 and 4.5 assume that successive rainfall events are independent. This is not strictly true in winter in south-east Spain, but on the whole there is little antecedent moisture.

The hydrological model for extreme storm events derives from the work of Scoging and Thornes (1980). Infiltration is predicted from:

$$F_t = A + B/t \tag{4.6}$$

where F_t is the infiltration rate at time t, A is the final infiltrability of the soil in the standard ring infiltrometer test and B is the gradient of the infiltration curve through time. In our model (Fig. 4.1), if the rainfall intensity exceeds the infiltration capabilities of a soil, excess (Hortonian) overland flow occurs (although some water will infiltrate into storage). Even if rainfall intensity is low or the soil has high infiltration properties, or both, overland flow will occur as storage fills, i.e. as the soil becomes saturated. A digital simulation program for this process is presented in Thornes and Gilman (1983) (Fig. 4.1).

Both the extreme-event (Scoging–Thornes) model and the annual (Kirkby) model for bare slopes require that one estimates a typical storage volume for the soil or lithological type whose erosion potential is being assessed. This is obtained by integrating the area under the infiltration curve (see Fig. 4.2) between the values for $t = 1$ min and $F_t = A$ (the final infiltrability). The operation of the storm-event storage model is illustrated in Figure 4.3. Here the rainfall comes in two separate, well defined events. In the first storm, rapid infiltration takes place leading to an increase in the storage volume until storage capacity is reached, after which infiltration ceases and overland flow increases. In the second storm, storage is almost full and overland flow mirrors rainfall. Runoff estimated in this way is then used as p in equations 4.2 and 4.3.

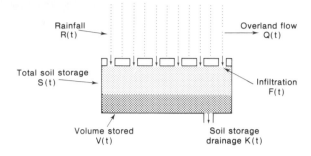

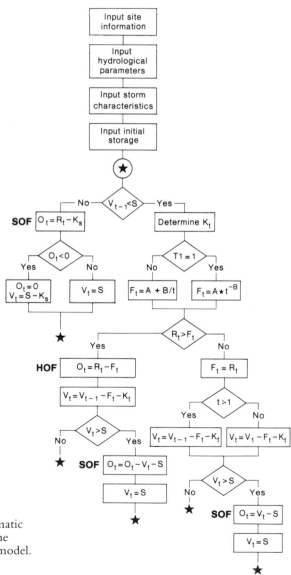

Figure 4.1 Schematic representation of the Scoging–Thornes model.

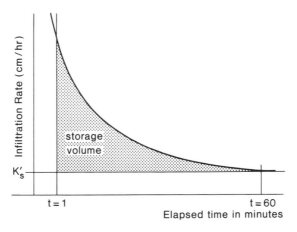

Figure 4.2 Infiltration curve defining storage volume.

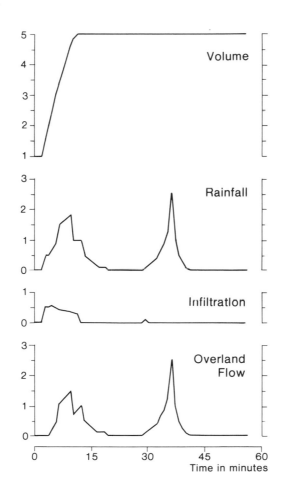

Figure 4.3 Simulated storm sequences.

Given that vegetation cover in south-east Spain is often sparse and that organic soils are often poorly developed, lithology and relief are particularly significant determinants of erosion. Accordingly, lithological maps were prepared for each site territory or intersecting set of site territories using the 1 : 50 000 topographic maps as a base and integrating field-checked information from air photographs and from the 1 : 50 000 and 1 : 200 000 geological maps published by IGME. These maps were used to stratify the sampling schemes by which other data were collected.

The lithologies are grouped under eight major headings. *Limestones* very largely comprise metamorphosed massive limestones, in places strongly dolomitised, and usually juxtaposed with two other hard-rock groups: *mica–schists* and mixed *metamorphics* (a residual category including quartzites, slates, granulites and so on). Throughout the area the intensively folded mica–schists form the dominant constituents of the mountain areas. More detailed analysis is contained in Thornes (1976) but it is worth noting that they weather easily and break down into platy angular fragments. In extreme cases they form impermeable debris surfaces but more usually they break down to give a thick and relatively porous regolith. Within the mixed metamorphics, the dominant type is a block brownish-coloured schist often accompanied by large numbers of quartz bands. During the middle and later Tertiary these lithologies were weathered and eroded to produce the basal *conglomerates* that occur around the margins of the inland and coastal basins. The character of these conglomerates is heavily conditioned by the source materials. Where they are formed of mica–schists with a relatively poor calcareous cement, they break up readily. Elsewhere they form strong ridges flanking the mountains. During the Pliocene, extensive spreads of marginal conglomerates were built up on the pediments formed in the basins, often over the underlying slightly folded Lower Miocene sediments. Where these have been strongly cemented, in Pliocene, Quaternary and Recent times, they are described here as *calichified conglomerates*. During the Lower and Upper Miocene, *Marls* were deposited throughout the interior basins, the facies varying according to position within the basin. Marginal facies tend to be more sandy whilst towards the centre of inland basins the marls are strongly gypsiferous or saliniferous. These marls are dominantly of silts and clays and puddle easily and quickly in heavy rainfall as a result of swelling; conversely they harden, crack and are subject to crusting when dry. Between the Lower and Upper Miocene some basins experienced tectonic activity and the latter, which are relatively little flexured, lie unconformably on the former. *Chalk*, a soft limestone with shear strengths higher than marls but lower than crystalline and metamorphosed limestones, occurs as folded but little altered deposits in the northern and western sectors of our study area. Finally, near the Mediterranean there are small areas of lava and ash which we group together as *volcanics*.

Within this stratification and consistent with a broad spatial coverage of the whole study area, some 40 locations were chosen at random in order to obtain infiltration measurements and bulk-density samples for each of the above lithologies. At each site four infiltration tests were carried out and bulk-density samples extracted from unvegetated, level tracts. After the initial series of 160 tests were completed, a further 60 were carried out in order to reduce the variance within certain lithological groups, the 15 locations again being chosen at random.

Topographic information was obtained by field measurements, from maps and from air photographs. Mean slope was measured from the $1:50\,000$ topographic maps using the contour intersection method at each of 25 cells $(1\ km^2)$ within each lithology in each of the site territories. Slope lengths were measured from air photographs using the same sample of locations. Both of these have been checked and calibrated against a programme of field measurements. Table 4.1 presents these measures.

Mean annual and monthly rainfall totals are available for many stations throughout south-east Spain, but information on the number of rainy days, like data on potential evapotranspiration (E_p in equation 4.5), are only available for provincial capitals. The E_p data are Penman values and for particular site territories they were either taken from the nearest provincial capitals or esti-mated from isolines (Elías Castillo & Giménez Ortiz 1965). Values for actual evapotranspiration (E_a in equation 4.5) are not published and were estimated from the difference between rainfall and the measured runoff at gauging stations in the river basins within which our site territories fall. This may be a significant source of error because the difference between rainfall and runoff is the result of more than just evapotranspiration. In particular, the abstraction of water which is extensively applied and reapplied for irrigation tends to raise our calculated values for E_a, and thereby inflates r_c in equation 4.5, causing soil storage to be underestimated and the amount of vegetation to be overestimated. This error should make our assessment of erosion under vegetated conditions closer to the situation that would have obtained over most of the past seven millennia when the vegetation of south-east Spain had not yet been degraded to its current level of sparseness.

The results of this work take the form of a set of annual and storm-event erosion values for areas within each site territory. These estimates are based on the description of lithologies and slopes within site territories, on the infor-mation about the hydrological characteristics of the various lithologies obtained from region-wide infiltration and bulk-density measurements and on climatic variables. The hydrological properties of the eight lithologies are indicated in Table 4.2. There are two well defined groups: the chalks and marls, on the one hand, and the mica–schists, limestones, conglomerates, calichified conglomer-ates and volcanics, on the other. The mixed metamorphics occupy an inter-mediate position. The marls and chalks have low storage volumes, because they have mostly finer grain sizes and lower overall porosities. This agrees with the results of Bork and Rohdenburg (1981), who carried out a detailed analysis of similar lithological groups near Zurgena (Almería). All the lithologies have high

Table 4.1 Derived data on slope lengths and on mean gradients.

(a) Slope lengths (m)

	L		MS	L/MS	MM	C		CC	M					CH	V
	1	2				1	2		1	2	3	4	5		
Almoloya		104							204	37					
Campico/Bastida		58		135		91		54	144	33	71	71			
Ceñuela															58
Mazarrón sites		119	100		69	99			40	148	129				
Ambrosio		149	58			100								136	
Canteras					65			144						135	
Virgen		183	100						102	68					
Malagón		183	74						60						
Picacho			49			55									
Oficio		102	62		123	43			29	62	99				
Vera basin sites					92	63									
Gatas			117	134	69				69						
Tabernas			118	97			54		36	48	41				
Enmedio			180	120		56	34		35						
Millares		133				51	157	256							
Barranquete								59		43					125
Culantrillo												111	66		
Guadix–Cardela		170						147	109					304	
Guadix–Negro									169	45	12			247	
Encina		268		265		168		193	84						
Nerja		148	84			187								172	
Alhama		279				107								126	
Montefrío		223				145								158	
Zuheros		227												313	

(b) Mean gradients (%)

	L 1	L 2	MS	L/MS	MM	C 1	C 2	CC	M 1	M 2	M 3	M 4	M 5	CH	V
Almoloya		30.8						6.0	8.5	20.3					
Campico		35.2				18.9		18.3	12.2	29.6	22.7				
Ceñuela				31.9								48.5			23.0
Mazarrón sites		17.2	37.0		30.9			7.0	34.7	7.5					
Ambrosio		27.3				20.1					24.8			19.6	
Canteras			21.9		25.9	15.5		24.7	11.8	21.6				20.1	
Virgen	24.8		10.9					5.5	19.0	3.4					
Malagón		36.1	25.5					7.4							
Picacho			10.0			20.3									
Oficio		49.0	29.6		41.9	20.9		15.0	22.1	15.8					
Vera basin sites		27.9			29.1	33.0		9.0			9.4				
Gatas			39.5	39.3		34.8	11.9		23.6						
Tabernas			33.8	33.8	32.4		22.2		37.4	24.5					
Enmedio			43.5	41.8			23.0		29.0		26.4				
Millares	35.0					30.0	5.6	35.0							
Barranquete								13.4		34.3					35.0
Culantrillo								6.6				22.2	28.4		
Guadix–Cardela		19.6						9.7	24.0					14.8 13.7	
Guadix–Negro		25.8				34.5		5.2 7.6	22.9	28.4	24.6				
Encina	47.3			42.7		34.8		19.9 3.0	31.9						
Nerja		22.4	43.6			26.1		10.8							
Alhama			31.2					15.5						18.0	
Montefrío		31.2												30.4 19.5	
Zuheros		32.7				24.1								17.0	

L = Limestone C = conglomerate MS = mica-schist CC = calichified conglomerate MM = mixed metamorphics M = marls CH = chalk
V = volcanics

Table 4.2   Soil storage volumes and parameters for runoff model.

Lithology	CH	M	MS	MM	L	C	CC	V
mean storage (mm)	24.7	28.5	56.5	38.6	47.3	56.4	59.9	57.2
deviation storage	16.0	29.8	66.8	22.7	33.5	76.2	54.2	26.7
final infiltrability	0.192	0.203	0.433	0.467	0.417	0.273	0.535	0.381
infiltration curve gradient	0.458	0.639	0.984	0.809	0.915	0.928	1.133	1.120
number of observations	38	59	41	18	28	30	8	7

coefficients of variation. This indicates that within any one lithology we are dealing with a very wide spectrum of storage conditions. The final infiltrabilities are too large to represent the natural hydraulic conductivities and simply reflect the shortcomings of the infiltrometer method. In the model we have assumed the conductivities to be negligibly small, i.e. they are at the dry limit of their soil moisture range. These final infiltrabilities are not used in the estimation of soil storage values.

Table 4.3 summarises the relevant rainfall data for the four provincial capitals within our study area, and indicates typical overland flows and sediment yields computed according to the annual (Kirkby) model, using the storage values from Table 4.2 and assuming that there is complete lack of vegetation cover. The greatest excesses are produced on the chalks and marls of the northern and western portions of our study area, near Granada. This reflects a combination of high rainfall, moderate intensities (large number of rainy days) and low storage. By contrast, the figures for Almería are relatively small. Conglomerates and calichified conglomerates, volcanics and mica–schists all have low relative erosion rates. This table essentially reflects the combination of climatic and storage parameters at work in the model on an annual, regular basis, the lengths and angles of slopes having been held constant.

Table 4.4 shows the relative magnitudes of erosion for the annual (Kirkby) model under vegetated conditions. The extremes represent the contrast between the extremely dry site territories of the southeastern coastal areas and the moister territories of the northwestern uplands. There is a sharp reduction in overland flow volumes and erosion amounts in comparison with the volumes and amounts on bare slopes and there is a strong difference between rilled and unrilled topographies. Table 4.5 shows that the excess water production using the storm-event (Scoging–Thornes) model is very different on different lithologies and that the response is very different depending on the intensity of the storms. For the lower-intensity storm ($60 \, \text{mm h}^{-1}$), the ratio of the highest to the lowest amounts of runoff is 392 : 1, while for the higher-intensity storm ($120 \, \text{mm h}^{-1}$) it is only 1.6 : 1.

Estimates of erosion in tonne km^{-2} yield the following summary results:

(a)   In the annual (Kirkby) model, on lithologies with low storage capabilities (marls and chalks), unvegetated gullied slopes would produce 50 to 5000 tonne $km^{-2} yr^{-1}$. Under similar conditions, high-storage lithologies produce 0.005 to 5 tonne $km^{-2} yr^{-1}$.

(b)   In the annual (Kirkby) model, vegetated ungullied slopes would produce 0 to 0.05 tonne $km^{-2} yr^{-1}$.

(c)   During a 60 mm storm event, the Scoging–Thornes model predicts losses of 5000 to 500 000 tonne km^{-2} on low-storage lithologies with bare gullied slopes and of 50 to 5000 tonne km^{-2} on high-storage lithologies and similar slopes.

(d)   During a 60 mm storm, 5 to 500 tonne km^{-2} would be lost on low-storage lithologies with vegetated gullied slopes, and 0.5 to 50 tonne km^{-2} would be lost under similar conditions on high-storage lithologies.

Only the results for a 60 mm storm on low-storage lithologies and bare gullied slopes are unrealistic. Apart from that high estimate, other results fall within the

Table 4.3 Relevant rainfall data for four provincial capitals, and typical overland flows and sediment yields computed according to the annual (Kirkby) model, using the storage values from Table 4.2.

(a)   Summary rainfall data (1934–60)

	Annual average (mm)	Days > 0.1 mm	Average rainfall per rainy day
Almería	233	42	5.547
Granada	473	77	6.142
Malaga	474	56	8.464
Murcia	304	47	6.46

(b) Overland flow ($l yr^{-1}$) and relative sediment yield (in brackets) for a 20 m long, 10° rilled bare slope on different lithologies. Erosion coefficient (k in equation 4.1) is set at 0.02. Annual figures based on Kirkby (1977); the model and storage volumes are described in the text

	L	MS	MM	C	CC	M	CH	V
Almería	0.92	0.18	4.0	0.18	0.095	27.0	NA	0.16
	(0.000 95)	(0.000 035)	(0.02)	(0.000 035)	(0.000 010)	(0.84)		(0.000 027)
Granada	4.3	0.907	18	0.97	55	91	170	NA
	(0.021)	(0.0011)	(0.34)	(0.0011)	(0.000 34)	(9.3)	(32.3)	
Malaga	35.0	12.0	NA	12	8.0	NA	NA	NA
	(1.4)	(0.2)		(0.2)	(0.08)			
Murcia	4.0	1	15	1	0.6	74	NA	1.0
	(0.018)	(0.0011)	(0.27)	(0.0011)	(0.000 37)	(6.17)		(0.001)

NA = not applicable.

Table 4.4 Annual overland flow and relative sediment yields delivered from rilled and unrilled 20 m, 10° vegetated slopes within site territories. $r_c = 100(E_a/E_p)^{0.5}$ using rainfall data from the most appropriate provincial capitals and evapotranspiration data derived from rainfall and from discharge measured at local stream gauging stations.

Site territories	Capitals	r_c	Overland flow (l yr^{-1})	Rilled slopes ($\times 10^{-4}$)	Unrilled slopes ($\times 10^{-6}$)
Vera basin sites, Gatas, El Oficio, Los Millares, Enmedio, El Barranquete	Almería	46	1.16	15	3.8
Tabernas	Almería	47	0.97	10	2.6
Almoloya	Murcia	51	2.28	58	14
Virgen	Granada	51	2.34	63	14
Mazarrón sites	Murcia	53	1.43	23	5.8
Campico/Bastida	Murcia	54	1.67	31	7.9
Ambrosio, Canteras	Granada	62	0.39	2	0.42
Culantrillo, Guadix sites	Almería	63	0.054	33	0.0083
Nerja	Malaga	64	0.49	270	4.0
Alhama, El Picacho	Granada	64	0.28	8.9	0.22
Malagón, Zuheros	Granada	65	0.24	0.61	1.4
Laborcillas, Montefrío	Granada	69	0.13	0.18	0.043
Encina	Granada	77	0.034	0.013	0.0033

Table 4.5 Estimated excess water production (mm) from 1 h storm with $K_t=0$ using the storm-event (Scoging–Thornes) model. K_t is the outflow from the base of the soil profile.

	Storm intensity	
	60 mm h^{-1}	120 mm h^{-1}
limestone (L)	12.7	72.7
mica–schist (MS)	3.5	63.5
mixed metamorphics (MM)	21.4	81.4
conglomerates (C)	3.6	63.6
calichified conglomerates (CC)	0.09	60.1
marls (M)	31.65	91.5
chalk (CH)	35.3	95.3
volcanics (V)	2.8	62.8

ranges reported by the literature for similar environments. Thus, the figure of 380 tonne $km^{-2}yr^{-1}$ given by Holeman (1968) for the Colorado River basin is comparable to the annual model for unvegetated slopes. The rates quoted by Young (1974) for surface wash in environments comparable to those of south-east Spain are 1000 tonne $km^{-2}yr^{-1}$ (from Schumm 1964) and 450 tonne $km^{-2}yr^{-1}$ (from Campbell 1970). The expected sediment yields for climatic conditions like those of our study area predicted by the Langbein and Schumm (1958) curve range from 200 to 400 tonne $km^{-2}yr^{-1}$. For the Guadix basin, estimates of sediment yield using the models of Fournier (1960), Carson and Kirkby (1972) and Jensen and Painter (1974) cluster around 25 tonne $km^{-2}yr^{-1}$. Measured rates based on the very limited data on suspended-sediment yields available from several river gauging stations in the region show values of about 16 tonne $km^{-2}yr^{-1}$, with a range between 7 and 72. One of these stations is located in the Culantrillo site territory where the annual model predicts that erosion rates for marls will range from 0.00005 tonne $km^{-2}yr^{-1}$ on vegetated ungullied slopes to 500 tonne $km^{-2}yr^{-1}$ on bare gullied slopes. Since only a little over half the Culantrillo territory consists of marls and only small areas of the marls are both unvegetated and gullied, the predictions of our models are of a similar order of magnitude to actual sediment yields.

All the rates calculated from the various empirical indices, from the limited available observations and from the 'vegetated' models outlined above indicate quite low rates of erosion for low-magnitude, high-frequency events in the south-east of Spain. This is consistent with the recently held general belief that in semi-arid environments virtually all the work on the landscape is done in extreme events. Only in highly localised, heavily gullied settings or under high-magnitude, low-frequency events do the rates reach significant proportions. In the great 1973 flood (with a recurrence of more than 500 years), Torre (1973) estimated ground losses of between 56 and 420 mm on mica–schists in the Alpujarras, the mean value of 41 locations being 151 mm. The values for mica–schists in the Nerja area for the 60 mm storm model are about 440 mm on gullied slopes. Although the model appears to overestimate the erosion rate, some of the discrepancies may be accounted for by the non-universality of gullying, on the one hand, and, on the other hand, by the steepness of slopes in the Nerja site territory (at 48%, much steeper than those in the Alpujarras). We reiterate the point made earlier: extreme cases of erosion are associated with intensive gully development on low-storage lithologies. Other rates are generally low and indicate only moderate amounts of erosion, mainly because of the relative paucity of runoff. This result is contrary to the expectations we held before our work and contrary to the first impression created by the visual impact of the landscape, and we shall return to it. First, however, we must address the question of the nature and age of gully growth in the region.

Studies of individual site settings

In the previous section we assessed the potential erosion losses on the various lithologies within the site territories under study. This analysis indicates that the areas that might be expected to have suffered the highest erosional losses would be the marls. Here the combination of a fairly susceptible lithology with extremely low storage and correspondingly high runoff potential favours the maximum possible erosion. The typical badlands morphology of much of the marls – high drainage densities, steep slopes, often with little vegetation cover and extensive gullying – supports the notion that erosion on low-storage lithologies has been catastrophic. It is surprising, therefore, to find reasonably intact archaeological sites in these areas, with *in situ* material 3500 to 6000 years old. The location of these sites along ridge tops and on river bluffs leaves little doubt that, although some erosion has taken place since they were occupied, the gross morphology of the landscape can have changed very little. In order to investigate this further, detailed studies were carried out in the vicinity of six of these sites. Three of them, Cerro del Gallo, Cuesta del Negro and El Culantrillo, are located in the vast badlands of the Guadix basin; the other three, La Gerundia, El Argar and El Gárcel, are located near Antas in the Vera basin.

At each site, geomorphological maps (Figs 4.5, 4.6, 4.8 & 4.10) were prepared at a scale of *ca*. 1 : 2500 in order to illustrate the relationship between the archaeological deposits and the landforms. At the three Guadix basin sites, topographical maps were also constructed using accurately surveyed spot heights interpolated with the aid of air photographs. In the geomorphological maps, symbols based on the system of Savigear (1965) represent the form of the land surface, with no implications regarding its formation or development. Breaks of slope were mapped first and identified as either sharp or smooth and either convex or concave. Ridge tops (always convex) were mapped using a slightly different symbol. Steep free faces and gully backwalls were also separately mapped since they constitute a distinctive and important element within the landscape. Other symbols, based in part on those of Cooke and Doornkamp (1974), distinguish various erosional processes (erosion by flowing water, especially on hill slopes) and various types of mass movement. Surface materials were also mapped to distinguish between erosional and depositional surfaces. River terraces and pediments are also identified.

Guadix basin sites   The three sites in our sample that are located in the Guadix area (Fig. 4.4) were selected for detailed study because that region shows some of the most intensive erosional topography in Spain and, indeed, the world. It is widely assumed that rates of erosion in the Guadix badlands are exceptionally high. As a result, here, if anywhere, there should have been appreciable change in the distribution of land available for agriculture.

The Tertiary basin to the north of the city of Guadix lies between the Sierra Nevada to the south, the Sierra Harana to the north-west and the Sierra de Gor

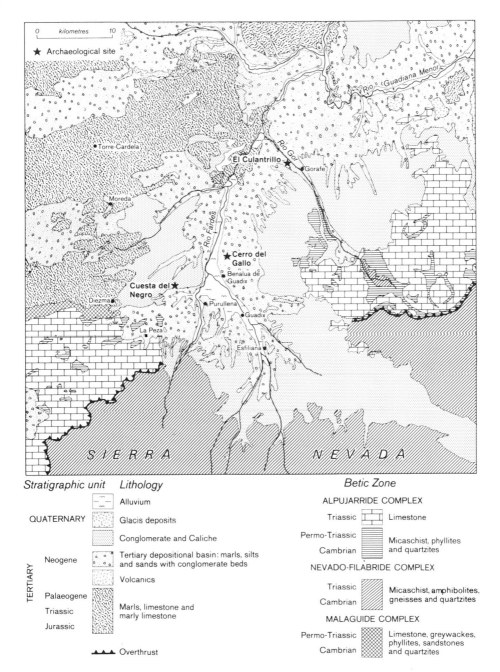

Figure 4.4 Geological map of the Guadix basin.

to the east (Fig. 4.4). The basin fill comprises marls and sands with conglomerate beds. Progressive subsidence has allowed the Tertiary fill to reach a thickness of several hundred metres (Vera 1970). The basin fill is capped by extensive caliche deposits presumed to be of Quaternary age. The long-term denudational history of the basin has been discussed by Birot and Solé Sabaris (1959), who conclude that it was closed until the breaching of the northern divide by the Guadiana Menor River in the upper Tertiary. This is thought to have initiated the wave of erosion that dissected the Tertiary basin. Three types of terrain can be distinguished within the basin as a whole:

(a) the hills and mountains of the Betic fold system
(b) the gently sloping upper surface of the Tertiary fill, which passes marginally onto pediplains cut across folded limestones and metamorphic rocks, and is extensively calichified
(c) the marl badlands formed by the dissection of the Tertiary fill

Drainage densities in this area are everywhere very high, but the form of the slopes varies from the escarpment edge (where the available relief is high and near-vertical free faces are the dominant shape form), to the major channels (where the relief becomes progressively more subdued and the slopes more convex), to the river valleys (where conical marl hills emerge from the alluvium). The three sites are located in a full range of these environments. Cuesta del Negro is near the edge of the escarpment, El Culantrillo in the middle of the badlands and Cerro del Gallo near the valley axis.

Rainfall within the Guadix basin is about 300 mm yr^{-1}, but it rises rapidly to 500 mm or more on the edges. Temperatures show large diurnal and seasonal ranges of about 25°C, and summer evaporation rates are very high. Climatic data suggest that some 17.8% of the rainfall appears as runoff (mainly in winter), a figure in reasonable agreement with the records from gauging stations (Negratín, 14.6%; Posito, 17.1%). 'Effective' rainfall for the basin edges is about 30% of the total. Rainfall intensities can be crudely estimated for stations near each of the archaeological sites. For a 30 min storm with a 2.33 year return rate, they are about 18 to 20 mm h^{-1}, and for a 100 year return storm about 90 to 150 mm h^{-1} (ICONA 1979). Using the techniques outlined earlier, the estimated volumetric storage of the marls is about 28 mm and of the calichified pediment about 58 mm. This suggests that saturated overland flows may occur, at least sporadically, most winters. Stream sediment load figures are, as we have noted on p. 61, low, the dominant transport mode being by solution (which is about eight times the suspended–load transport).

Cuesta del Negro   The site (Fig. 4.5) lies on a long spur descending from the flat plain east of Diezma down to the Fardes River. The plain itself, with thick caliche horizons at its surface, represents the almost unbroken top of the Tertiary fill of the basin. The surface is diachronous and impossible to date.

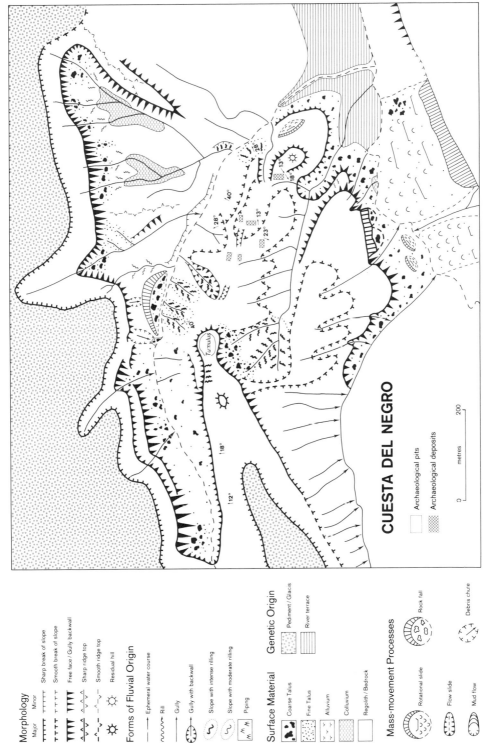

Morphology

Major   Minor

┬┬┬┬   ┬┬┬┬   Sharp break of slope

┬┬┬┬   ┬┬┬┬   Smooth break of slope

▜▜▜▜   ▜▜▜▜   Free face / Gully backwall

△△△   ⌃⌃⌃   Sharp ridge top

‿⌃‿   ‿⌃‿   Smooth ridge top

☼   Residual hill

Forms of Fluvial Origin

——————   Ephemeral water course

∿∿∿   Rill

〰〰   Gully

⌒⌒⌒   Gully with backwall

ى   Slope with intense rilling

ى   Slope with moderate rilling

ʍ ʍ ʍ   Piping

Surface Material   Genetic Origin

Coarse Talus

Fine Talus

Alluvium

Colluvium

Regolith / Bedrock

Pediment / Glacis

River terrace

Mass-movement Processes

Rotational slide

Rock fall

Flow slide

Debris chute

Mud flow

CUESTA DEL NEGRO

☐ Archaeological pits

▨ Archaeological deposits

0   metres   200

Figure 4.5 Geomorphological map of Cuesta del Negro.

Figure 4.6   Geomorphological map of El Culantrillo.

Shallow depressions in the plain lead to the escarpment edge, where the drainage lines are controlled in their descent to the Fardes by the many sandstone and conglomerate lenses found in the marl series. The drainage pattern at the edge of the plain is dominated by those channels that have captured some of the drainage on the upper surface and hence have obtained a competitive advantage (cf. Faulkner 1976).

   The site itself has three distinct parts: a large mound of settlement debris at the top of the spur ('tumulus' on Fig. 4.5), an upper excavated area and a lower excavated area. The upper area is on a rounded knoll with steep slopes which to the south have *in situ* structures. The lower area is a shallow embayment crossed by a depression with house structures on either side. Steep gullies and evident recent erosion occur on this, the southern side of the slope. Cuesta del Negro was excavated in 1971–72 by the Department of Prehistory, University of Granada, and the materials from site A have been published (Molina González &

Pareja López 1975). There are two main phases of occupation, Argaric and Late Bronze Age. The large mound at the head of the spur yielded Argaric remains (Carrasco Rus, personal communication).

The remaining archaeological debris is in places over 2 m thick and exhibits structures that run parallel to the slope. Although some materials have moved down hill, the *in situ* structures and the distribution of remains (such as the position of the tumulus) show that the overall shape of the spur and its superficial deposits have changed very little since Argaric times, some 3500 years ago. The main changes have evidently been in the headward extension of

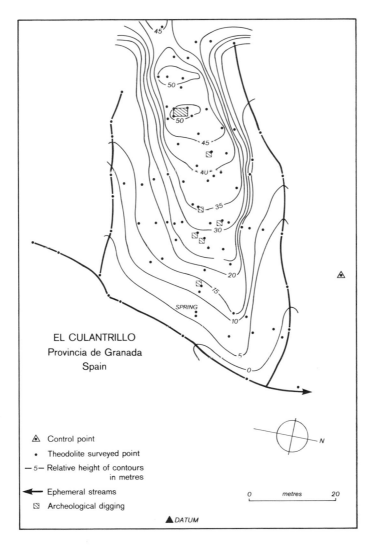

Figure 4.7 Contour map of El Culantrillo.

some south-facing gullies, mainly along the line of a road up the spur, which was used until the 1930s and is now significantly dissected.

The two streams adjacent to the site have well developed alluvial fills, now incised to a depth of about 3 m. The upper surface of the fill continues on as a river terrace to the streams' junction with the River Fardes. The fill consists of buff-coloured silts with a slightly coarser mean grain size than the marls forming the bedrock. Dating of the terraces has not been carried out. They may represent sustained, slow aggradation or a single season of heavy storm deposition that was subsequently incised.

El Culantrillo   El Culantrillo (Figs 4.6 & 4.7) north-west of Gorafe, occupies an intermediate position between the escarpment edge of the dissected infill and the River Gor. The bedrock is marked by strong sandstone lenses which separate thicker bands of marls. The marls are more highly cemented and the sandstone bands further apart than at Cuesta del Negro. As a result the bedrock can sustain deep canyons with vertical walls 15 to 20 m high. The site itself (Fig. 4.7) is a broad interfluve on either side of which streams have cut deep V-shaped notches which rise to near vertical sandstone cliffs. The site is separated from the spur above it by a low col.

The main dating points at the site are provided by a dozen Argaric burials excavated by García Sánchez (1963) (see p. 137 below for discussion of the dating evidence). These demonstrate an Argaric occupation between 4000 and 3500 years ago. The burials, clearly *in situ*, extend along the entire slope of the spur. Tomb 1, which yielded three chalices, is particularly important: it is located on the steep south-east slope of the spur, below the point where the slope dips sharply towards the stream below; since the tomb can only have been dug into an existing slope, it provides a *terminus ante quem* for the general configuration of the spur.

The principal stream at the foot of the El Culantrillo spur has a small terrace and evidence of slight alluvial filling followed by entrenchment. The stream passes through a small gap before joining the Gor. The river has a strongly developed terrace 6 m above its bed. The terrace can be easily traced up and down stream. At the junction of the stream draining the site and the River Gor, however, both channels cut into folded and steeply dipping bedrock. This suggests that while there was some incision during or before the site's occupation, there has been little or no change since. As at Cuesta del Negro, the bases of the marl cliffs near the site are buried in talus; this suggests that mass movement is one of the main processes generating material for the alluvium.

South of El Culantrillo, a large series of megalithic tombs stretch along both sides of the Gor canyon (García Sánchez & Spahni 1959). Typologically datable grave goods are scarce, but the tombs' contents indicate use in Copper Age times, as much as 5000 years ago. Many of the 198 tombs are located along the edge of the escarpment, an apparently intentional alignment which suggests that the upper parts of the steep (30° and above) canyon slopes have remained stationary for five millennia. This is confirmed by the presence of megaliths on the slopes immediately below the caliche edge of the escarpment. The Sabina 14 and 15 tombs, 750 m south of the site, for example, are located on slopes of 27° to 32°. The morphology here is complex, but the stability of the escarpment since later prehistoric times cannot be doubted.

Cerro del Gallo   Cerro del Gallo (Figs 4.8 & 4.9) is located near the centre of the Guadix basin at the junction of the San Torcuato and Chamarro *ramblas*, which cut through the marl badlands to the Fardes River. The site occupies over 2 ha of the broad interfluve running east–west between the *ramblas*. The lithologies here are largely marls and silty clays. Higher surrounding interfluves, such as those

Figure 4.8   Geomorphological map of Cerro del Gallo.

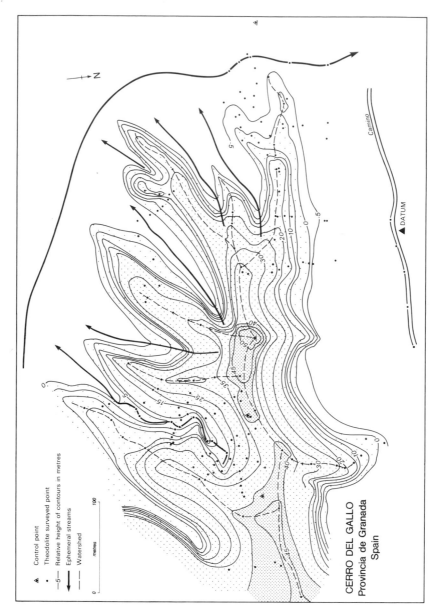

Figure 4.9 Contour map of Cerro del Gallo.

CERRO DEL GALLO
Provincia de Granada
Spain

▲ Control point
• Theodolite surveyed point
—5— Relative height of contours in metres
↓ Ephemeral streams
--- Watershed

metres
0   100

beyond the Chamorro to the south, are capped with calichified conglomerates. On the site itself, however, materials are fine grained.

At the site itself and throughout its vicinity there is a marked contrast between north- and south-facing slopes. On the south-facing slopes there is little vegetation cover and the slopes are strongly gullied. The north-facing slopes have nearly complete grass cover and an organic soil, and show almost no evidence of surface erosion. These slopes are steep because of arcuate failures at the base of the slope. This contrast has been noted in other semi-arid areas and is attributable to variations in hydrological budget and runoff due to microclimate (Thornes 1982).

The foot slopes of the steep spurs surrounding the site show well developed, gently sloping (about 9°) glacis. These extend laterally into the gullies that penetrate the south- and southwest-facing slopes and eventually merge with the fans from these gullies, passing without a sharp break onto the alluvial fill of the *ramblas*. There is a striking parallel here with the two earlier sites in that all three are above terraced streams with minor incisions into the alluvial fill.

The archaeological deposit occurs along the interfluve and on the generally dissected slopes to the south, with none being found on the ungullied northern slope. No full excavation of the site has been carried out, but the description of artifacts found here makes it clear that it is of Argaric age (see pp. 137–8). As the geomorphological map (Fig. 4.8) clearly indicates, the archaeological deposit is being eroded away in many places as the generally smooth concave embayments are dissected by the gully systems. Many of the gullies are very deep (up to 5 m) with steep back- and sidewalls, and erosion of these slopes is clearly progressing by the headward extension of these gully networks rather than by a lowering of the surface as a whole.

Notwithstanding the degree of rilling and gullying, a large area of archaeological material remains evident on the site and in places is 2–3 m thick. As the topographic map (Fig. 4.9) shows, material is found on steep side slopes as well as on interfluves. At the point indicated by an asterisk in Figure 4.9, the intact mouth of a pottery vessel was observed, exposed by the slight incision of a rill. This was presumed to be *in situ*, since transport down the steep slope by the rill would almost certainly have broken the rim of the vessel. This, too, implies that the gully configuration at Cerro del Gallo has been fairly stable over the 3500 years since the site's occupation.

Vera basin sites   The sites of El Gárcel, La Gerundia and El Argar (Fig. 4.10) are located in close proximity to one another on river bluffs on the left bank of the River Antas opposite the town of the same name near the centre of the Vera basin in coastal Almería province. The basin is filled with sedimentary deposits of Tertiary age and is bounded to the north, west and east by the faulted margins of mountain chains of the Betic system (Völk 1967). The predominant lithology within the basin is marl, which has been overlaid in places along the margins by conglomerates. These are still intact around the basin margins where they abut

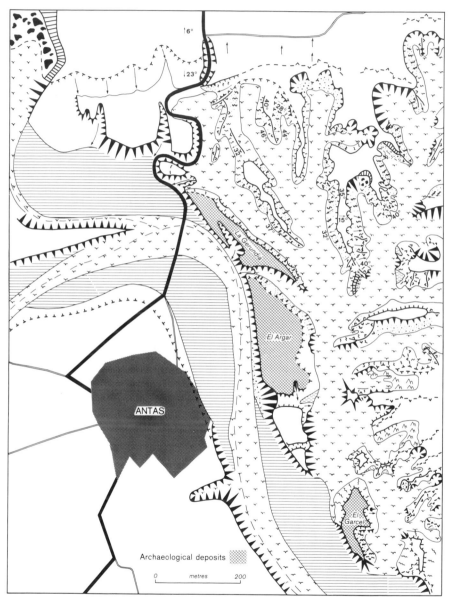

Figure 4.10 Geomorphological map of El Argar, La Gerundia and El Gárcel.

against the mountains, but have been breached by the drainage systems of the Rivers Almanzora, Antas and Aguas.

Towards the centre of the basin this conglomerate has been largely removed and remains only in small patches capping residual hills. Elsewhere the landscape is dominated by marl slopes, sometimes intensely dissected to form badlands. Near the site the Lower Miocene marls and conglomerates are steeply folded into monoclinal ridges but the Upper Miocene, Pliocene and Quaternary deposits are less deformed. The Upper Miocene marls here are fine textured and with poorly developed bedding characteristic of deposition in relatively still water. To the south of the site is a well developed escarpment of Pliocene conglomerates (e.g. Völk 1967) which sheds coarse debris to the north towards the Vera–Huercal Overa road. These colluvial materials are heavily calichified.

The south- and southeastern-facing scarp and glacis are well defined, the latter forming a well developed and probably diachronous surface truncated towards the axis of the depression by the River Antas and dissected by a dense network of gullies cut into the marl glacis. The sites (Fig. 4.10) are placed on the glacis between the Antas and the ridge of uplifted marls to the north-east in the area of deep dissection. Elsewhere in this part of the basin the marls have a very subdued relief with smooth convexo-concave slopes. The badlands near the sites have steep-walled flat-floored gullies whose slopes become more gentle towards the Antas. The steep faces at the head of the *ramblas* may exceed 15 m in height and are dominated by piping and mass movement. Towards the Antas, slopes range from 25° to 40° and are characterised by rilling and slope wash. At the mouths of the gullies their alluvium grades into a terrace a few metres above the contemporary bed of the River Antas.

The ridge tops on which the sites lie are surrounded on all sides by steep slopes showing clear evidence of rilling and mass movement. The sides bordering the stream are near-vertical and are clearly being trimmed at the base by the Rio Antas. The sites of La Gerundia and El Argar are separated by a divide formed by the headwards erosion of a steep gully draining into the Antas. The sites of El Argar and El Gárcel are separated by the mouth of the main *rambla* of the badland drainage system. Each site contains distinct archaeological assemblages belonging to different phases of the prehistoric sequence. The archaeological evidence, excavated by Siret and Siret (1887), is reviewed on p. 105. El Gárcel dates to the Late Neolithic and/or Early Copper Age, La Gerundia to the later Copper Age, and El Argar to the Bronze Age (of which it is the regional type site). Thus, the sites date to the fourth, third and second millennia BC, respectively. Given the proximity of these sites, it seems unlikely that the materials from each millennium should be largely segregated on separate hilltops unless the hilltops were separated, as they are now, at the time of the sites' occupations. The lack of any archaeological deposits on any of the nearby hilltops similarly suggests that the *rambla* system behind the sites was present when they were occupied. Thus, the archaeological evidence from these sites suggests that the gross morphology of this badland area has changed very little since the occupation of the site at El Gárcel some 6000 years ago.

At this point we may summarise the evidence. First, there is the visual appearance of the spectacular marl badlands of the Guadix and other Tertiary depositional basins in south-east Spain. Their high drainage densities and steep, sparsely vegetated valley side slopes, coupled with the semi-arid climate, lead one to expect very rapid rates of erosion. The estimates of erosion rates and the limited available sediment load data indicate, however, erosion rates that are quite modest in global terms (Fournier 1960). In the Guadix basin they are of the order of only 25 tonne km^{-2} yr^{-1}. The *in situ* archaeological deposits also imply greater slope stability and less rapid erosion than the visual evidence suggests. The four core areas of site territories that we have studied in detail are not isolated examples by any means. Tres Cabezos and Campos, Terrera Ventura, Cerro de la Virgen, La Bastida and Cerro de la Encina are other sites located on marl bluffs and promontories defined by highly dissected drainages. The positioning of the remains at all of these sites suggests the considerable geomorphological stability of their surroundings.

The sparse vegetation cover resulting from a harsh climate and from over-grazing reveals clearly every geomorphic detail and thereby creates a misleading impression of catastrophic erosion. The apparent contrast between the 'hard' Palaeozoic and Mesozoic rocks and the Tertiary deposits reinforces this impression although closer inspection reveals the marls to be well cemented and capable of maintaining nearly vertical slopes. All the same, extremely high drainage densities and steep slopes appear difficult to reconcile with low erosion rates.

The simplest explanation for this anomaly is that the erosion rates obtained by simulations and from available records are incorrect and should be higher. Observations are few in number, unreliable in quality, and recorded only for a short period. Moreover, human activities, such as the construction of earth banks across *ramblas* to trap flood water and sediments, may have suppressed sediment yield figures below those which would occur naturally. (At the same time, however, the recent widespread neglect of terracing, a result of the reduction of rural population over the past 25 years, may have caused unusually *high* erosion rates in the period for which we have records of sediment yields.) The estimates based on our models agree very well with the published yield data in the Guadix area, but this may partly reflect the use of the same basic parameters in all models. Furthermore, the models use parameters based on long-term climatic means, whereas in south-east Spain the large variations that occur over the short term are probably more important.

A second explanation is that rates were much higher in the past because the climate was different. The models of Langbein and Schumm (1958) and Carson and Kirkby (1972) are very sensitive to small changes in the values of climatic inputs under semi-arid conditions. The limited available evidence on past climates implies, however, relatively stable conditions over the past several thousand years. The argument that widespread erosion in Mediterranean lands is the result of forest clearance and other such agricultural activities is incompatible with the archaeological evidence (see discussion in Davidson (1980)). Thus, if a change in climate is the explanation for higher erosion rates in the past, since the present patterns of slopes, gullies and channels was in existence before later prehistoric sites were occupied, the climatic changes responsible must have been Quaternary in age.

The most likely explanation of the low erosion rates in spectacularly eroded settings is the long-term denudational history of basins in south-east Spain. In the Guadix area, the breaching of the endorrheic basin in late Tertiary times, coupled with progressive uplift, may have led to outward propagation of the network from the principal channels by headward erosion. Parker (1977) has shown experimentally that this tends to occur by the addition of first-order channels when there is continued basal incision. This addition tends to be cyclical, accompanied by alternately high and low sediment yields with an exponential decay in yields between the peaks. The present-day restriction of erosion to minor extensions in headwater areas, the development of fills with only slight incision along the main valley axes, and the relative atrophy of forms near the centre of the basin appear consistent with the hypothesis that the Guadix drainage system is an ancient and mature one. Even if one assumes the pre-existence of a network that was subsequently entrenched in the headwater areas with aggradation occurring downstream, the incision of the high-density network would lead to convex slopes with basal incision and removal of deposits. These conditions are conducive to slopes that are stable in response to runoff events and unlikely to be dissected (Smith & Bretherton 1972, Kirkby 1980b). This explanation is consistent with the observation that uplift has occurred over the entire Guadix basin since Pliocene times. It is also in agreement with observations elsewhere in the region that the impact of the 1973 flood was predominantly on the channel margins, through land slides, or (in upland areas) in the channels themselves (Thornes 1976), which suggests that coupling of hillslope and channel erosion is poor.

If we accept that a long history of denudation explains the low erosion rates in the Guadix badlands, how likely is it that other areas of extensive badlands in south-east Spain are similarly undergoing only modest change at the present and recently? Observations at some reservoirs certainly indicate a high rate of sedimentation (López Bermúdez 1973, López Bermúdez & Gutiérrez Escudo 1982), although this might be due to channel trenching rather than hillslope dissection. The historical–empirical record alone is unlikely ever to be complete enough to resolve these problems conclusively for every area of south-east Spain. For the moment we have shown that, in the Guadix and Vera basins, major development of gullies occurred before sites were occupied several thousand years ago. Here, and probably elsewhere, subsequent adjustments have been through local headward erosion and some channel incision

rather than by hillslope dissection and major gully development and extension.

Erosion: conclusions

Our investigations concerning the magnitude of erosion in south-east Spain
inform our reconstruction of prehistoric land use in two ways. First, they
indicate that the overall proportions of landforms within the site territories has
been fairly stable over the past several thousand years. Flat or gently sloping
interfluves suitable for farming have not been lost on any large scale to the
progressive encroachment of badland gullies, even on lithologies whose low
moisture storage/high runoff potentials make them particularly susceptible to
erosion. Even if we set aside the findings suggested by our detailed examination
of the settings of archaeological sites in badland areas, it would be difficult to
envisage great changes in landforms as a result of regolith loss. On the
assumption that the escarpment at the top of a slope is level, the retreat of the
escarpment may be estimated by:

$$R = D_1/\sin \theta_1 \qquad\qquad (4.7)$$

where R is the escarpment retreat (in mm yr^{-1}), D_1 is the depth (in mm yr^{-1}) of
lost regolith on slopes of a given lithology in a given site territory and θ_1 is the
mean slope angle on that lithology in that territory. Now on ungullied,
vegetated slopes R is negligible when it is multiplied by the number of years
since a site was in use. Significant amounts of escarpment retreat (in terms of the
area of the interfluves) begin to be generated on low-storage lithologies (marls
and chalks) when these have been bare and gullied for a millennium or more.
Areas that may have fulfilled these conditions (south-facing badland slopes) are
too small and too few to change the areas of *monte* and *secano* sufficiently to make
a difference to our analysis of contrasts in the proportions of land uses within
and between site territories.

Secondly, our analysis shows that regolith loss has taken place on a scale
sufficient to make consideration of modern soil quality (or, in some areas,
presence) irrelevant to an assessment of ancient land-use potential. Following
the extreme-event (Scoging–Thornes) model, 60 mm h^{-1} storms (with a recurrence of 75 to 150 years depending on the region of south-east Spain) would
produce over several millennia measurable results on susceptible lithologies
even if these were vegetated and ungullied. If vegetation were removed
seasonally, as by cultivation, or permanently, as by overgrazing, the effects of
storms at least in the arid sector would become even more dramatic. As a result
of several thousand years of storms of varying magnitude, agriculture in
south-east Spain by and large involves either direct exploitation of the C horizon
or cultivation of intensively tended, terraced plots with anthropogenic organic
soils. We can only assume that, several millennia ago when the settlements of

early farmers were founded, most land level enough for cultivation, even that which now has a surface of bare limestone or caliche or exfoliating schist, would have had some arable potential. For this reason the distinction between *monte* and *secano* on our land-use potential maps has been based on topography.

Water diversion potential

Our general problem involves contrasting the irrigation potential of land near Neolithic through Bronze Age sites in both the arid lowlands of south-east Spain and *Hochandalusien*. Irrigation potential is determined not just by the amount of water available, of course, but also by the availability of suitable land, the quality of the available water and the technical means available for capturing the water. Given the primitive technical means available in later prehistoric times, irrigation would essentially be limited to areas with surface flows from springs and along water courses. Information on spring flows within the site territories is available from the *Inventario de Puntos de Agua* prepared by IGME. In most areas of the south-east, however, surface flows of water along streams are reduced, and in the arid sector almost eliminated, by abstraction for irrigation. The Almanzora, the Ándarax, the Guadalentín, and so on, are so thoroughly converted to human purposes that they carry water only in relatively large storms, so that it is difficult to determine by measurement today what amounts of water they would make available for palaeotechnic diversion. Estimation of surface flows in stream channels during winter (the growing season for the staple grains cultivated in prehistoric times) is, therefore, an essential step in comparing the irrigation potential of the territories around the sites under study.

The extent to which water yields today are comparable to those of the past is a function, naturally, of the changes that have occurred in climate, vegetation and soils. These may not have been very large, as we have argued, but they certainly have been complex and spatially variable. Runoff is more sensitive to changes in these variables than are soil cover or gully development, and the response time to change is more rapid. It has to be admitted, furthermore, that the effects of vegetation removal on hydrological response are still, rather surprisingly, very poorly understood. We take present-day winter water yields as a baseline from which to consider the likely spatial variations in later prehistoric times in the belief that spatial contrasts at the present time are probably much greater than the likely differences since ancient times.

Winter water yield refers to the average rate of flow past a given point in a stream channel between 1 October and 30 April. Our selection of this measure is dictated partly by choice and partly by data constraints. The total volume of water determines the upper bound of the amount that can be put into storage, both artificial (for example, reservoirs) and natural (for example, in gravels beneath the river bed), but it tells us nothing of the timing and intensity of flows, variables of interest with respect to water use. The use of average winter yield has the advantage, however, that the total volume of flows is less sensitive than their timing and intensity to the changes outlined in the previous paragraph. The model we have used has as its primary input mean annual precipitation; in this respect we follow Schumm's (1965) predilection for effective runoff. Our choice of the period October–April simply reflects the fact that in south-east Spain over 90% of all rainfall (by volume) occurs in these months, so that winter runoff is both more persistent and easier to use because of the higher proportion of base flow. In the arid south-east, irrigation is mainly directed towards success in obtaining primary winter crops. It is only in the uplands and in highly favoured lowland spots that irrigation is applied to extending the growing season into summer by double cropping.

We have tackled the problem of estimating winter water yield empirically. An alternative would have been to simulate the flows using deterministic or stochastic models of individual events, but this approach faces certain difficulties. The problem of routing in large ephemeral channel systems has not yet been adequately investigated, and the larger channels in our study area have catchments of several thousand square kilometres. There are also data constraints. Good information on rainfall intensity is restricted to a few unrepresentative stations (the provincial capitals). Although daily stream flow data are available from gauging stations and are of good quality, the interpretation of their autographic records presents severe problems. Finally, we lack good data on channel routing (necessary for kinematic models, for example) and on subsurface storage. These problems would be compounded by the extremely varied nature of the terrain and the consequent difficulty of sampling the catchment basins. Accordingly, since fairly good rainfall and runoff data are available, an empirical approach offers the best prospect of meeting our goal.

The approach we have used is a variant of the so-called 'rational' method, in which discharge for individual storms is expressed as a function of rainfall intensity and basin area (Linsley *et al.* 1975). This is a black–box technique in the extreme and avoids all questions of interception, storage and routing. That we obtain a regional correlation between mean rainfall and runoff has the advantage of incorporating within the regression and its attendant error factors those contrasts produced by regional differences. The correlation will incorporate, for example, the differing transmission losses that will occur in larger and smaller streams. This approach may, however, also incorporate unwanted biases.

We have regressed specific yield (mean annual discharge per unit area as measured at stream gauging stations) against mean annual rainfall in those areas. Then we have applied this regression to catchments without gauging stations, multiplying the specific yield by area to obtain estimates of mean annual flow. That is,

$$Q_i = A_i Y_i \tag{4.8}$$

where

$$Y_i = kp_i^n \qquad (4.9)$$

in which Q_i is the mean winter discharge (in l s^{-1}), A_i is the area of the ith catchment basin (in square kilometres), p_i is the mean annual precipitation (in millimetres) and k and n are regression coefficients.

Data were collected from river gauging stations of the three water authorities

Table 4.6 Master list of gauging stations used in analysis.

Station ref.	Name and location	Length of record (yr)	Specific yield (l s^{-1}km^{-2})	Area (km^2)	Rainfall annual (mm)	Flashiness
5012	Guadalquivir, El Doctor	41	51.65	28	1393	3.7
5019	Guadiana Menos, Manzano	34	2.37	4144	451	2.6
5023	Posito	56	3.12	7180	490	3.1
5038	Aguas Blancas, Puente Blanqueo	34	9.17	50	700	2.9
5039	Monachil, Presa	23	18.59	48	1229	2.3
5042	Velillos, Pinos Puente	25	10.04	382	600	5.1
5045	Genil, Loja	58	4.54	4210	490	2.7
5047	Puente Genil	58	5.94	6162	600	2.4
6005	Ugijar, Las Tosquillas	36	4.04	120	608	2.9
6013	Sabar, Alfarnatejo	16	13.69	39	769	7.2
6014	Guaro, Cortijo el Monte	39	12.00	119	689	4.8
6015	Salia, La Vinuela	40	9.04	67	776	5.0
6016	Bermuza, Los Gonzalez	40	25.57	13	769	4.1
6017	Almuhares, Grandillos	39	13.39	12	750	4.0
6018	Rabita, Hoya del Bujo	38	9.00	47	723	5.8
6020	Algarrobo, La Umbria	33	7.69	67	642	4.6
6022	Guadalmedina, Casabermeja	13	8.16	59	650	4.7
6023	Nacimiento, El Choro	29	0.58	616	429	1.4
6027	Janto, Alfaix	34	0.39	70	279	3.5
6031	Guadalmedina, Pantano	38	10.17	153	608	6.4
6042	Durcal, Los Sauces	41	16.09	20	1050	1.6
6043	Izbor, Presa Melegis	41	6.78	328	646	1.6
6067	Almanzora, Cantoria	16	1.11	1100	406	5.0
6073	Santa Barbara	19	0.84	1850	380	3.9
7006	Segura, Almadenes	53	2.16	7111	470	2.08
7016	Cieza	65	2.38	8026	452	2.03
7018	Archena	65	1.92	8754	430	2.0
7025	Guadalentín, Paso de los Carros	30	0.006	3225	210	–
7028	Segura, Orihuela	70	1.18	13603	369	2.6
7029	Rojales	53	0.58	14893	357	6.0
7030	Guadarmar	52	0.40	14925	357	8.10
7040	Rambla de Algeciras, Librilla	29	1.01	52	385	–

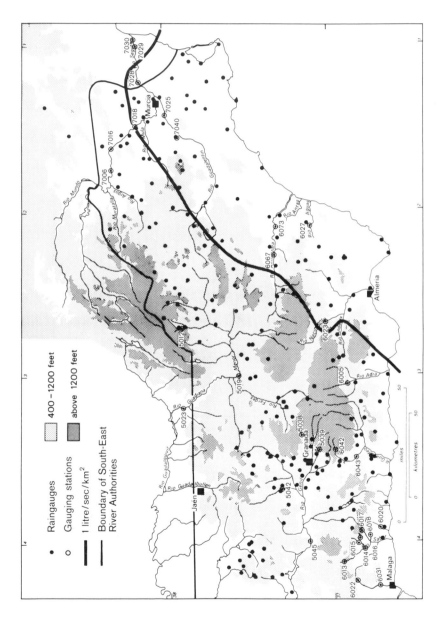

Figure 4.11 Map of south-east Spain with locations of stream gauging stations, rain gauging stations and the 400 mm isohyet.

in south-east Spain (Cuencas del Sur, Cuenca del Guadalquivir and Cuenca de la Segura). The location of the gauging stations used in the analysis is shown in Figure 4.11, together with the rainfall stations used to obtain estimates of runoff on ungauged streams within the site territories. Initially some 2000 station-years of runoff data were examined, but some stations had to be excluded because of reservoirs, canals and other strong human interference or because the lengths of their records were too short. In the event, only stations with records longer than 10 years were selected because shorter records tend to be dominated by runs of exceptionally wet or dry years. The final selection of 32 stations, given in Table 4.6, was also based on the homogeneity of their data. A detailed study of three of the longest records showed that individual flow events (and hence specific yields) have a strong negative skew, a Pearson type III distribution reflecting the dominance of flows in the smallest size class. The annual means of these flow events are log-normally distributed, and so we have transformed the data prior to analysis.

The plot of specific yields against rainfall is shown in Figure 4.12. Regression of this distribution results in the equation:

$$Y = 10^{-10.075} p^{3.866} \qquad (4.10)$$

in which Y is specific yield ($l\ s^{-1}\ km^{-2}$) and p is mean annual rainfall (mm). This function rises steeply above 400 mm precipitation. This reflects the reduced evapotranspirational losses in upland catchments coupled with the lower trans-mission losses in the smaller channels. It must also to some extent reflect lower abstraction for irrigation. The Pearson correlation value is 0.917 and the standard error of Y is 0.304. Roughly speaking the latter means that there is a 68% probability that the true specific yield will lie between double and half the predicted value.

Equations 4.8 and 4.10 have been used to generate estimates of winter water yields for the streams within the archaeological site territories. To do this, 1:50 000 scale topographic maps of the site territories were used to define all permanent and ephemeral stream channels. The accuracy with which these were mapped determined the lower bound of the flows that could be estimated. At each confluence in the stream network, the area in the catchment upstream was obtained from the topographic maps (for large streams arising beyond the site territories 1:200 000 scale maps were used). To obtain rainfall for the areas, all available rain gauging stations have been used and the mean annual rainfall established from Thiessen polygons between the stations. Where the number of stations permitted, large catchments were subdivided into more homogeneous sub-areas taking into account the overall relief of the landscape. Mean precipi-tation for each sub-area of a catchment was then calculated before obtaining the specific yields from the regression equations. Flows in a downstream direction are, therefore, not simple additions of flows from upstream. This is to be expected since it reflects the non-linearity of the processes involved.

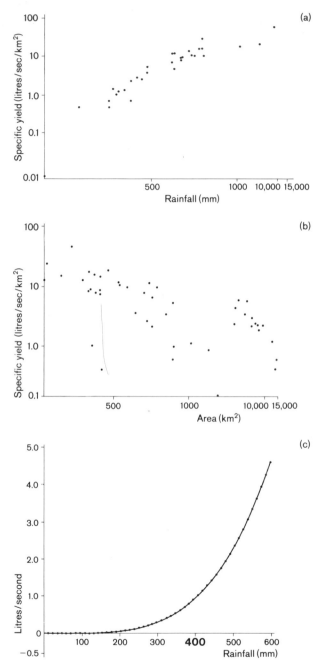

Figure 4.12 Scattergram of specific yields at the 32 gauging stations vs rainfall.

Figure 4.11 shows the line separating areas in which winter yields are higher and lower than $1 \ s^{-1} \ km^{-2}$ (west and east of the line, respectively). This division is critical hydrologically because above this threshold there is sharp increase of runoff with respect to rainfall. The value of this threshold corresponds to a rainfall of $404 \ mm \ yr^{-1}$, so that the 400 mm isohyet is quite suitable for its demarcation. It lies a little outside the line defining the arid south-east according to Geiger (1973) and close to the line defining the natural boundary of the evergreen oak, *Quercus ilex*, according to Freitag (1971, p. 286). The results are also very close to those produced by Langbein *et al.* (1949) expressing the relation between rainfall, runoff and mean annual temperature. This is somewhat surprising given the level of human activity in south-east Spain, but to some extent justifies the rough-and-ready procedures we have adopted.

Maps presenting the average winter yield along streams in each site territory or intersecting set of site territories are presented in the next chapter. With certain anomalies, which we shall discuss in detail below, the magnitudes of the predicted values correspond well to the present-day distribution of irrigation once one has allowed for areas fed by groundwater supplies. The capacity to use the flows we have estimated depends, as we have stated earlier, not just on the absolute volume of water available but also on the quality of the water, on the availability and quality of land to which the water may be diverted, and on the storage capabilities of the irrigators. Indeed, where flows are flashy, storage capabilities become critical for expanding irrigation, so that for a primitive technology there is an upper as well as a lower bound to the amount of usable water. What is encouraging for our purposes is the strength of the contrasts that emerge both within and between site territories in the magnitude of the surface flows available for irrigating winter grain crops. Once adjustment for the factors we have just mentioned has been made, the contrasts in irrigation potential seem more than large enough to resist serious distortions by the imponderable errors introduced by landscape changes since Argaric times.

5   Site territories

This chapter describes the sites under study and their territories, and analyses the proportions of the several land-use categories within the territories. For each site or group of sites we briefly describe the environmental setting and review the archaeological evidence for the age and settlement function of the locality. Table 5.1 then presents the area (ha) of each of the land-use potential categories – *monte, secano,* terraced, *boquera* and *regadío* – for each of the successive time zones from core to periphery – 0 to 12 min, 12 to 30 min, 30 to 60 min and 60 to 120 min – of each site territory. These areas, the primary results of our research, have been obtained from maps that integrate the present distribution of land uses with the evidence developed on recent changes in agricultural practice, on erosional potential and on water diversion potential. To construct maps of land-use potential has required the case-by-case weighing of several lines of evidence so as to convert the distribution of land uses observable today to a distribution of land-use potentials relevant to the economy and technology of the later prehistoric period. In considering the evidence at particular sites, we have tried to bear in mind the outcome that our overall theory concerning prehistoric irrigation in south-east Spain would propose for that site given its age and environment. That is to say, we would predict that during the Neolithic and Copper Age sites would be oriented to *regadío* in the arid, but not in the moist, sector of the south-east, but that Bronze Age sites would be so oriented in both sectors. Where the evidence indicates that adjustments might reasonably be made either in favour or against our hypothesis, we have made the adjustment against our hypothesis in order to strengthen our final conclusions. In this chapter, we discuss case-by-case how the evidence was assessed and how the final mapping of land-use potential diverges from present-day land-use distributions. Winter water yield diagrams for the streams within each territory or group of territories are presented, together with the final land-use potential maps for the 1 h territory of each site.

Our analysis of the distribution of land-use categories within each site territory proceeds along simple lines. We examine the relative proportions of the various land-use categories in the areas near the sites (the 12 and 30 min territories) against the proportions in the peripheral zones of the 2 h territories. Those land uses present in higher proportions near a site are those favoured by the site's location. At some sites the comparison of core and periphery leads to no clear conclusion as to the land-use preferences embodied in the site's location. This may occur when more than one agricultural land-use category is more frequent near a site or when all agricultural land uses are more frequent far from a site. In the former case we choose as the preferred land use that one showing the greatest contrast between the zones close to the site and those farther away.

In the latter case we compare the proportions of the several agricultural land-use categories in the site vicinity to see which is most abundant. The conclusions so drawn are considered against the available economic evidence from the sites.

La Almoloya

The site is located at the summit of a limestone hill (elevation 585 m), one of the northern outliers of the Sierra Espuña. Its location dominates the valley of the River Pliego to the west and plains of caliche-topped marls to the east. Mean annual rainfall at the town of Pliego, 4 km to the north, is 283 mm, but in the sierra to the south it rises rapidly to over 500 mm (León Llamazares *et al.* 1974). The climax vegetation of most of the site territory would consist of a chaparral formation of kermes oak, mastic tree, and so on. On the higher elevations of Espuña there would have been *encinar*, of which a few relict stands still remain (Freitag 1971, p. 231). Within the site territory the natural vegetation has either been replaced by cultivation or been reduced to a low scrub (which in many areas, including the vicinity of the site, has been reforested with Aleppo pine).

The site was tested in 1944 by Cuadrado Díaz (1945–46). He uncovered cist and urn burials with grave goods including plain carinated vessels, a small riveted dagger and other typical Argaric materials. Cuadrado Díaz's pits were placed on the cliff-surrounded 50 m by 80 m plateau at the top of the hill. The range of materials, including querns, serrated flint sickle blades, loom weights and abundant potsherds, clearly indicate that the site was used as a settlement.

The upper slopes of the hill, just below the summit, are terraced and have ceramics on the surface. Since terracing is only found towards the top of the hill (and elsewhere in the vicinity is not used to extend cultivation to steeper slopes), it must be part of the settlement complex, so that the total extent of the site may be over 2 ha.

The basic lithologies of the site territory are the limestones of Espuña and its northern outliers and marls of Tertiary age, capped by a caliche surface, but exposed by the drainage network incision. The erosion potential on the marls is high: the material lost on an unvegetated, gullied marl slope would be enough over a millennium to cause an escarpment retreat of 25 to 50 m. The limit of *secano* interfluves have been adjusted to that extent on south-facing marl slopes.

The general distribution of *secano* and *regadío* by district, as indicated in the 1757 *Relación Particular* for Pliego, is similar to that of the present. The bulk of the *regadío* was near the town of Pliego itself, with the rest of the municipal territory being either *monte* or *secano*, except for small irrigated areas in the bottom of the drainages that dissect the marls east of the limestone hills on which the site is located. The total area of *regadío* reported in the 1757 *Respuesta General* is, however, considerably smaller than the present-day irrigated area. The main source of water for the Pliego *huerta* was the Fuente de las Anguilas, located 30 min north-west of the site, a spring of highly irregular production

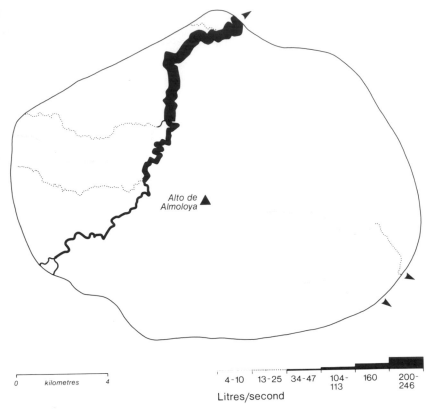

Alto de
Almoloya ▲

0   kilometres   4

4-10   13-25   34-47   104-   160   200-
                         113   246

Litres/second

Figure 5.1   Mean winter water yields within the 2 h territory of La Almoloya.

(Mádoz 1846–50, XIII, pp. 87–8). This has now been replaced at the same location by a deep well, which produces a regular flow. Since the increased size of the Pliego *huerta* can be explained as a result of the improved water supply, we have reduced the irrigated area in our land-use map to its 1757 extent, with the exception of areas along the Rivers Pliego and Mula, whose considerable flows (indicated in Fig. 5.1) would have provided water for them.

Whatever the adjustments, however, it is apparent that the Almoloya settlement is situated so as to exploit *secano*. As the land-use map (Fig. 5.2) shows, one does not reach any *regadío* until one is almost half an hour away from the site and the highest proportion of *regadío* occurs between the 30 min and 1 h time contours. The defensive emplacement of the site at the top of a hill naturally means that there is a high proportion of *monte* in the immediate vicinity. In the 30 min territory of the site, however, *monte* is less frequent than in the area beyond 30 min distance (39% vs 53%). Terracing in the Almoloya site territory also increases in importance as one moves away from the site: its principal function in this area is to retain moisture and check erosion along drainage lines in the marls, and in the areas close to the site the marls are not exposed beneath their caliche capping. *Secano*, however, has its highest proportion of the total land area (60%) within 30 min of the site, a proportion which declines to 37% in the area between 1 h and 2 h distance. The shifting proportions of the various land-use categories clearly indicate that the site of La Almoloya is best located for the exploitation of dry arable land.

Campico de Lébor, La Bastida

Both sites are located along the Rambla de Lébor: Campico (elevation 310 m) is 500 m upstream from the *rambla*'s opening onto the plain of the Guadalentín river; La Bastida (elevation 400 m) is on a 40 m high marl bluff 2 km further upstream. Mean annual rainfall at Totana (4 km east of the sites) is 260 mm (León Llamazares *et al.* 1974). The gypsiferous marls in the vicinity of the sites, along the north side of the Guadalentín plain, would have carried a specialised vegetation of shrubs such as saltwort (*Salsola papillosa*) and glasswort (*Anabasis mucronata*), but most of the sites' territories would be covered with a chaparral plant community with such species as kermes oak, mastic tree, oleaster and

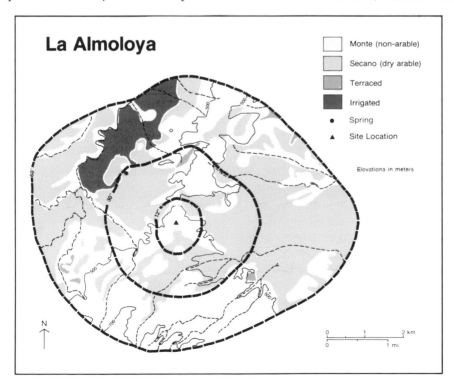

Figure 5.2   Land-use potential within the 1 h territory of La Almoloya.

Aleppo pine (Freitag 1971). Except for areas being reforested with pines, this is now reduced to garrigue or put to cultivation.

La Bastida has been well known since the 19th century, thanks to excavations by Inchaurrandieta in 1869 (Martínez Santa Olalla *et al.* 1947, pp. 31–40) and by Siret and Siret (1887, pp. 107–8) and to extensive pothunting thereafter. In 1944 the Seminario de Historia Primitiva excavated the site (Martínez Santa Olalla *et al.* 1947) and tested other nearby localities, including Campico (Val Caturla 1948). La Bastida is a classic Argaric site with terraced rectangular structures covering more than a hectare of the hill slope above the bluff overlooking the *rambla*. There is abundant domestic and industrial debris, including abundant ceramics, querns and copper slag. The (over 100) jar and cist burials underneath the house floors have yielded a full range of characteristic Argaric finds: halberds, axes, riveted daggers, carinated bowls, chalices, and so on. At Campico, which has now been destroyed by bulldozers making new agricultural terraces, excavations uncovered five large pits containing domestic debris, such as potsherds, querns, stone axes, and a lithic industry including both geometric microliths and bifacially flaked arrow heads. These latter elements indicate a Millaran date for the site, although the geometric microliths and the absence of metal may point to an earlier, 'Almerian' time. The nearby sepulchral cave of Los Blanquizares (Cuadrado Ruiz 1930, Arribas 1953), with its 92 burials and rich Millaran grave goods (anthropomorphic figurines of stone and bone, bone combs, ceramics and lithics similar to those in the settlement), has produced a Bell Beaker, a clear, later Copper Age diagnostic (Arribas 1953, Fig. 61).

The lithologies that predominate within the site territories – the Quaternary alluvium of the Guadalentín plain and the mica–schists and conglomerates of the Sierra de Manilla to the west and of the outliers and pediment of Sierra Espuña to the north – have low erosional potentials. In the immediate vicinity of the sites, however, are marl badlands, which have disastrous erosional potential. The present degree of dissection, however, is probably the product of long-term denudation associated with the subsidence of the Guadalentín valley. Indeed, that La Bastida is placed to exploit the defensive possibilities afforded by a marl bluff above the Rambla de Lébor suggests that the general configuration of the landscape has remained fairly stable over the past several thousand years (cf. pp. 62–74). Los Picarios, 2.5 km south-west of La Bastida, is another (unexcavated) prehistoric site (Martínez Santa Olalla *et al.* 1947, p. 17) located defensively on top of a steep-sided promontory in the same area of marls.

Agriculture within the site territories has been extensively modernised in recent years. Deep wells have extended irrigation to most of the Guadalentín plain. The 1956 air photographs indicate that this extension had only just begun. Even before this, the 18th-century Puentes and 19th-century Valdeinfierno reservoirs upstream on the Guadalentín drainage had permitted gravity-fed irrigation to be extended well beyond Lorca and as far as the southwestern sector of the 2 h territories. At the same time that irrigation has been greatly expanded

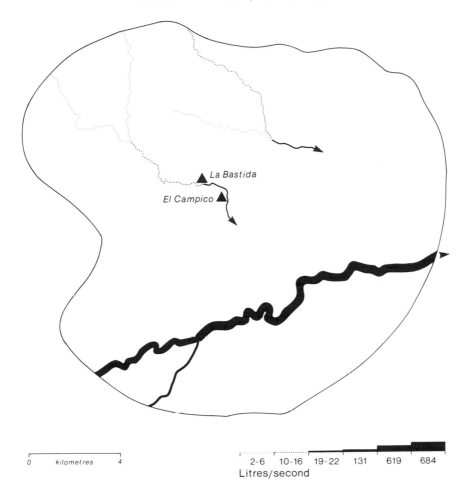

Figure 5.3 Mean winter water yields within the overlapping 2 h territories of La Bastida and El Campico de Lébor.

in areas formerly dry-farmed, the greater availability of water has caused the abandonment of older, less effective hydraulic facilities. The 1757 Ensenada *Respuesta General* for Totana–Aledo lists six *boqueras* along the Rambla de Lébor, none of which are in operation now.[1] Indeed, even the irrigation system that captured the not-insignificant flows along the Lébor (whose winter water yield we estimate at 19 to $22 \, \mathrm{l \, s^{-1}}$) at its opening onto the Guadalentín plain has been abandoned since 1956.

In the light of these changes, we have made the following adjustments in the distribution of land-use categories. Within the municipal territories of Totana and Aledo we have restricted *regadío* to the 2494 ha reported in the 1757 *Respuesta*. All of the 1757 irrigated area would have fallen within our site

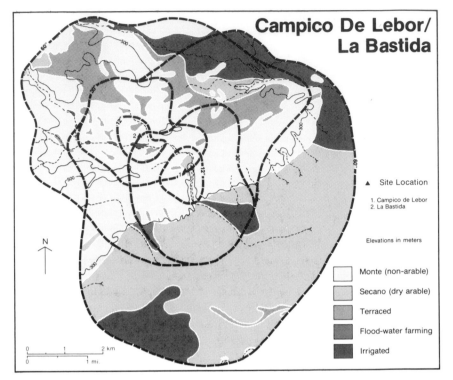

Figure 5.4 Land–use potential within the overlapping 1 h territories of La Bastida and El Campico de Lébor.

territory, and we have adjusted the distribution of *regadío* by eliminating areas on the Guadalentín plain furthest down stream along the principal water source, the Rambla de los Molinos. We have retained, however, the evidently palaeo-technic irrigated area now out of use at the mouth of the Lébor. The *regadío* on the Guadalentín plain in the southwestern sector of the territories, an area receiving its irrigation water from the above-mentioned reservoirs, has been mapped at its 1956 extent. In the absence of upstream damming, the Gua-dalentín (which now only has flows during very large storm events) would carry large winter flows, which would be available for irrigation in the southern peripheries of the site territories (Fig. 5.3). At the same time, short of an exhaustive analysis of the massive *Respuesta Particular* for all of the very large municipal territory of Lorca (within which the irrigated area under consider-ation lies), an accurate assessment of the extent of pre-reservoir *regadío* within the site territories is impossible. Since any reduction of the extent of irrigated land in the peripheral areas of the site territories would tend to favour our hypothesis (that Copper and Bronze Age sites in the arid zone of south-east Spain were located so as to exploit irrigable land) by increasing the relative proportion of irrigated land in the core areas of the territories, we have mapped the *regadío* in the southwestern sector at its 1956 extent. For the same reason, we have not added *boquera* land along the Lébor: only exhaustive analysis of the Totana–Aledo *Relación General* would permit determination of the extent of *boquera*-fed land near the sites, and any arbitrary addition of *boquera* area to the core of the territories would favour our hypothesis.

Because both Campico and Bastida are located in an area of marl badlands, *monte* is the predominant land-use category in the core of their territories (see Fig. 5.4): it forms 56% of the Campico and 82% of the Bastida 30 min territories, but only 30% and 39% respectively of the 2 h territories as wholes. By the same token, the proportion of most agricultural land-use categories increases as one moves away from the sites. The exception is terraced land, which is more abundant in the 30 min territories (8% of the total area at Campico, 14% at Bastida) than in the 2 h territories (5% and 6% respectively). This occurs because the principal lithology near the site is marl, on which terracing is particularly necessary to check soil loss. The Rambla de Lébor, along which both sites are situated, is (as Fig. 5.3 indicates) one of the three principal sources of water in the territories, but the narrow canyon through which it flows provides little land for irrigation above the point where the stream reaches the Guadalentín plain. The Guadalentín River in the southern periphery of the site territories has far more abundant flows (although a large ephemeral stream wandering across its floodplain during highly irregular events may have been difficult to control with prehistoric technology). The Rambla de los Molinos in the north-east sector of the territories not only has more water than the Lébor (besides its estimated winter water yield of 19 to $221 s^{-1}$, it is fed by springs with an aggregate and year-round flow of $141 s^{-1}$), but also has more land accessible to gravity-fed irrigation. While Campico and Bastida are located in the vicinity of significant hydraulic resources (which have been more heavily used in the recent past than they are now), it is clear that the overall distribution of land and water would make other locations in the area even more suitable for irrigation agriculture. Near the sites dry-farmed land (preferably terraced) is the dominant potential land use.

The Mazarrón sites: La Ceñuela, Ifre, Parazuelos, Cabezo Negro de Pastrana, Zapata

The sites of the Mazarrón group are located in coastal Murcia province on the seaward side of the Sierra de la Almenara. La Ceñuela (elevation 240 m) is located on a marl hillock above the Rambla del Puntarrón, and Parazuelos (elevation 88 m) on a conglomerate outcrop beside the Rambla de Ramonete. These two *ramblas* are, as Figure 5.5 indicates, two of the principal streams draining the Almenara chain. Ifre (elevation 219 m), Zapata (elevation 360 m) and Cabezo Negro (elevation 360 m) are also located near streams, but are on the summits of calcareous ridges, outliers of the *sierra*. There are no raingauge

Figure 5.5 Mean winter water yields within the overlapping 2h territories of the Mazarrón sites.

stations within the site territory, but it is clear that along the immediate coast mean annual precipitation would be under 200 mm: at Águilas, on the coast to the south-west, mean precipitation is 177 mm yr^{-1}, while at Cabo Tiñoso to the east it is 151 mm yr^{-1} (León Llamazares *et al.* 1974). Totals would rise rapidly as one moves up into the *sierra*, which reaches a height of almost 900 m. The area along the immediate coast would have a climax vegetation of thorny bushes, a scrub community including such species as the palmetto and the boxthorn. Most of the rest of the site territories would be covered with a chaparral formation like that described for the Campico–Bastida territories immediately to the north (p. 87). The limits of the Zapata and Cabezo Negro 2 h territories reach the heights of La Almenara, where stands of evergreen oak might be expected. While fairly intact areas of scrub and chaparral are still present within the territories, most areas are either cleared for cultivation or overgrazed to a sparse cover of aromatics.

The Sirets' (1887, pp. 45–50, plates 6–8) excavations of the 30 to 60 cm deep deposit at Parazuelos uncovered a large, subrectangular, stone-walled structure (38 m × 16 m) and an artifact inventory of residential debris (potsherds, querns) which included such Millaran elements as bifacially flaked points, large flint blades and a copper awl. The four other sites in this group are all Argaric. Ifre, also excavated by the Sirets (1887, pp. 85–96, plates 17 & 18), is located on a ridge towering over 100 m above the *rambla* at its base. The acropolis covers about 0.2 ha; the closely packed stone structures (walls were found standing to a height of 1 m) and domestic debris (ceramics, querns, loom weights, bone awls, a possible bread oven) indicate that the site was used not just as a temporary refuge but as a permanent habitation. The jar burials underneath the floors yielded classic Bronze Age diagnostics (chalices, carinated vases, flat copper axes, and so on). Zapata, another of the Sirets' sites (1887, pp. 101–6, plates 19–21), is also located on a high hill, over 80 m above the Rambla del Rio Amir. The summit has 1 to 2 m of settlement debris, including hearths, pottery and loom weights. Cist burials were found on the summit and also on the southern slopes of the hill. Since Argaric burials are typically located under house floors, the settlement may have covered more than the *ca.* 0.1 ha at the summit. The burials contained such typical Argaric elements as chalices and riveted daggers.

At La Ceñuela the Sirets (1887, p. 107) reported prehistoric materials from two low hillocks 100 m apart. Excavations in 1973–74 at the southern hillock by Zamora Camellada (1976) revealed two constructional levels of stone-walled houses with burnt wattle-and-daub from the collapsed roofs. No burials were found, but the ceramics from the site included fragments of chalices; a flat copper axe also indicated an Argaric age.

Cabezo Negro de Pastrana was excavated in 1977 by a team from the Universities of Barcelona and Murcia (Aubet *et al.* 1979). The site covers the hill slope at the end of the ridge separating the drainages of the Rambla de Pastrana and the Barranco de la Cañada. Test pits uncovered 1.5 m of archaeological deposits with abundant domestic debris (including ceramics, querns and a raised silo with carbonised grain). The metal objects and the pottery clearly indicate an Argaric occupation (cf. the intact chalice – Aubet *et al.* 1979, Fig. 3).

The various lithologies within the site territory are located in different topographic settings. The *sierra* and its outliers consist of limestones, mica–schists, mixed metamorphics and volcanics. Conglomerates, sometimes cali-chified, form pediments at the base of the ridges, while the valleys are filled with marls and Quaternary alluvium. None of these lithologies have more than moderate erosion potential. This is because the hard rocks and conglomerates have relatively high infiltrabilities and the marls have relatively low relief. On the marls, erosion is now checked by terracing along drainage lines (see Fig. 5.6).

The agricultural landscape in these site territories has changed greatly in the past 25 years. The absence of frost in this coastal area has led to the widespread growing of winter vegetables for urban markets. Water for these farming operations has been obtained from deep wells, which have caused the water table to drop 50 to 100 m, so that springs throughout the area have dried up. In the municipality of Mazarrón in the 1960s only five springs were still flowing in the area covered by the site territories (Navarro Alvargonzález & Figueras

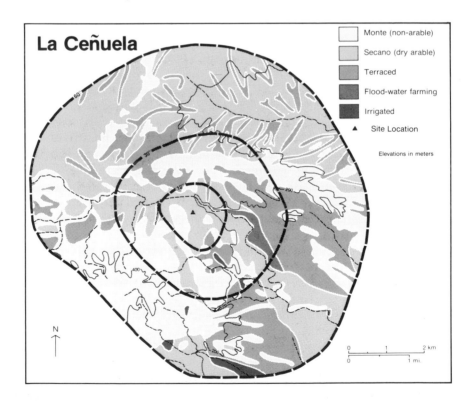

Figure 5.6   Land-use potential within the 1 h territory of La Ceñuela.

Molina, undated), and *none* are recorded in the current IGME *Inventario de Puntos de Agua*. Fortunately, the destruction of the hydraulic base of the traditional irrigation in this area post-dates the 1956 air photographs, which still reveal the 'many farmhouses with plots of irrigated land thanks to the springs which come from the nearby mountains' mentioned by Madoz (1846–50, X, p. 376), as well as the areas of floodwater farming traditional to the area (cf. Madoz 1846–50, XI, p. 322). It is clear that the area of irrigation within the site territories must have increased greatly from the mid-18th to the mid-20th centuries, however: the 1757 Ensenada *Respuesta General* for Mazarrón reports only 21.7 ha of *regadío* within a municipal territory larger than, but only partially overlapping with, the site territories. The increase over the past two centuries took place entirely on the basis of a traditional, gravity-fed technology, so that the expansion can be seen as a realisation of irrigation potential during a period of rapid population increase. Accordingly, the distribution of irrigated land in the 1956 air photographs (verified in the field by the on-the-spot inspection of each place where a dark patch appeared on the air photographs) forms the basis of our mapping of *regadío* potential.

Parazuelos is located immediately beside the Rambla de Ramonete. As Figure 5.7 shows, most categories of arable land are more abundant in the core than in the periphery of the site territory. Since the site is on an outcrop in the *rambla* floodplain at a distance from steeper, mountainous slopes, *monte* forms only 33% of the 30 min territory, but 61% of the area between 30 min and 2 h distance. The corresponding figures for *secano* are 54% and 33%, for *boquera*-fed land 6% and 3%, and for *regadío* 5.5% and 0.7%. Terraced land, more abundant on steeper slopes, is the only agricultural land use more abundant in the periphery (1.9%) than in the core (1.5%). Because the site is located alongside a major watercourse, *regadío* and *boquera*-fed land are more important than *secano* within the 30 min territory. Irrigated and floodwater-farmed land together form 24% of the land within 12 min of the site, but only 9% of the area between 12 and 30 min, the corresponding proportions for *secano* being 42% and 56%. It is clear, then, that the location of this Copper Age site responds to climatic constraints and favours hydraulic over dry farming.[2]

Le Ceñuela is located on a low marl ridge at the base of the Sierra de la Almenara. Because the marls near the site have a lower erosional base point than marls at lower elevations, terracing is more important within the 30 min territory (25%) than in the area from 30 min to 2 h distance (9%) (see Fig. 5.6). Where the Rambla del Puntarrón emerges from its narrow upper valley near the site, its flows are diverted by *boqueras*; thus, floodwater-farmed land also is relatively more abundant in the 30 min territory (3.5%) than in the peripheral zone (0.9%). *Secano*, however, forms a higher proportion of the land surface (66%) at a distance from the site than in the 30 min territory (37%). If the availability of land for dry farming were the critical factor determining settlement placement, La Ceñuela's settlers would have located their dwellings elsewhere. Water for irrigation along the Guadalentín river to the north would

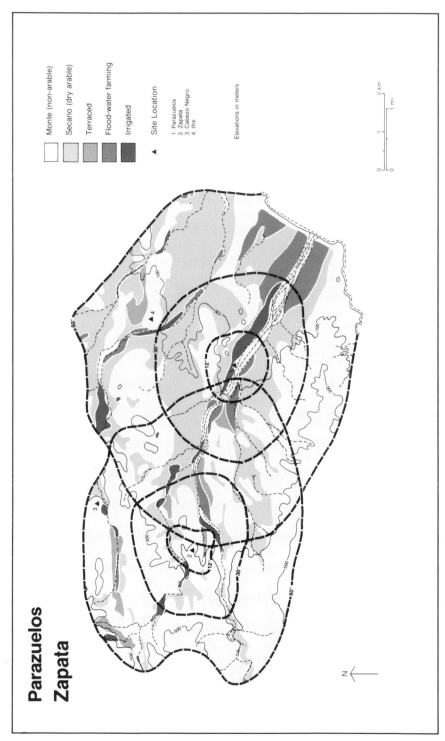

Figure 5.7 Land-use potential within the overlapping 1 h territories of Parazuelos and Zapata.

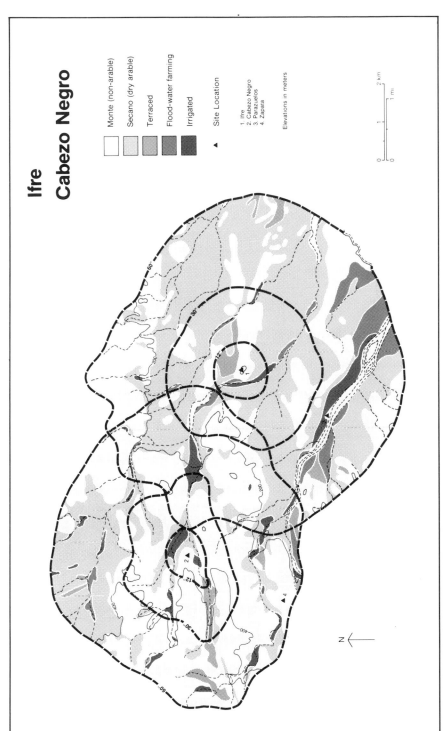

Figure 5.8 Land-use potential within the overlapping 1h territories of Ifre and Cabezo Negro de Pastrana.

be much more abundant, but harder to control (cf. p. 91). Thus, the location of the site near a *rambla* with a smaller, but significant, water diversion potential (the mean winter water yield of $71s^{-1}$ indicated in Figure 5.5 would be concentrated in larger flows capable of watering a large area thoroughly) may represent a maximisation of irrigation potential under palaeotechnic conditions.

The remaining Bronze Age sites in the Mazarrón group are situated in extreme defensive positions, so that least-cost access to agricultural land cannot have been a primary consideration in their placement. In all of them, however, the location of the site favours hydraulic more than dry farming. In the Ifre site territory (Fig. 5.8), the *secano* and terraced categories form a higher proportion of the 30 min territory (66% and 3%, respectively) than in the rest of the 2 h territory (34% and 2%), while *regadío* and *boquera*-fed land is somewhat less frequent in the core (1.5% and 2.6%) than in the periphery (2.3% and 3.3%) of the site territory. The high ridge on which Ifre is located dominates the Rambla de Pastrana, a stream with significant winter flows (see Fig. 5.5), just at a point where a bedrock bar across the stream bed produces a resurgence of the watercourse's flow. (Until recently this was the location of a water mill, mentioned both by the Sirets (1887, p. 85) and in the 1757 *Respuesta General* for Lorca.) Thanks to this water source, the proportion of *regadío* is higher within the 12 min territory than in any other more distant time zone of the site territory. The irrigated land in its immediate vicinity would have provided the necessary base for secure agricultural production to meet the needs of this small site's inhabitants.[3] In short, Ifre is appropriately situated for both hydraulic and (in the occasional rainy year) dry farming.

Zapata is located on top of a high hill near the main body of the Sierra de la Almenara and overlooking the Rambla del Rio Amir. The broken topography in the site's vicinity means that *monte* predominates within the core of the site territory: it forms 70% of the land within 30 min of the site, but only 63% of the area between 30 min and 2 h distance. The corresponding proportions of land suitable for *secano* are 20% and 31%. Among the agricultural land uses, terraced and *regadío* are both relatively more abundant in the core than in the periphery: they form 3.2% and 3.7%, respectively, of the 30 min territory, but 1.4% and 2.3% of the more distant zone. Within the site territory as a whole, then, many localities would be better placed for dry farming than Zapata. By contrast, even though the site's placement is obviously governed by defensive considerations, the possibilities for hydraulic farming are still somewhat better in Zapata's vicinity than in the site territory as a whole.

At Cabezo Negro de Pastrana, the proportions of *monte* and *secano* in the core and the periphery of the site territory are almost the same as those at Zapata, but the *regadío* potential in the site's immediate vicinity is much higher. As Figure 5.8 shows, the site is located at the end of a ridge separating two *ramblas*, both of which have some irrigated land along their sides, as well as a *huerta* at their confluence. *Monte* forms 71% of the 30 min territory and 60% of the area between 30 min and 2 h distance; the corresponding proportions of *secano* are

19% and 35%. *Regadío*, by contrast, forms 25% of the area within 12 min of the site (6% of the land within 30 min), but only 2% of the peripheral zone. Here, then, the defensive considerations governing Argaric site placement have been satisfied at little sacrifice to the potential for secure, irrigation-based farming.

Vera basin sites

The Vera basin lies between the Mediterranean coast and the Sierras Cabrera (to the south), de los Filabres (to the west), de Almagro (to the north) and Almagrera and de los Pinos (both to the north-east). The low-lying areas between these elements of the Betic fold system are filled with Tertiary marine and Quaternary alluvial–colluvial deposits. The climate of the basin has been described on p. 71. At Cuevas, in its centre, mean annual rainfall is 255 mm, with a median of 221 mm (Kleinpenning 1965, p. 26), but in the *sierras* rainfall is much higher. The precipitation at higher elevations feeds the three major streams that cross the basin (Fig. 5.9): from north to south, the Rivers Alman-zora (with its tributary, the Rambla de Canalejas), Antas and Aguas. The Sirets were based at the mines of Herrerías at the confluence of the Almanzora and Canalejas, so that the archaeological resources of the basin were well canvassed early on. All nine sites in our sample were originally published in *Les Premiers Ages du Metal* (Siret & Siret 1887).

Because of the aridity of the climate, evergreen forest would not form the climax vegetation anywhere within the site territories. Areas at low elevations (below 200 m) would be covered with thorny scrub (Freitag 1971, Völk 1973), while higher elevations (900 m is reached within the site territories) would be covered with a chaparral formation. Both communities have been described above. Although overgrazing and cultivation have degraded or eliminated the original vegetation over much of the site territories, relict stands of the climax communities still remain intact in several places within the site territories (Freitag 1971, pp. 254, 264). The acorns the Sirets report from Lugarico Viejo (1887, plate 16) suggest that the kermes oak element of the chaparral formation was present in the lower areas of the basin (from which it has been eliminated now). The importance of mastic tree, pine and olive in the samples of charcoal fragments recovered from the recent excavations at Fuente Alamo indicate that the reconstructed climax vegetation of chaparral was in fact abundantly distributed in the hills around the Vera basin in Bronze Age times (Scoch & Schweingruber 1982).

The arid climate also contributes to the moderate erosion potential of the principal lithologies within the site territories. The hard-rock lithologies of the mountains ringing the basin and the conglomerate pediments extending from them all have high infiltrabilities, but even on the relatively impermeable marls erosion potential is not catastrophic, essentially because runoff sufficient to accomplish extensive work on slopes occurs on few occasions and slopes are

Figure 5.9 Mean winter water yields in the overlapping 2 h territories of sites in the Vera basin.

low. On bare, gullied slopes our estimates of annual soil loss would lead to an escarpment retreat of only a few metres per millennium (cf. equation 4.7). This finding suggests why, in spite of the fact that soils throughout the basin consist of relic C horizons (Völk 1973, p. 273), the siting of ancient settlements can suggest that the general configuration of the landscape has changed little over the past several millennia (cf. pp. 71–74).

El Oficio (elevation 235 m) is located on the southernmost extension of the

Sierra de los Pinos and dominates the plain at its base by 100 m. The Sirets (1887, pp. 179–97, plates 60–63) reported 1.5 m of deposits amid the rectangular structures at the summit. The stone buildings, abundant ceramics, querns and loom weights found in the acropolis suggest its use as a permanent habitation. The Sirets also reported some (unexcavated) structures on the gentler, eastern slope of the hill, so that the total size of the settlement may have been larger than the 0.25 ha at the top. The cist and jar burials found beneath the house floors yielded a classic Argaric inventory including halberds, riveted daggers, chalices, and so on.

The El Oficio site territory is in the northern portion of the Vera basin and comprises the northern portion of the municipality of Cuevas and the southern portion of Pulpí, formerly part of Vera, the town south-west of Cuevas. Kleinpenning's (1965) detailed review of agricultural practice within Cuevas makes it clear that, apart from some 230 ha of new irrigated land watered by artesian wells as of 1961, farming in the northern sector of the municipality was entirely traditional in character. A few springs at the base of Sierra de Almagro and the surface and subsurface flows along the Rambla de Canalejas provided some irrigated and floodwater-farmed land, but the rest was either *monte* or *secano* (often terraced). The 1956 air photographs provide, then, a reliable guide to traditional land uses within the El Oficio site territory.[4]

Because of El Oficio's extreme defensive position, *monte* forms a higher proportion of the 30 min territory (67%) than of the area between 30 min and 2 h distance (53%). At the same time, as Figure 5.10 shows, the proportion of agricultural land-use categories increases as one moves away from the site. Irrigated land is somewhat more abundant in the core than in the periphery (1.2% vs 0.7%), but the highest proportion of *regadío* occurs in the 30 min to 1 h zone (2.7%), at a considerable distance from the site. *Secano*, terraced and *boquera*-fed land are all more abundant in the periphery of the site territory. The defensive preoccupations that led the inhabitants to settle on a site which, on its most approachable side, must almost be scaled, clearly were more important than any consideration of least-cost access to farmland. Within the 30 min territory, however, the most abundant land-use category is *secano*.

Campos and Tres Cabezos (elevation 100 m) are located on a dissected terrace 20 m above the floodplain of the Almanzora River immediately opposite the town of Cuevas. Both sites were excavated by the Sirets (1887, pp. 21–8, 53–61, plates 3 & 9–11). Campos has been re-excavated by Martín Socas in 1976, 1977 and 1980 (Ministerio de Cultura 1981, p. 38). The Sirets' excavations at Campos revealed a fortified structure with bastions at the end of the dissected terrace. (This positioning suggests, of course, that the ravines cutting through the 20 m terrace antedate the site). The interior of the bastion structure contained 1.5 m of deposits with miscellaneous occupational debris (ceramics, bone awls, post-holes, burnt fragments of wattle-and-daub). The recent campaigns at the site have revealed round hut floors. The lithic industry of bifacially flaked points and large blades, the phalange idol, and the copper implements illustrated by the

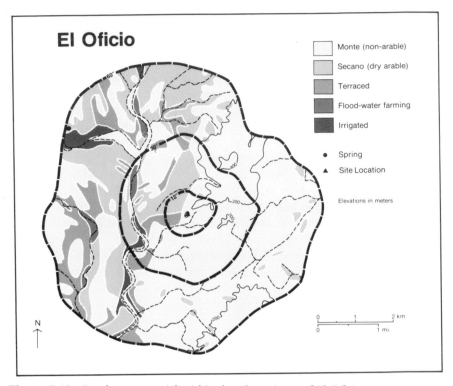

Figure 5.10   Land-use potential within the 1 h territory of El Oficio.

Sirets, as well as the painted and incised objects reported from the most recent excavations, point clearly to a Copper Age date for the site.

The Sirets' excavations at Tres Cabezos (across the ravine from the Campos bastion structure) revealed 10 shallow pits with dark soil. These yielded plain pottery and ground stone axes. The absence of metal or other chronologically diagnostic artifacts led the Sirets to assign the site to the Neolithic. It is possible, however, that the lack of distinctive pieces may reflect a functional, rather than a temporal, contrast to the Campos series.

Within the past 15 years, the sinking of deep wells to tap the Ballabona aquifer south-west of Cuevas has permitted irrigation to be extended to areas previously *secano* throughout the centre of the Vera basin. This expansion of *regadío* post-dates Kleinpenning's (1965) study of agriculture within Cuevas, as well as the 1956–57 air photographs for the area. While it is easy to control the effects of this recent modernisation, it is more difficult to assess the extent of recent changes in traditional farming. The *huerta* of the Almanzora is now divided into two areas (Kleinpenning 1965, pp. 30–7). The *tierras de huerta* receive about $1001 s^{-1}$ year-round from the 'Fuente de Overa', a spring 17 km up the Almanzora, and from the 'Alumbramiento del Cebollar', a 3 km long underground gallery tapping the Almanzora's subsurface flow. The *tierras de rio*, a larger area down stream from the *tierras de huerta*, is fed by the Almanzora's periodic surface flows, captured by large *boqueras*. Although it is not possible to arrive at quantitative estimates of 18th-century land uses along the Almanzora,[5] the 1752 Ensenada *Respuesta General* for Cuevas makes the distinction between *tierras de huerta* and *de rio*. On the one hand, it is obvious that the development of the Overa and Cebollar water sources would have been beyond prehistoric technical competences and investment levels. On the other hand, the $100\,\mathrm{l\,s^{-1}}$ flow from these sources is relatively small compared to the mean winter water yields we have estimated for the lower Almanzora (over $800\,\mathrm{l\,s^{-1}}$) (Fig. 5.9). Thus, while the Overa and Cebollar water sources provide stability in the water supply, the overall area of land that might be usefully prepared for hydraulic farming has not been greatly increased by their construction. Within the site territories we have counted the *tierras de huerta* as *regadío* and the *tierras de rio* as *boquera*-fed land in token of the degree of permanence of their water sources, but it is clear that any prehistoric hydraulic farming would have used the occasional surface flows only, so that for our purposes the two categories must be considered together.

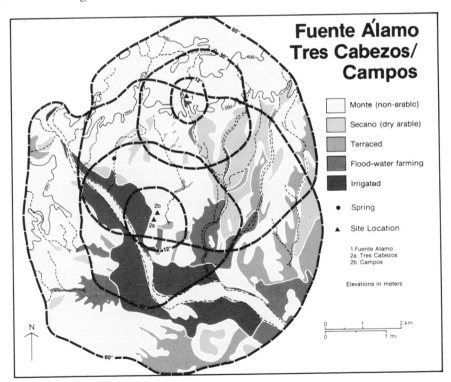

Figure 5.11 Land-use potential within the overlapping 1 h territories of Tres Cabezos–Campos and Fuente Álamo.

Campos and Tres Cabezos are well situated to exploit water diversion potential. '... This is a site location where one of the three main rivers is entering the Vera basin; in fact, about 2 km above the prehistoric sites, the river emerges from narrower, more deeply incised reaches to widen out forming over 1 km of alluvium at Cuevas before changing direction to flow down to the coast' (Chapman 1978, p. 270). As Figure 5.11 shows, within the 30 min territory 45% of the land is irrigated or floodwater-farmed (the latter includes some *tierra de rio*, but is mostly land fed by small *boqueras* along the *ramblas* leading down from the Sierra de Almagro to the north). This percentage is higher than that of any other land-use category in the core of the site territory, and much higher than the proportion of *regadío* and *boquera*-fed land in the area between 30 min and 2 h distance from the site (11%). By contrast, the proportions of the land surface devoted to *monte, secano* and terraced land increase as one moves from core to periphery of the sites' territories. The arid climate demands that the grain, which we know was grown by the inhabitants of these sites (Siret & Siret 1887, plate 11), be irrigated, and the location of the sites maximises the potential for doing so.

Fuente Álamo (elevation 250 m) is located on a hilltop at the base of Sierra de Almagro. The top of the site is 65 m above the spring of the same name. The flow of $0.5 l s^{-1}$ (in the Sirets' time) has fed a small, irrigated area below the site. First excavated by the Sirets (1887, pp. 199–209, plates 64–68), Fuente Álamo has been the object of extensive work in 1977 and 1979 by the Deutsches Archäolo-gisches Institut (Schubart & Arteaga 1978, 1980). The acropolis at the top of the hill has an area of 0.2 ha with settlement debris up to 4 m thick. The south-facing slope of the hill is covered with rubble, so that the total area of this unquestion-able settlement may be 1 ha. The site is a classic Argaric locality with cist and jar burials containing grave goods such as silver jewellery, riveted daggers, chalices, and so on. The faience beads from Tomb 9 provided one of the principal pre-radiocarbon dating points for the Bronze Age of south-east Spain (Siret & Siret 1887, p. 205). The recent excavations have isolated a post-Argaric, Late Bronze Age component at the summit of the stratigraphic sequence; the precise chronology of the Argaric components has yet to be worked out.

The Fuente Álamo site territory overlaps substantially, as Figure 5.11 indi-cates, with that of Campos and Tres Cabezos. It is clear that the placement of this site was a response primarily to defensive considerations. Irrigated land (along the Almanzora), floodwater-farmed land (along the Almanzora and down stream along the *ramblas* draining Sierra de Almagro) and terraced land all are relatively more frequent as one moves from the 30 min territory to the areas at a greater distance from the site. Potential *secano* forms a somewhat higher proportion of the 30 min territory (20%) than of the peripheral zones (11%), but, as Kleinpenning (1965) makes clear, such land was of very little worth before water from the Ballabona aquifer became available. The spring at the site provides for some limited hydraulic agriculture, but unless it flowed much more abundantly in prehistoric than in recent times, the population of the site, which must have numbered in the hundreds, cannot have supported itself on the agricultural resources in its immediate vicinity. Dry-farmed land, the most abundant type of land near the site, would not have been reliable enough.

El Argar, El Garcel, La Gerundia, Fuente Vermeja and Lugarico Viejo are located along the River Antas, which drains the eastern portion of the Sierra de los Filabres. The first three of these sites are so close to one another that they may be seen as having essentially identical site territories. All three are located at an elevation of 100 m on dissected marl mesas just below where the Rambla de Cajete joins the Antas. The site's location and its geomorphological significance have been discussed on pp. 71–74. Fuente Vermeja (elevation 190 m) is located 3.5 km west of these sites on a slope descending from the conglomerate pediment through which the Antas has cut its bed. The site is immediately above both the river and the spring that gives the locality its name (and which in 1973 produced a flow of $2 l s^{-1}$). Lugarico Viejo (elevation 210 m) is 0.75 km further up stream, on the gently sloping summit of a hill immediately above the river.

All five of the Antas River sites were first excavated by the Sirets (1887, pp. 1–9, 71–83, 111–64, plates 1, 13–16 & 22–56). Some of Louis Siret's post-1887 finds at El Argar and El Gárcel have been published (by Ruiz-Gálvez (1977) and Gossé (1941), respectively). Further excavations conducted at El Gárcel in 1973 have been described only briefly (Acosta 1976).

El Gárcel, like La Gerundia and El Argar, is on top of a marl mesa defined by drainage lines descending from the north to the Antas. Archaeological materials were found in a layer of dark soil at the surface (Siret & Siret 1887, p. 3) and in pits sunk into the marl subsoil (Gossé 1941). Querns, pottery and plant remains indicate that the locality was a settlement (the surface of the mesa is 0.4 ha). The presence of geometric microliths (an archaic, 'Mesolithic' trait) and of abundant undecorated pottery led the Sirets to place the site's occupation in the Neolithic (although the presence of copper slag suggests continued use of the locality into later times). Since this attribution, like that for Tres Cabezos, depends more on the absence of Copper Age type fossils than on the presence of distinctively Neolithic features, some authorities, such as Acosta (1976), interpret El Gárcel as an impoverished Copper Age habitation site. It is clear, however, that at least the El Gárcel lithic series is quite unlike the stone tool assemblages from unquestionable Copper Age localities.

The mesa top of La Gerundia covers 0.9 ha. Archaeological finds were concentrated in the dark topsoil. The Sirets reported no structures, but the finds include such settlement debris as potsherds and ground stone loom weights and axes. Tanged copper points, bifacially flaked points and Beaker sherds are clear Copper Age diagnostics.

El Argar covers 1.5 ha. The Sirets excavated deposits up to 2.5 m thick with rectangular structures (Siret & Siret 1887, Fig. XV) and abundant occupational debris of all kinds. The (more than 1000) earth, cist and jar burials provided a full panoply of the distinctive artifacts that make this the type site of the Bronze Age

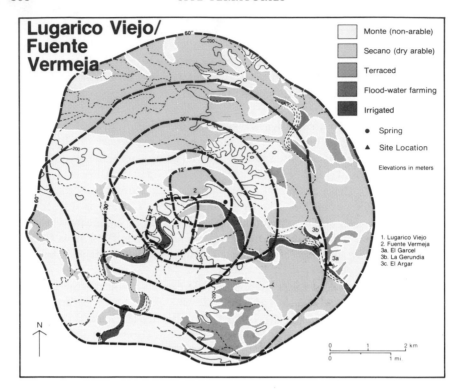

Figure 5.12 Land-use potential within the overlapping 1 h territories of Lugarico Viejo and Fuente Vermeja.

in south-east Spain. A few Beaker sherds (Siret & Siret 1887, Fig. XVII/10) suggest, however, that occupation of the locality may have begun in the preceding period.

Chapman (1981a) has demonstrated that the Siret collection procedures at Los Millares involved the careful retention of a full range of the stylistically distinctive fraction of the assemblages. Each of these three localities, located only a few hundred metres from one another, produced materials whose central stylistic tendencies are entirely distinct from those of the other two. Unless the Sirets were much more biased in their selection procedures in their early work than they were later on, it seems clear that the three localities belong to successive stages of the south-east's prehistory.

The slopes on which the site of Fuente Vermeja is situated covers about 0.8 ha. The Sirets excavated rectangular stone structures with abundant potsherds, querns and other domestic debris. Burials from the site yielded riveted daggers, carinated vessels and other typical, Argaric materials.

The hilltop of Lugarico Viejo covers about 1.3 ha, of which the Sirets excavated only a small portion. Their work uncovered occupational debris – potsherds, querns, loom weights, storage vessels with carbonised grain – and burials with riveted daggers and other Argaric elements. The ceramics include incised wares of Late Bronze Age character, so that the occupations of Lugarico Viejo and Fuente Vermeja may not have been entirely contemporaneous.

The drilling of deep wells to exploit the Ballabona aquifer has transformed farming in the Antas valley. On the one hand, the pumped water has permitted irrigation to expand onto previous *secano* and to be intensified on existent *regadío*. On the other hand, the consequent drop in the water table has eliminated many traditional water sources. Three galleries along the Antas between Fuente Vermeja and El Argar produced $100\,\mathrm{l\,s}^{-1}$ of flow in 1973 and are now dry. Not all changes are so recent, however. Water from one of these galleries (indicated as a spring on Figures 5.12 and 5.13) was brought by aqueducts across the Rambla de Cajete to wide areas west and south of the town of Vera and across the Antas to areas south of the town of the same name. This is clearly a 19th-century elaboration of irrigation: the 1752 *Respuestas Generales* for Antas and Vera (including the now separated townships of Pulpí and Los Gallardos) report only 193 ha of *regadío*, far less than would have been fed by the aqueducts. We have mapped as *regadío* only those areas immediately beside springs and along the Antas floodplain where relatively small-scale works suffice to supply

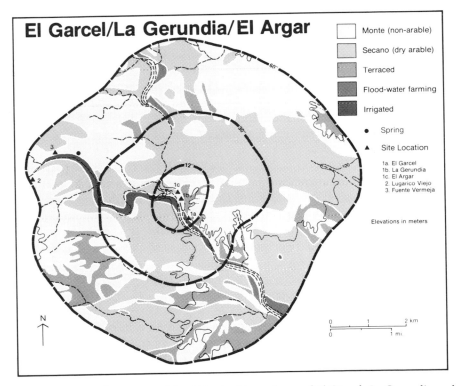

Figure 5.13 Land-use potential within the 1 h territory of El Gárcel, La Gerundia and El Argar.

water to the fields. The total *regadío* area for the Lugarico Viejo territory, which overlaps with most of the Antas and Vera municipalities, is 266.75 ha. This suggests that our *regadío* total is still larger than the amount irrigated in the 18th century. The expansion of irrigation during the 19th century involved not just the construction of large-scale works like the aqueducts, but the expansion of small-scale operations as well.

As shown in Figures 5.12 and 5.13, the distribution of land uses within all three site territories indicates that the sites were situated to exploit hydraulic resources preferentially. This is simply because all of the sites are located along one of the Vera basin's major watercourses.[6] As a result, the proportion of *regadío* in each of the 30 min territories is higher than in the area between 30 min and 2 h distance: at Lugarico Viejo 6% vs 1%; Fuente Vermeja 6% vs 3%; El Argar and nearby sites 5% vs 4%. The lessening magnitude of the contrast as one moves down the Antas valley is due to the fact that the downstream sites' 2 h territories reach the irrigated area of the Almanzora valley to the north-east. The percentage of irrigated land in the El Argar site territory is only 1% in the 30 min to 1 h time zone, but rises to 4.7% in the area beyond 1 h from the site.

Boqueras are used in these site territories partly to exploit the hydraulic opportunities along smaller streams. They are also used in the areas furthest down stream along the Antas, which would only be reached by larger, less frequent flows (the water from lesser events having been completely captured up stream). Thus, *boquera*-fed land increases steadily as one moves from core to periphery of each of the site territories. Terraced land in these territories is located along drainage lines on marls so as to check erosion and retain moisture. Marls are more frequent in the lower-lying central areas of the basin. For this reason, the proportion of terraced land is higher at a distance from the sites than closer to them and highest overall in the El Argar site territory, the lowest and most central of the three.

The same topographical considerations govern the relative proportions of *monte* and *secano*. Lugarico Viejo is the westernmost of the sites, located in the foothills at the edge of the basin. Thus, *monte* decreases as one moves away from the site (from 72% in the 30 min territory to 53% in the peripheral zones), while *secano* increases (the corresponding proportions are 21% and 36%). In the territory of El Argar and its neighbours, closer to the centre of the basin and with a less precipitous topography in its vicinity, the proportions of *secano* and *monte* in the 30 min territories are 60% and 24%, respectively; in the peripheral zones the corresponding proportions are 35% and 43%. In the El Argar site territory, then, *secano*, as well as *regadío*, is emphasised within the core. If, however, one excludes from consideration the 1 to 2 h zone of the site territory, the relatively better location of the El Argar group of sites for hydraulic than for dry-farming becomes apparent. *Regadío* is 12% of the 12 min zone, 4% of the 12 to 30 min zone and 1% of the 30 min to 1 h zone; *secano*'s corresponding proportions are 39%, 63% and 41%. Quite simply, the Quaternary terraces north and south of the Antas valley provide better dry-farming opportunities than the Antas valley, in which the sites are situated. To sum up, none of the Antas sites are in extreme defensive positions; all of them have easy access to arable land. At Lugarico Viejo and Fuente Vermeja, *regadío* is the most favoured agricultural land-use category. Within the site territory of the El Argar cluster, both potential *regadío* and potential *secano* are favoured in the core.

Gatas (elevation 230 m) is located on the sloping top of a limestone hill at the foot of Sierra Cabrera at the southern edge of the Vera basin. The site was subjected to limited excavation by the Sirets (1887, pp. 165–77, plates 57–59). The 0.7 ha surface of the slope is covered with the rubble of stone structures, and the finds reported by the Sirets – potsherds, querns and so on – clearly indicate the site's settlement function. Several burials revealed materials of Argaric character: one urn, for example, included a silver diadem and a riveted dagger as grave goods.

The southern portion of the Vera basin, distant from the Ballabona aquifer, has undergone no great changes in agricultural exploitation patterns in the past 25 years. Cultivation is still palaeotechnic in character and the same land-use distributions are present today as in the 1956–57 air photographs. In the 18th century, the site territory was included within the municipal jurisdictions of

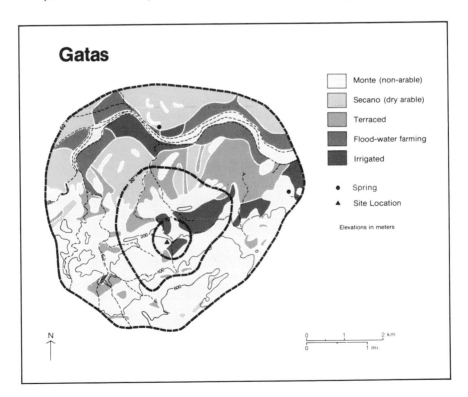

Figure 5.14 Land-use potential within the 1 h territory of Gatas.

Vera, Turre and Mojácar. Since it is apparent that municipal boundaries today are not those reported in the Ensenada survey, and since the 1752 land–use measure for Turre was the variably sized *fanega de puño*,[7] it is difficult to estimate precisely how much irrigation has expanded over the past two centuries. Mojácar's *Respuesta General* reports 39 ha of *regadío*, compared to about 155 ha now. At any rate, the large increase in irrigation that no doubt took place was achieved by the addition of small–scale, essentially palaeotechnic, hydraulic works, so that we feel justified in taking the present-day situation as a fairly complete realisation of traditional irrigation potential.

The limestone massif of the Sierra Cabrera produces a number of springs, all of which are used to irrigate larger or smaller areas. Within the Gatas 30 min territory there are 12 springs and short galleries, which together produce a flow of $12 \, \mathrm{ls}^{-1}$. Thus, as Figure 5.14 shows, *regadío* forms 14% of the 30 min territory (36% of the area within 12 min of the site). In the area between 30 min and 2 h distance, the proportion of *regadío* is only 3%. By contrast the proportion of *secano* increases as one moves away from the site (12% of the 30 min territory, 30% of the peripheral zones). Terracing is used within the territory both to extend cultivation to the steeper slopes of Sierra Cabrera and to check erosion and retain moisture along drainage lines in the marls of the northern portion of the territory, closer to the centre of the basin. Terracing is present, therefore, in similar proportions in both core and periphery (17% and 14%, respectively). *Boquera*-fed land is located mainly along the River Aguas. Of the land in the peripheral zones of the Gatas territory, 7% is floodwater farmed, but there is no floodwater farming in the 30 min territory. Clearly, then, Gatas is a Bronze Age site in which defensive considerations were able to be satisfied in a manner compatible with rational exploitation of agricultural resources. This is an arid–zone site whose location maximises hydraulic potential.

Terrera Ventura

Terrera Ventura (elevation 370 m) is located at the southwestern extremity of the Campo de Tabernas, the plain between the Sierras Alhamilla and de los Filabres, which respectively limit the site territory to the south and to the north. In 1951–59 mean rainfall at Tabernas, 1 km north-east of the site, was $250 \, \mathrm{mm \, yr}^{-1}$, with a median of 222 mm,[8] but precipitation would be much more abundant at greater elevations (the site territory reaches the 1000 m contour in Sierra Alhamilla). Because of the low rainfall, the bulk of the site territory would be covered with a chaparral formation of the kind described above (cf. Freitag 1971). As Driesch and Morales (1977, pp. 29–33) point out, the abundance and variety of wild species in the Terrera Ventura faunal series confirm the widespread presence of such a plant community at the time of the site's occupation. Some *Quercus ilex* forest still survives on the heights of the *sierras*. For the most part, where the natural vegetation has not been replaced by cultivation, it has been overgrazed and cut to a degraded scrub, which in turn accentuates the desert quality of the landscape.

The lithologies over most of the site territory – limestones, mica–schists, metamorphics and conglomerates of the *sierras* and their outliers; the Quaternary alluvium of the Campo de Tabernas – have moderate to negligible erosion potential, either because of their high infiltrabilities or low slopes. Even the relatively impermeable Tertiary marls in the southwestern quadrant of the Terrera Ventura territory lack potential for catastrophic change, essentially for the same reasons discussed in reference to the Vera basin marls: low rainfall leads to few flows capable of performing extensive work on slopes. Terrera Ventura itself is located on top of a marl bluff 80 m above the Rambla de los Molinos. While the escarpment may have retreated since the site's occupation by some metres (Gusi Jener (1975, p. 312) estimates 10 m), Terrera Ventura's placement suggests that the 6 to 8 m of escarpment retreat per millennium above bare, gullied marl slopes indicated by equation 4.7 overestimates the amount of change in the distribution of landforms caused by erosion. Severe regolith loss has occurred on all lithologies, of course, but not to the extent of affecting our mapping of land-use categories.

Terrera Ventura has been excavated in 1950 by Cuadrado Ruiz (Topp & Arribas 1965), in 1961 by Martínez Santa Olalla (unpublished) and in 1973–74 by Gusi Jener (1975, 1976). The site covers 0.8 ha (and may have measured 1 ha before the retreat of the bluff). Gusi Jener's stratigraphic excavation of the 2.5 m of deposits revealed four successive levels. The basal layer (I) has some red ware similar to the *almagra* pottery of the Cultura de las Cuevas Neolithic. The uppermost layer (IV) has Beaker sherds and a few metal pieces, as well as bifacially flaked points. The intervening layers (II, III) contain undecorated pottery and few stylistically distinctive elements (apart from some 'idols' reported from III). Round structures in layers I and II are replaced by rectilinear structures in layer III. The precise associations of the 3rd millennium BC radiocarbon determinations obtained by Gusi Jener (cf. p. 19) have not yet been published. The *almagra* ware from the basal level of the Gusi Jener excavations and the early 4th millennium BC radiocarbon date taken from the section of the Cuadrado Ruiz or Martínez Santa Olalla excavations (cf. p. 19) are the most solid evidence available for assigning any site in the arid south-east to a pre-Millaran, Late Neolithic phase.[9] It would appear, then, that the occupation of Terrera Ventura spans the period between 4000 and 2000 BC.

The site territory of Terrera Ventura coincides fairly closely with the municipal territory of Tabernas. The 1752 Ensenada *Respuesta General* for Tabernas reported 212 *fanegas de puño* of *regadío* and 5000 of *secano* (cultivated on a three- to nine-year fallow cycle) in a total of 12 000 *fanegas* in the municipality as a whole. The proportions of *regadío* : *secano* : *monte* (2 : 42 : 57) are quite similar to the proportions of (*regadío* and *boquera*-fed) : (terraced and *secano*) : *monte* within the site territory (2 : 39 : 59), which we have obtained from air photographs and fieldwork. The essential limitation on farming in this extremely arid sector is the

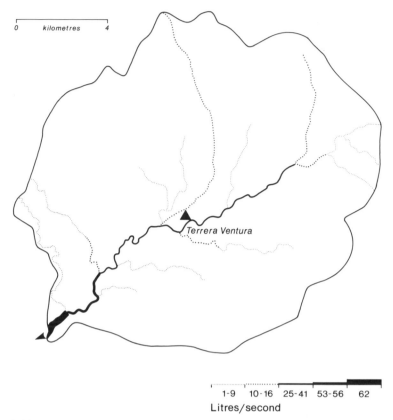

0   kilometres   4

Terrera Ventura

1-9   10-16   25-41   53-56   62
Litres/second

Figure 5.15   Mean winter water yields within the 2 h territory of Terrera Ventura.

lack of water: there are very few springs within the site territory (only one of which produces as much as $5 l s^{-1}$) and *rambla* flows are so sporadic (and subsurface flows so sparse) that they can only be exploited by *boqueras*. The possibilities for hydraulic farming are so limited that even in the 18th century they seem to have been fully exploited. Since the 1956–57 air photographs were taken, a few deep wells have been sunk in the northeastern quadrant of the site territory and now irrigate parts of the Campo de Tabernas, but these entirely modern operations are easily discounted from the potential palaeotechnic total.

Terrera Ventura is located above the Rambla de los Molinos near the point where it is joined by several other dry washes (see Fig. 5.15). As a result, *boquera*-fed land forms a higher proportion of the 30 min territory (6%) than in the area between 30 min and 2 h distance (2%). A spring at the southeastern edge of the 30 min territory (see Fig. 5.16) feeds a small irrigated area, so that *regadío* (although negligible in all areas of the territory) is also somewhat more abundant in the core than in the periphery (0.8% vs 0.1%). Terracing is used in the Tabernas territory, as in other areas of the arid south-east, to retain moisture in dry-farmed fields and to check soil loss. The concentration of terracing in the core of the Terrera Ventura territory (where it forms 28% of the land area vs 3% in the peripheral zones) is due, however, to the ancient site's proximity to the modern village of Tabernas. Least-cost considerations have led the recent inhabitants to build terraces near their homes and, thus, near the site as well. Both *monte* and unterraced *secano* increase as one moves away from the site. Clearly, in as arid a territory as that of Terrera Ventura, capital intensification in the form of terracing or hydraulic works is essential to successful agricultural production. The concentration of terracing in the core of the site territory is an artifact of Terrera Ventura's closeness to a present-day settlement. It is the hydraulic aspect of intensification which, therefore, must be given most importance in the site's placement. The fauna from Terrera Ventura tends to confirm the importance of hydraulic farming to the site's inhabitants. Sheep and goats, capable of exploiting the arid rangeland near the site, form 34% of the assemblage, but cattle and pigs, both of which would require considerably more water, form 30.5% and 18% respectively (Driesch & Morales 1977; see Table 2.2). The faunal series supports the notion that the inhabitants of Terrera Ventura practised an intensive agriculture for which hydraulic operations would be essential and for which the settlement's location was well suited.

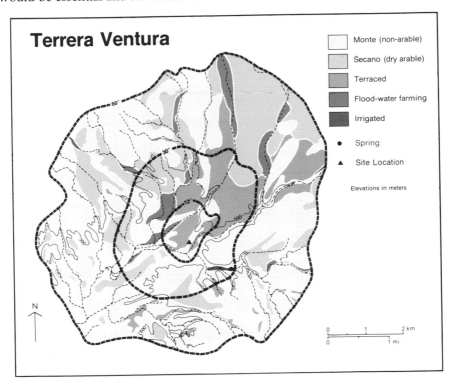

Figure 5.16 Land-use potential within the 1 h territory of Terrera Ventura.

Los Millares, Cerro Enmedio

Los Millares (elevation 250 m) is located on a promontory some 60 m above the river Ándarax, where it is joined by the Rambla de Huéchar. The site has been excavated, in 1891–92 by Louis Siret's foreman, Pedro Flores (Siret 1893), in 1953–56 (Almagro Basch & Arribas 1963) and since 1979 by a University of Granada team (Arribas *et al.* 1979). The Los Millares site has three parts. The tip of the promontory, enclosed by a wall with bastions (Almagro Basch & Arribas 1963, pp. 34, 273), covers an area of about 5 ha. The 1950s excavations cleared a small portion of the area inside the wall and uncovered curvilinear structures and rather nondescript occupational debris (querns, undecorated potsherds, and so on) (*ibid.*, pp. 39–46). The extent of contemporaneous occupation of the settlement area is undetermined, however: the University of Granada excavations have revealed a second line of fortifications (and possibly a third) inside the first. The over 2 m of deposits uncovered by these later investigations may help clarify the chronology of the settlement's occupation, which must have been well under way by 3000 BC (see our discussion of Los Millares' radio-carbon dates on p. 20). Distributed over the base of the promontory outside the wall is a megalithic cemetery of at least 85 tombs (Chapman 1981a): 75 of these, excavated by Flores, were published by the Leisners (1943); 21 were excavated (or re-excavated) by Almagro Basch and Arribas. The tombs have produced the range of characteristic materials that make Los Millares the type site of the Copper Age of south-east Spain. Finally, Siret reported four 'forts' on hills overlooking the promontory from the south, and recent work by the University of Granada team has identified more possible lookout towers on heights east of the Rambla de Huéchar (Arribas *et al.* 1979, Fig. 1). The surface of the largest of the forts has been cleared to reveal its layout during the most recent campaign and the material collected during the process of that work indicate the structure's contemporaneity with the settlement (Arribas & Molina 1982). Los Millares is, thus, the largest and most complex prehistoric settlement and burial complex in south-east Spain (and, in its time, western Europe), and understand-ably has come to be regarded as the 'central place' of Spanish Copper Age.

Cerro de Enmedio (elevation 400 m) is a limestone hill at the base of Sierra Alhamilla, where the limestones and mica–schists of the mountain range meet the marls and conglomerates of the lower Ándarax basin. The hilltop, protected by cliffs to the south and east, is enclosed by walls on the north and west. The 0.6 ha within the walls was surveyed by a University of Granada team and reveals rectangular structures at the surface (Molina *et al.* 1980). Amateur exca-vations in the 1950s produced carinated vessels, an archer's wristguard and a tanged point, materials which Schubart (1980) attributed to the 'A' phase of the El Argar Culture.

The lower Ándarax valley, in which the overlapping territories of both these sites are situated, is a region of extremely arid climate. Almería city, outside the territories to the south, has a mean annual rainfall total of 223 mm; Rioja (elevation 125 m), along the Ándarax midway between the sites, receives a mean of 215 mm yr^{-1} (Sáenz Lorite 1977, pp. 377, 385). As one moves up into the Sierra Alhamilla (north of Enmedio) and the Sierra de Gádor (south-west of Los Millares), rainfall rises rapidly: Alhama (elevation 520 m), in the southern portion of the Los Millares territory, receives 274 mm yr^{-1} and the highest elevations within the territories (1340 m in Sierra Alhamilla) must receive over 400 mm yr^{-1}. Because of the dry climate, areas below about 300 m within the territories would have a climax vegetation consisting of Freitag's (1971) *Mediterrane Trockenbusch* (thorny scrub) formation. At higher elevations, the climax formation would be a chaparral community, and *encinar* is still present at the summit of Sierra Alhamilla. This, however, is all the natural vegetation that still survives several millennia of grazing and charcoal burning.

In these site territories, as in others in the arid sector of the south-east, our modelling of erosional potential suggests that there have been no catastrophic changes in landforms (and thus in the land uses they may support) since later prehistoric times. The mica–schists, limestones and conglomerates (sometimes calichified), which predominate within the site territories, all have high infiltrabilities and low potential for regolith loss. For the same reasons as in other arid-sector site territories (the lack of a sufficient number of large flows), even the marls, which on the north side of the Ándarax downstream from Los Millares are dissected into badlands, cannot have changed significantly since the sites' occupations. Large amounts of surface materials have been removed from all lithologies, but nowhere in sufficient quantities to change measurably the distribution of cultivable surfaces. Indeed, at Los Millares itself, the positioning of the town wall with respect to the ravines cutting into the promontory clearly indicates that the latter antedate the former (Chapman 1978, p. 270).

As Sáenz Lorite (1977) makes clear, the principal recent changes in agricultural practices in the lower Ándarax all involve the introduction of techniques to expand the extent of irrigation for market-oriented farming. In the past 25 years the sinking of deep wells at the base of Sierra de Gádor has permitted irrigation to be extended to previously dry-farmed terraces descending to the Ándarax. The development of a foreign market for Ohanes table grapes goes back to the early 19th century, however, so that the expansion of irrigation is not simply a recent phenomenon. In Gádor, a municipality 2.5 km down stream from Los Millares, *regadío* expanded from 121 ha in 1752 to 382 ha in 1932 and 385 ha in 1973 (Sáenz Lorite 1973, p. 689). Comparison of the amounts of *regadío* reported in the Ensenada *Respuestas Generales* for other townships along the lower Ándarax (Benahadux, Pechina, Rioja, Santa Fe de Mondújar) with the extent of irrigated land visible in the 1956–57 air photographs indicates a similar increase. This expansion is the result of the construction of galleries in the bed of the Ándarax to tap its subsurface flow. According to the IGME *Inventario de Puntos de Agua*, between Los Millares and the downstream limit of the territories, seven galleries up to 4 km long together produce a flow of 1040 l s^{-1}. This is a substantial proportion of the 1700 to 1800 l s^{-1} of mean winter water yield that

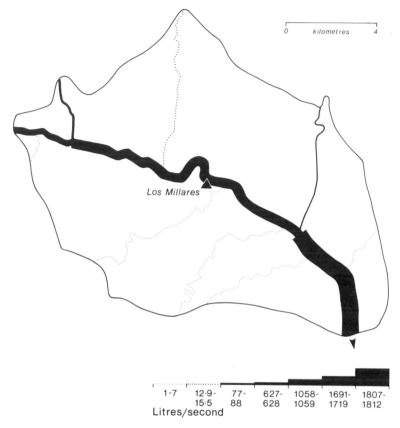

Figure 5.17   Mean winter water yields within the 2h territory of Los Millares.

we estimate for that stretch of the river (see Figs 5.17 & 5.18). This surface flow would, of course, be irregular in winter and absent in summer (when the galleries still produce $800 \, \mathrm{l \, s^{-1}}$). The *Respuestas Generales* for the municipalities mentioned above and the *Relación Particular* for Santa Fe de Mondújar (which we have examined in detail) make it clear that in the mid-18th century all their *regadío* was fed by the winter flows of the Ándarax and its tributary *ramblas* and that practically no irrigation water was available in summer. Thus, the construction of the galleries (a task beyond palaeotechnic capabilities) post-dates the 18th century and permitted the expansion of *regadío*. Accordingly, within these municipalities we have mapped irrigated land at its 1752 extent.[10] Within the core of the Los Millares site territory, our detailed reconstruction of the extent and distribution of the various land uses from the plot-by-plot descriptions of the *Relación Particular* for Santa Fe de Mondújar (where the site is situated) forms the basis of our mapping.

Municipalities upstream from Los Millares along the Ándarax (Alhama, Alicún, Alsodux, Bentarique, Huécija, Terque) did not report the extent of their various land uses in their responses to the Ensenada questionnaire. Here, as elsewhere in the arid south-east, there has also been expansion of the extent of irrigation since the 18th century. These townships are all situated in the western periphery of the Los Millares site territory. Thus, any reduction (by an imponderable amount) of the extent of *regadío* in this sector would tend to favour our hypothesis that Los Millares, a Copper Age site in the arid south-east, was situated so as to exploit hydraulic potential. Accordingly, up stream from Santa Fe we have mapped *regadío* at its 1956–57 extent. Besides the irrigated land along the Ándarax and its affluents, there are patches of *regadío* near springs at the base of Sierra Alhamilla (in the Enmedio territory) and the Sierra de Gádor (in the Los Millares territory). The Ensenada data make clear that these springs were also exploited in the 18th century, and we have mapped the extent of *regadío* in their vicinity by the 1956–57 air photographs.

The Ándarax, which drains the northern slope of the Sierra de Gádor, the eastern face of the Sierra Nevada and the southern slope of the Sierra de los Filabres, is the largest stream in the arid sector of our study area. The location of Los Millares immediately above this river clearly favours the practice of hydraulic farming. Indeed, as Figure 5.19 indicates, although the size and precipitousness of the Los Millares promontory limits the amount of *regadío*

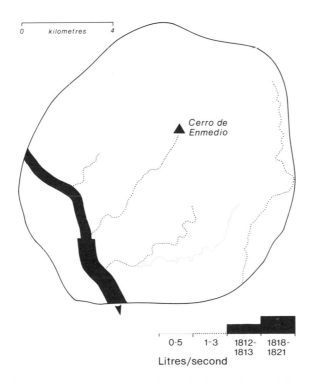

Figure 5.18   Mean winter water yields within the 2h territory of Cerro de Enmedio.

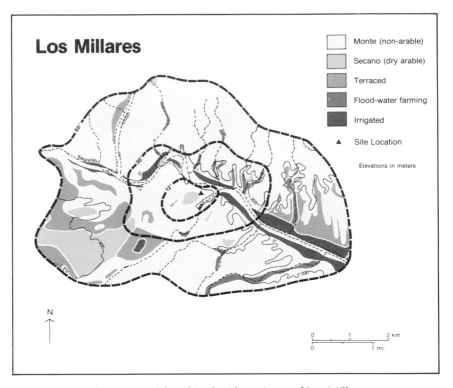

Figure 5.19   Land-use potential within the 1 h territory of Los Millares.

within 12 min of the site, *regadío* is the only agricultural land-use category more abundant within the 30 min territory (where it forms 9% of the land surface) than within the area between 30 min and 2 h distance (where the proportion is 5%). Dry farming (on the less steep interfluves) and floodwater farming (along the smaller drainages) are equally available in the core and the periphery, while terraced land (mainly used to extend cultivation to the lower slopes of the Sierra de Gádor) increases in frequency at a distance from the site. At the largest Copper Age site in south-east Spain (and indeed western Europe), the irrigation hypothesis is clearly confirmed.

Cerro de Enmedio is located near several important springs. The largest, indicated on Figure 5.20, produces a year-round flow of $15 \, \mathrm{l \, s^{-1}}$, and additional sources (some with short galleries) within the 30 min territory produce a collective flow of $12.5 \, \mathrm{l \, s^{-1}}$ (IGME, *Inventario de Puntos de Agua*). As a result, there is considerable irrigation potential in the immediate vicinity of the site (18% of the 30 min territory is *regadío*), more than in the farther reaches of the site territory (where the proportion of irrigated land, mostly located along the Ándarax over 1 h away, is 6%). All other agricultural land uses are proportionally more frequent in the periphery than in the core of the site territory.

Here, as at Gatas, the defensive considerations that governed the placement of Argaric sites was conveniently combined with easy access to irrigable land.

El Tarajal

The settlement of El Tarajal (elevation 40 m) and its associated megalithic cemetery, El Barranquete, are located on opposite banks of the Rambla de Morales, 1 km up stream from its confluence with the Rambla del Hacho. Mean annual rainfall at Cabo de Gata (on the coast, 8 km to the south-west) is 201 mm (Sáenz Lorite 1977, p. 383), but more would be expected at higher elevations within the site territory (which reach 435 m). The entirety of the Barranquete–Tarajal site territory falls within the Campo de Níjar, the core of the Níjar Desert. All of the plains would have a climax vegetation of thorny scrub, with chaparral on the higher slopes of the hills in the eastern and southern portions of the site territory (Freitag 1971). The conglomerates and volcanic rocks, which are the basic lithologies over most of the site territory, have low erosion potential.

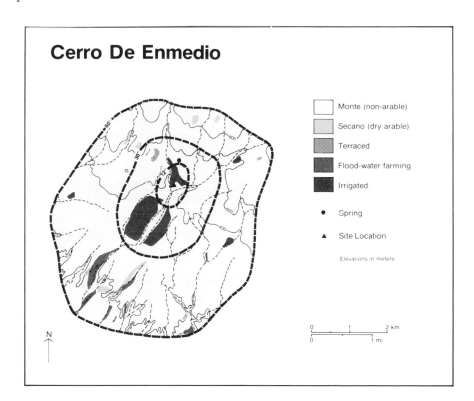

Figure 5.20 Land-use potential within the 1 h territory of Cerro de Enmedio.

Almagro Gorbea excavated the megalithic tombs in 1969–72 and the settlement (El Tarajal) in 1974 (Almagro Gorbea 1973, 1976, 1977). The necropolis consists of corbelled-vaulted, dry-stone-walled passage graves very similar to those at Los Millares and Almizaraque (Almagro Gorbea 1965). The 11 tombs excavated yielded a Copper Age inventory including copper axes, geometric microliths and bifacially flaked points, undecorated ceramics and one Beaker bowl. Elements such as the riveted dagger from Tomb 4 and the chalice from Tomb 5 indicate that use of the tombs continued into Argaric times. As we have seen (p. 20), radiocarbon dates place the construction of Tomb 7 in the early third millennium BC. Finds from the single test pit in the settlement have not been described in full, but include such characteristic Copper Age elements as painted pottery, bifacially flaked points and a tanged copper dagger. The over 3 m of deposits contained several constructional levels. In 1975 the 0.3 ha terrace on which the settlement was located was bulldozed and converted to a tomato field.

In recent years, deep wells (which now produce an aggregate flow of $1100 \, \mathrm{l \, s^{-1}}$) have greatly increased the extent of irrigation in the Campo de Níjar: the irrigated, sand-mulched vegetable fields alone now cover 3300 ha (Sáenz Lorite 1977, pp. 122, 255). By contrast the Ensenada *Respuesta* for Níjar (within whose limits most of the site territory falls) indicates that only 60 ha were irrigated in 1752 (20 000 *fanegas de puño* were put to grain on a three- to nine-year fallow cycle, and 130 000 were left uncultivated). It is apparent that, even before the modern development of deep wells, the extent of *regadío* had expanded considerably since 1752. We have included in the *regadío* total those areas that show irrigation in the 1956–57 air photographs and whose water supply depends on springs and water courses. The 350 ha of *regadío* we have mapped along the lower Rambla de Morales is, for example, in reasonable correspondence to the $180 \, \mathrm{l \, s^{-1}}$ that we estimate as the Morales' winter flow (Fig. 5.21). Two centuries ago the inland settlement pattern of this part of the coast (Sáenz Lorite 1977, pp. 260–2) would have made intensive exploitation of this area impracticable. As the population of Níjar increased from 2100 in 1752 to 5090 in 1850 and over 14 000 in 1900 (*ibid.*, pp. 280–301), the possibilities for traditional irrigation came to be fully exploited. It is clear, however, that areas now irrigated by non-traditional means would in the past have been either *secano* or uncultivated.

The distribution of land uses within the site territory clearly indicates that El Barranquete–El Tarajal was suitably located for irrigation farming (see Fig. 5.22). The proportion of *regadío* within the 30 min territory is 4.7%; in the area beyond 30 min distance it is 1.5%. *Secano*, however, is less frequent within the 30 min territory than in the outer zone (44% vs 66%). That land watered by *boqueras* is only found in the periphery of the site territory reflects the fact that Barranquete–Tarajal is located along the main drainage in the Campo de Níjar, the Morales–Hacho, practically the only water source within the territory sufficiently abundant to support irrigation (see Fig. 5.21), while the *boqueras* take

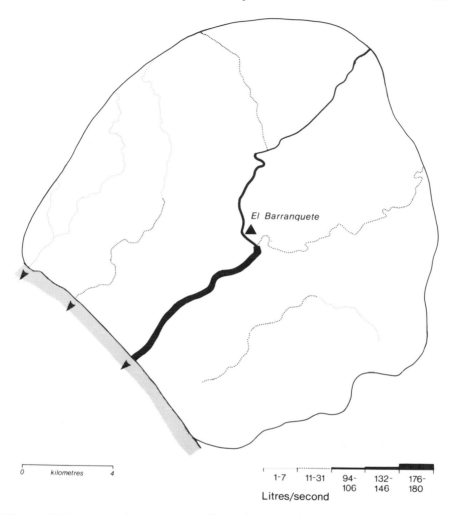

Figure 5.21 Mean winter water yields within the 2h territory of El Tarajal–El Barranquete.

advantage of the much smaller and more infrequent flows along small, peripheral drainages.

The only available excavated evidence on subsistence is the animal bones from the El Barranquete tombs (Driesch 1973b). The very high proportion of cattle (50% of the fragments from economically significant species) is no doubt due to the ritual context of the finds, but this context also underlines the *perceived* importance of cattle in the subsistence practices of the tombs' users. To maintain cattle in an environment as arid as the Níjar Desert would require that one grow fodder for them. Caprines, however, can graze on the available scrub. Given the lesser cost of producing caprines than cattle and their equal value as sources of

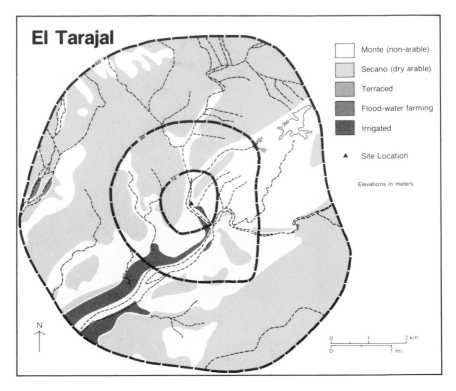

Figure 5.22   Land-use potential within the 1 h territory of El Tarajal–El Barranquete.

food, one must conclude that the importance of cattle to their husbanders (an importance sufficient to warrant ritual expression) would have been as sources of traction power. The importance of this 'secondary product' (Sherratt 1981) can only be understood as part of an intensive agriculture, for which the site's location is well suited.

Cueva de Ambrosio

This large rock shelter (elevation 1030 m) is located in a limestone cliff immediately above the Arroyo del Moral at the point where this small stream emerges from a narrow canyon. There are no rainfall stations within the site territory, but the mean annual rainfall figures of 404 mm for Topares (elevation 1196 m, 14 km to the north-west), 291 mm for the Valdeinfierno Reservoir (elevation 689 m, 14 km to the east) (León Llamazares *et al.* 1974) and 426 mm for Vélez Blanco (elevation 1074 m, 18 km to the south) probably give a representative range of precipitation values. Given these fairly high rainfall totals, the climax vegetation over most of the site territory would consist of evergreen oak and Aleppo pine forest, with deciduous oaks at higher elevations (1332 m within the site territory), and chaparral at its lower, drier, eastern extremity. Although some *encinar* survives here and there, most of the territory is now converted to cultivation, reduced to scrub or reforested with pine.

The 0.04 ha interior of the shelter contained a 60 cm Neolithic layer above the Upper Palaeolithic (Solutrean) deposits. The upper stratum was excavated completely in 1944 by Jiménez Navarro (1962), and the Palaeolithic deposits were partly excavated in 1958 and 1960 by Ripoll Perelló (1960–61). The incised and punctated wares found in the upper level affiliate its assemblage with the Cultura de las Cuevas (cf. Navarrete Enciso 1976, I, pp. 397–8). The upper level consisted of a dark midden with ash lenses, potsherds, animal bones (including rabbit, cattle, goat and deer: *ibid.*) and querns, all indicative of a domestic occupation.

Geologically, the Ambrosio territory consists of strongly tilted calcareous deposits. The harder limestone bands with high infiltrabilities have only moderate potential for erosion (see Appendices B and C). Given the high rainfall levels, however, the more impermeable, softer marl and chalk horizons have the potential for catastrophic erosion (which the rapid filling of the Valdeinfierno reservoir in the 19th century suggests has been in part fulfilled). Equation 4.7

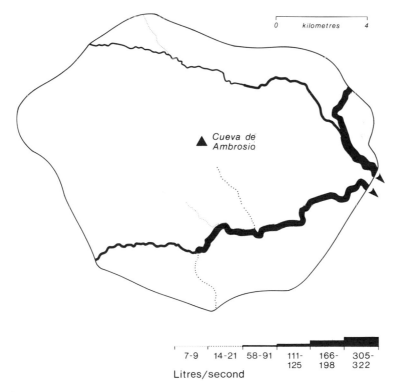

Figure 5.23 indicates kilometres scale 0 to 4

7-9   14-21   58-91   111-   166-   305-
                      125   198   322
Litres/second

Figure 5.23   Mean winter water yields within the 2 h territory of Cueva de Ambrosio.

suggests that a bare, gullied marl slope would lose enough material to cause its top edge to retreat about 250 m over a millennium; the corresponding figure on ungullied marls is 100 m. Since the landscape shows extensive evidence of ravining on the softer lithologies, and since south-facing slopes may reasonably be expected to have been stripped of vegetation for as much as one millennium of the six since the site was occupied, we have made the above adjustments to the extent of *secano* where topographically warranted.

The Cueva de Ambrosio territory falls inside the boundaries of the very large municipality of Vélez Blanco. As far as one can tell from the Ensenada *Respuesta General*, in 1752 intensive cultivation seems to have been concentrated in the vicinity of the town itself, with outlying districts composed either of *secano* (7800 ha) or *monte* (45 400 ha, of which some 30 000 were still forested). In this outlying district of the municipality, the main changes in land use since 1752 involve, on the one hand, extensive land clearance for cultivation (the ratio of *secano* to *monte* is now about 1 : 2 instead of 1 : 6) and, on the other hand, a limited development of *regadío* near springs and along streams. One such irrigated patch (which has fallen into disuse since our first visit to Cueva de Ambrosio in 1974) is in the immediate vicinity of the site. On the whole, however, the considerable

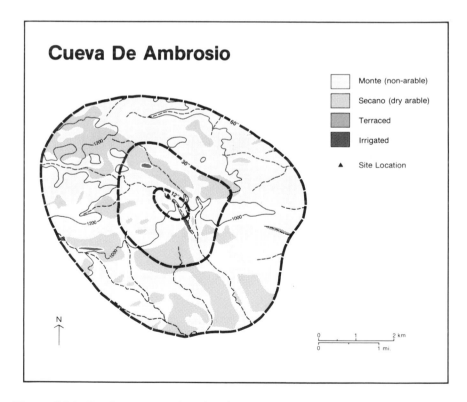

Figure 5.24 Land-use potential within the 1 h territory of Cueva de Ambrosio.

water diversion potential of the streams running through the site territory (see Fig. 5.23) remains greatly underexploited: the Rambla Mayor in the northern portion of the site territory has no *regadío*; the River Caramel in the southern portion has less than 60 ha of irrigated land. Our hypothesis for this relatively moist Neolithic site is that the site location would not maximise irrigation potential. Since the unfulfilled potential for irrigation is along streams that run through peripheral areas of the site territory, so that adjustments (whose precise extent would be difficult to determine) to increase present *regadío* would favour our hypothesis, our mapping of irrigated land reflects the current, underexploited situation.

As a result of the proximity of Cueva de Ambrosio to the irrigated patch near its eponymous farmhouse, the proportion of *regadío* within the 30 min territory of the site is higher than in the site territory as a whole (1.2% vs 0.6%) (see Fig. 5.24). *Secano* also forms a higher proportion of the 30 min than of the whole site territory (37% vs 32%). Since both *secano* and *regadío* are relatively more important in the core than in the periphery of the site territory, and since our estimates of water diversion potential suggest that the amount of *regadío* in the periphery of the site territory is appreciably below potential, we believe it is justifiable to interpret the distribution of land-use types within the territory as indicating that the inhabitants of Cueva de Ambrosio emphasised *secano* (or *monte*) in their subsistence activities.

Cerro de las Canteras

The site (elevation 790 m) is located on a small hill immediately above the River Claro and at the downstream extremity of the irrigated terraces that descend from Vélez Blanco, 5 km to the west. Mean annual rainfall at Tirieza (elevation 790 m), 5 km east of the site, is 332 mm (León Llamazares *et al.* 1974); at Vélez Blanco (elevation 1074 m), 426 mm; at Vélez Rubio (elevation 839 m), 5 km to the south-west, 469 mm. The approximately 400 mm yr^{-1} received in the vicinity of the site itself would rise substantially as one moves up into the Sierra de Maimón to the west and the Sierra de Gigantes to the north (the highest elevation within the site territory is 1600 m).

The climax vegetation over the bulk of the site territory would consist of evergreen oak and pine forests (*encinar* and *pinar*), but a chaparral formation may have been present in the lower, drier area near the eastern margin of the 2 h territory. As late as 1752, the Ensenada *Respuesta* for Vélez Blanco (whose municipal territory is much larger than the area of the site territory) reports 20 000 ha of oak and pine forest. In the higher areas of the *sierras*, forest of deciduous oaks may have been present. The principal lithologies in the site territory – limestones, mica-schists, metamorphics, conglomerates – all have low erosion potential, and the small area of chalk in the northwestern periphery shows no evidence of extensive ravining.

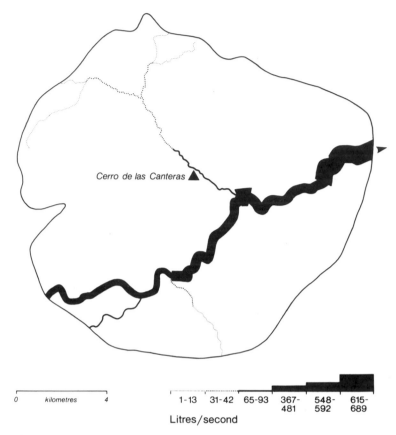

Litres/second

Figure 5.25   Mean winter water yields within the 2 h territory of Cerro de las Canteras.

The site was excavated by Motos (1918) in the earlier part of this century. A variety of diagnostic artifacts (phalange idols, incised ceramics with 'oculi' (*Symbolkeramik*), bifacially flaked arrowheads, a tanged copper dagger) clearly point to a Millaran (Copper Age) date. Two phases of occupation are reported on the site, but this division cannot be related to reliable assemblages. The site is clearly a settlement, with round and oval huts reported and a variety of artifacts of domestic character (querns, abundant sherds, etc.). Motos concentrated his work at the 36 m by 20 m summit of the hill, but reported structures along the southern slope as well.

Cerro de las Canteras's site territory lies at the boundary of the large municipalities of Vélez Blanco, Vélez Rubio and Lorca, so that the land-use reports of the Ensenada *Respuestas* cannot be clearly applied to the area that concerns us. The present agricultural landscape shows little evidence of recent modernisation – all irrigation in the territory is gravity fed from accessible sources – but does present certain problems of interpretation. The main sources of water for irrigation are, on the one hand, a series of springs at the base of the Sierra de Maimón, which collectively produce $220 \, \mathrm{l \, s^{-1}}$ (IGME, *Inventario de Puntos de Agua*), and, on the other hand, the water available in the main stream drainages (the River Claro by the site, and the Rambla de Chirivel, which after its confluence with Claro 2.5 km below the site becomes the River Corneros), whose winter flows are estimated in Figure 5.25. The Maimón springs feed an extensive *huerta* which extends to the vicinity of the site. This large irrigated area is the incremental product of centuries of investment in the land. Thus, much of the irrigated land west of the site up to the limit of the 1 h territory would not be potentially irrigable unless the springs had already been extensively exploited. At the same time, the irrigable potential of the River Corneros, in the 1 h to 2 h time zone east of the site, is underexploited today because the water is reserved by the Lorca irrigation cooperative for the Puentes reservoir down stream, which feeds the *huerta* near the city of Lorca itself. Thus, the distribution of present land uses tends to overestimate the amount of irrigable land that would have been present close to the site at the time of its occupation and to underestimate the amount of irrigable land available in the peripheral areas of the site territory. The hypothesis we are investigating would predict that in a

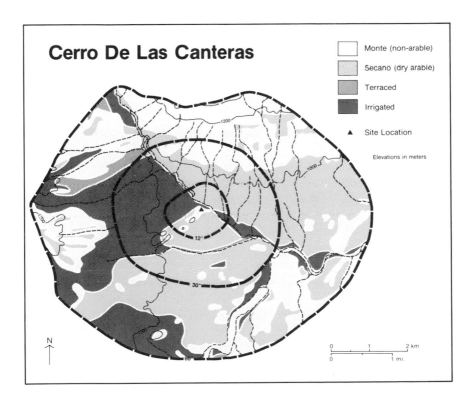

Figure 5.26 Land-use potential within the 1 h territory of Cerro de las Canteras.

relatively moist Copper Age site territory, such as Cerro de las Canteras, the site would not need to be located so as to maximise irrigation potential. Rather than adjust the distribution of land uses in favour of the hypothesis, we have, with one exception,[11] used the present situation as the basis of our land-use potential map.

Cerro de las Canteras is located at the bottom of the Corneros valley and, accordingly, naturally arable land, both *secano* and *regadío*, forms a high proportion of the core of the site territory (see Fig. 5.26). As one moves away from the site, one reaches the steeper mountain slopes and the amount of *monte* increases (from 10% of the area within 30 min of the site to 70% of the area from 1 h to 2 h distance). Terraced land, which in the Canteras territory is mainly used to extend cultivation to steeper slopes, also is relatively more frequent further away from the site. By contrast, *regadío* and *secano* form respectively 31% and 57% of the 30 min territory, but only 9% and 18% of the area from 1 h to 2 h distance. Since the rates of decline in the proportion of both *regadío* and *secano* from core to periphery of the site territory are very similar, and since, as we have seen, our measures of land-use potential overestimate the amount of *regadío* in the core and underestimate it in the periphery, we consider that the site's location is mainly oriented towards the exploitation of *secano*. To put matters another way, the location of the site anywhere at the bottom of the valley would maximise the amount of *secano* available, but the location of the site near the River Claro, instead of near the Chirivel or Corneros or near the springs at the base of Maimón, does not maximise irrigation potential.

El Picacho

The site (elevation 880 m) is located at the summit of a steep limestone hill that towers 80 m above the Rambla de Oria, precisely at the southern end of the 'Boca de Oria', the canyon by which the *rambla* passes through the Sierra de las Estancias. Mean annual rainfall at Oria (elevation 1023 m), 5 km to the west of the site, is 565 mm, but the median figure of 404 mm is probably more representative of the amount of precipitation over most of the site territory.

The potential vegetation over most of the site territory would consist of *encinar* with deciduous oaks and *carrasco* (Bordeaux) pines at higher elevations in the Sierra de las Estancias (which reaches almost 1400 m within the site territory) (Freitag 1971). Although in 1752 some stands of *carrascos* were reported in the Oria *Respuesta* as being reserved for exploitation by the Spanish navy, the natural vegetation is now fairly uniformly degraded to scrub. The principal lithologies within the site territory – limestones, mica–schists and conglomerates – all have relatively low erosion potential, so that large-scale geomorphological change is unlikely.

El Picacho was excavated in 1971–72 by Hernández Hernández and Dug Godoy (1975). The site is a typical Argaric settlement of rectangular houses with burials under the floors. Diagnostic artifact types (mostly found as grave goods) include chalices, carinated vessels, riveted copper or bronze daggers and archers' wrist guards. The radiocarbon determinations from the site (see p. 23) confirm that it was occupied during the earlier part of the 2nd millennium BC. The excavators (Hernández Hernández and Dug Godoy 1975, p. 115) suggest that the locality was only occupied in times of danger:

> ... Both on account of its strategic emplacement and on account of the scanty food remains found within the walls, we are inclined to believe that this settlement was regarded as refuge rather than a permanent dwelling place.

The well made stone constructions and the presence of artifacts devoted to daily maintenance activities (e.g. querns, loom weights) suggest, however, a permanent occupation of the *ca.* 0.13 ha summit.

The agricultural landscape within the Picacho site territory today presents an entirely traditional façade. Irrigation is entirely gravity fed from accessible

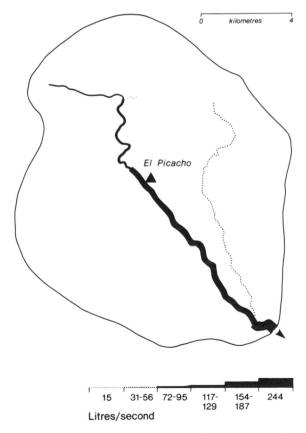

Figure 5.27 Mean winter water yields within the 2 h territory of El Picacho.

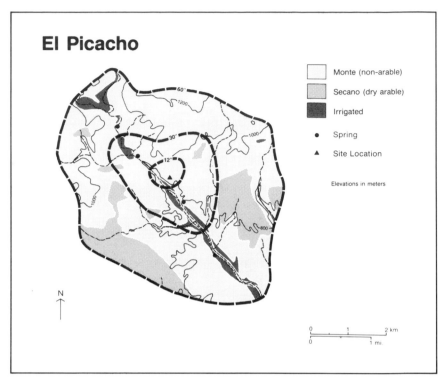

Figure 5.28   Land-use potential within the 1 h territory of El Picacho.

sources, springs and *rambla* flows (see Figure 5.27 for our estimate of the magnitude of the latter). The 1752 Oria *Respuesta* covers an area considerably larger than the Picacho 2 h territory, which it almost completely encloses. The reported total of *regadío* in 1752 is 246 ha, just over a third of the area of *regadío* that we have measured within the 2 h territory. Now the amount of irrigated land (43.25 ha) along the Rambla de Oria, the *regadío* closest to the site, is not larger than the estimated flows along the water course (154 to $1871 s^{-1}$) would support. Irrigation in the 30 min territory of the site is limited, not by the amount of water available to an archaic irrigation technology, but by the limited amount of land to which the water can be conveniently brought. Thus, any reduction in the area of *regadío* to bring the modern situation in line with the Ensenada reported total would have to be made in the peripheral areas of the site territory. Such an adjustment would only tend to strengthen the confirmation of the prediction for this site territory that our line of thinking would tend to make: namely, that the Argaric inhabitants of El Picacho practised hydraulic agriculture and located their dwellings as conveniently for that activity as defensive considerations would permit. Accordingly, rather than adjust the totals of *regadío*, as it were, in our favour (by amounts whose scale would be difficult to establish), we prefer to assume either that the estimates in the Ensenada *Respuesta* were too low or that the increase in irrigated land represents a realisation of a potential available to, but not actually exploited by, cultivators with an archaic technology. Thus, we take the present distribution of land uses as our guide to the potential land uses within this territory without adjustment.

Over 94% of the El Picacho 2h territory comprises *monte* and *secano*. The location of the site in an extreme defensive location at the foot of the Sierra de las Estancias ensures that *monte* will decline as one moves from core to periphery of the site territory and that *secano* will increase as one moves away from the site (and the mountains) to areas of lower relief more suitable for dry farming. *Regadío* constitutes 8% of the land surface within 30 min of the site, but under 5% of the total from 30 min to 2h distance. Thus, even without adjusting *regadío* land areas to conform to 18th-century evidence, the distribution of irrigated land indicates the site's favourable placement to exploit it. This is confirmed if we examine the 30 min territory in detail. We know that El Picacho's inhabitants were farmers, because the excavators report carbonised barley from the site (Hernández Hernández & Dug Godoy 1975, p. 114). Of the arable land close to the site (within 30 min walk), 69% is *regadío*, and the little *secano* that is present is located at the periphery of the time zone (see Fig. 5.28). It is reasonable to conclude, therefore, that the barley was grown on the irrigable land.

El Malagón

The site is located at an elevation of 1180 m at the extreme eastern edge of the Guadix–Baza endorrheic basin. Consistent rainfall records have not been collected from stations within the site territory, but Chirivel (elevation 1041 m), 15 km to the east, has a mean of 462 mm yr^{-1}, while Cúllar-Baza (elevation 891 m), 15 km to the west, has a mean of 317 mm yr^{-1}. Mean annual rainfall for the site territory is, therefore, above 400 mm.

Most of the site territory would have a climax vegetation of evergreen oak forest (*encinar* still covers the hills immediately east of the site), but with cold-tolerant elements such as deciduous oak (*quejigo*) (*Quercus faginea*) and Bordeaux pine (*carrasco*) (*Pinus pinaster*) at higher elevations in the Sierra de María to the north and the Sierra de las Estancias to the south (Rivas Goday & Rivas Martínez 1971). The limestones and mica–schists of the hills and mountains within the site territory and the conglomerate pediments extending from them all have low erosional potential. At the western extremity of the 2h territory, the drainage system cuts into Tertiary marl fill of the endorrheic basin, and the steep gullied slopes above the *ramblas* have much higher erosional potential. Even here, however, the potential changes would not be enough to alter to a significant degree global land-use distributions within the territory.

El Malagón was excavated by a University of Granada team in 1975 (Arribas *et al.* 1977, 1978). The finds include such elements as bifacially flaked projectile points, large flint blades, a tanged copper dagger, an ivory statuette (Arribas

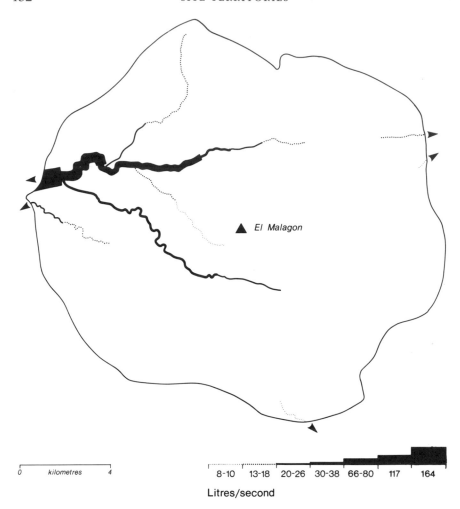

▲ El Malagon

```
┌──────────────────┐
0    kilometres    4
```

```
8-10   13-18  20-26  30-38  66-80   117    164
```
Litres/second

Figure 5.29 Mean winter water yields within the 2h territory of El Malagón.

1977) and a variety of undecorated ceramics, all of which point to a pre- (or non-) Beaker, Millaran (Copper Age) date for the site. Indeed, recent radio-carbon dates point to an occupation during the early 3rd millennium BC (see p. 22). The excavators note that the frequency of copper finds at El Malagón seems to be higher than in the settlement debris of other Copper Age villages (e.g. Los Millares) (Arribas *et al*. 1978, p. 89). The settlement has three construc-tional phases of approximately circular huts over a depth of deposits of 1.5 m. A possible fortification is reported on the northern edge of the excavated area, as well as a possible Los Millares-like fort on the hill immediately east of the settlement (Molina Gonzalez 1983, p. 73).

Changes in the agricultural practices in the region over the past centuries have not affected land-use potentials. The 1752 *Respuesta* for Cúllar-Baza, within whose boundaries most of the site territory falls, indicates that cultivation was concentrated near the town itself with outlying *secano* cultivated on a one-year-in-seven fallow cycle and much uncleared land. Indeed, land clearance is in progress even near El Malagón itself. The *regadío* and *boquera*-fed land along the *ramblas* and near springs is small scale, entirely proportionate to palaeotechnically available water sources (see Fig. 5.29) and traditional in character. Changes over the past 250 years involve the actualisation of land-use potential, which can, therefore, be readily delineated from the modern landscape.

Over 98% of the land in the Malagón 2 h territory consists of *monte* and *secano*, with *regadío* and floodwater-farmed land forming 1.7% of the total. Low as the proportion of regularly or occasionally irrigable land is in the site territory as a whole, it is even lower (1.3%) in the area within 30 min of the site (see Fig. 5.30). *Secano*, on the other hand, forms 80% of the 30 min territory, but 74% of the 2 h territory. A small spring today provides water for domestic use and for a small irrigated plot at the farmstead 200 m from the site itself, but, on the whole, the location of the site maximises the use of dry arable land (just as the principal operations of the present-day *cortijo* are all on *secano*).

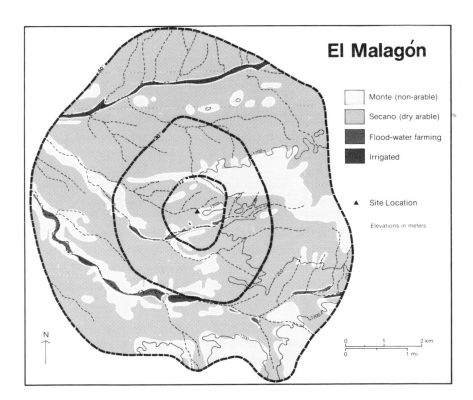

El Malagón

☐ Monte (non-arable)

▨ Secano (dry arable)

▨ Flood-water farming

■ Irrigated

▲ Site Location

Elevations in meters

Figure 5.30 Land-use potential within the 1 h territory of El Malagón.

Cerro de la Virgen

The site (elevation 920 m) is located on a marl promontory jutting into the floodplain of the River Orce, which cuts through the plains of the northeastern portion of the Guadix–Baza inland basin. The mean annual rainfall at Galera (4 km to the west) is 289 mm and at Orce (3 km to the east), 294 mm, but in the Sierra de Orce (which within the site territory rises to over 1500 m) to the south-east, it is much higher.

Wilhelm Schüle directed excavations on the site in 1963, 1965, 1967 and 1970 (Schüle & Pellicer 1966, Schüle 1980). The site covers 1.2 ha and has up to 6 m of archaeological deposits. There are three main prehistoric phases of occupation: pre-Beaker Copper Age (Level I), Beaker Copper Age (Level II) and Argaric Bronze Age (Level III), clearly dated not only by artifactual type fossils (the main diagnostics are described by Schüle (1980, pp. 33–8)) but also by radiocarbon determinations (see pp. 22 and 23). From its earliest occupation the settlement was protected by a wall across the southern end of the promontory where it joins the marl slopes of the valley sides (*ibid.*, p. 29). The site was unquestionably used as a habitation, since there is abundant domestic garbage and (in the Copper Age) round house floors (Kalb 1969). The irrigation canal reported by Schüle (1967) runs along the western side of the promontory and is clearly dated to the Copper Age (both by the Beaker sherd included in the upper silts in the ditch and by the Argaric burial placed over the ditch after it fell into disuse).

The climax vegetation within the Cerro de la Virgen 2 h territory would comprise four major communities (Rivas Goday & Rivas Martínez 1971). Along the floodplains of the major streams (the Rivers Orce and Huéscar, which join to form the River Galera) there would be a gallery forest of elms and poplars. The marl slopes of the valley sides, which towards the southwestern limit of the site territory become an area of extensive badlands, would support a chaparral community of kermes oak, buckthorn, etc. The rest of the site territory would be covered with evergreen oak woodland (*encinar*), but deciduous oak forest would occur at higher elevations in the Sierra de Orce.

The lithologies within the Cerro de la Virgen territory consist primarily of the limestones of the mountains in the south-east of the territory (these have a relatively low erosional potential) and the Pliocene and Early Quaternary marls that fill the Guadix–Baza endorrheic basin, marls often capped by caliches and now cut through by *ramblas*. The marls have a considerable potential for erosion (equation 4.7 indicates that a bare gullied slope might lose enough material over a millennium to push back its top edge 75 to 100 m). In spite of this, several ancient sites survive on dissected marl promontories and hillocks: not just Cerro de la Virgen itself, but also the 1st millennium BC settlement of Cerro del Real near Galera (Pellicer & Schüle 1962, 1966, Schüle 1980) and its associated necropolis of Tutugi (Cabré Aguiló 1920), which suggests that here, as near Guadix and Antas (see pp. 62–74), the marls have been relatively stable for the past several millennia. In spite of the existence of badlands in the western periphery of the site territory, we conclude that the overall proportions of landforms have not changed markedly over recent millennia.

The landscape of the present day shows little evidence of recent capital intensification. The *Respuestas Generales* of 1752 for the municipalities of Orce, Galera and Huéscar do not report land uses in measures convertible to a metric standard, but it is apparent that the area of both *secano* and *regadío* was much smaller than it is now. Much *secano* is reported as 'unfruitful through neglect' or was cultivated on a very long fallow cycle (up to six years in Huéscar). Since the amount of *regadío* in 1752 can hardly have been limited by the available water supply (streams within the site territory have an estimated winter flow of 40 to $2001\,s^{-1}$ – see Fig. 5.31 – and the six largest springs within the site territory together produce flows of between 435 and $11941\,s^{-1}$ (IGME, *Inventario de*

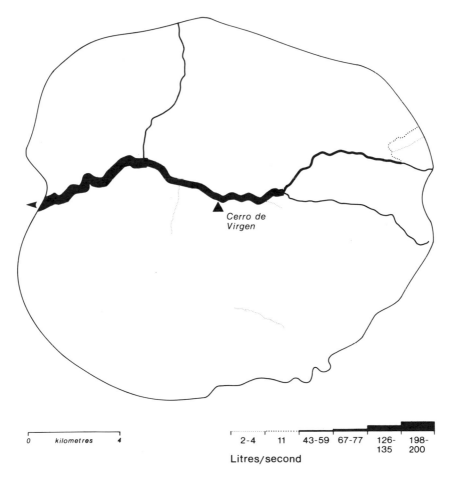

Figure 5.31   Mean winter water yields in the 2h territory of Cerro de la Virgen.

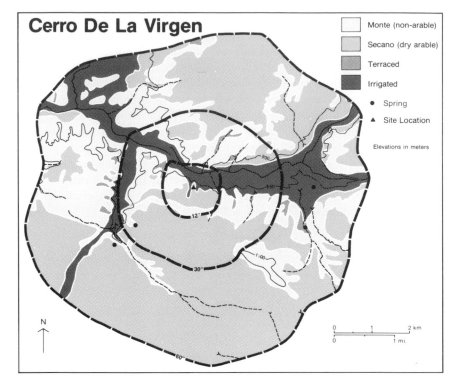

Figure 5.32   Land-use potential within the 1 h territory of Cerro de la Virgen.

Puntos de Agua)), and since present irrigation is all gravity fed from accessible sources nearby, it seems reasonable to take the extent of *regadío* visible in the 1956–57 air photographs as an approximation of palaeotechnic irrigation potential.

The distribution of land-use proportions within the site territory clearly indicates that Cerro de la Virgen was located for the preferential exploitation of *regadío* (see Fig. 5.32). Because the site is located on a promontory at the edge of a river floodplain, the proportion of *regadío* declines from 33.9% to 12.1% as one moves from the area within 12 min of the site to the area beyond 60 min walking distance. The proportion of *secano*, however, increases as one moves away from the site. *Monte*, which includes both dissected marl slopes along drainage lines and the steeper slopes in the mountains, and terracing, which is placed along drainage lines in the marls so as to retain moisture and check erosion, show no great increase or decrease with distance from the site.

Cerro de la Virgen is, of course, one of the localities that provide excavated evidence for intensive farming. First, of course, there is the irrigation ditch itself. Secondly, there is the faunal evidence (see Table 2.2 and pp. 25–27). This indicates that the proportion of cattle and horses (draft animals) is high and increases over the span of the site's occupation and that pigs, whose most suitable habitat would have been the gallery forest on the floodplain, decline over time, presumably as the area near the river was converted to irrigated terraces. The site was initially found in a setting potentially suitable for capital-intensive farming and the excavated evidence indicates persuasively that this potential was utilised over the course of the site's occupation.

El Culantrillo, Cerro del Gallo, Cuesta del Negro

These three localities are situated in the southwestern portion of the Guadix-Baza basin, an area whose principal geomorphological and climatic character-istics have been described on pp. 62–71. Following Rivas Goday and Rivas Martínez (1971), the site territories would have a climax vegetation consisting of three principal communities. On the badland slopes of the Guadix formation, generally below about 1000 m and receiving less than 350 mm yr^{-1} of precipi-tation, there would be a chaparral formation (see p. 134), now largely reduced to a cover of esparto grass and other shrubs. In the valley bottoms in the immediate vicinity of streams with year-round flows of water, there would be a gallery forest of elm and poplar. Such floodplain areas are now entirely put to irrigated cultivation. On the calichified surface of the marl fill of the basin and on the lower slopes of the mountains at the margins of the territories, where rainfall is generally above 400 mm yr^{-1}, there would be an evergreen oak forest. These encinares still survive in places, but mostly they have been cleared for cultivation. The spectacular badlands of the Guadix formation have suggested to many authorities that erosion has caused extensive changes in the distribution of landforms in the basin within recent times. Our studies at these sites (cf. pp. 62–71, see also Wise et al. 1982) and our general modelling of erosion potential on the various lithologies within the territories suggest, however, that the general configuration of the landscape in these site territories has remained relatively stable in the three to four millennia since the sites were occupied.

All three sites were occupied during the Bronze Age. El Culantrillo was tested in 1955 by García Sánchez (1963) in the wake of extensive operations by pothunters. The site (elevation 840 m) is located on a spur on the southern escarpment of the Gor River canyon. A series of burials produced carinated bowls, riveted daggers and other materials of Argaric character. The abun-dance of stony rubble on the surface and the surface finds of querns indicate that the 0.175 ha flat top of the spur was used not just for burials but also as a settlement.

The Cerro del Gallo site (elevation 880 m) is distributed over more than 2 ha along the top and sides of a marl interfluve above the confluence of two ramblas about 1 km above the point where the drainage system reaches the floodplain of the Fardes River. The site has not been formally excavated, but the pits made by clandestine excavators reveal stone structures and substantial (in places at least

60 cm thick) archaeological deposits. Collections from the site in the possession
of the schoolmaster at Benalúa include carinated vessels, chalices and archers'
wristguards, all Argaric diagnostics (Torre Peña & Aguayo de Hoyos 1976).

   Cuesta del Negro (elevation 950–1000 m) was excavated by a University of
Granada team in 1971–72. The archaeological remains are distributed over some
300 m of a spur descending towards the Fardes River. A round mound of debris,
the remains of an Argaric fort (Carrasco Rus, personal communication), is at the
top of the spur, and several areas of settlement have been identified on the slopes
below it. One of these habitation areas has been published (Molina González &
Pareja López 1975), and its stratigraphy reveals two main phases of occupation.
The upper levels have rectangular structures and an artifact assemblage including incised pottery. This is a Late Bronze Age component, radiocarbon dated to
the later 2nd millennium BC (see p. 24). Below this are two Early Bronze Age

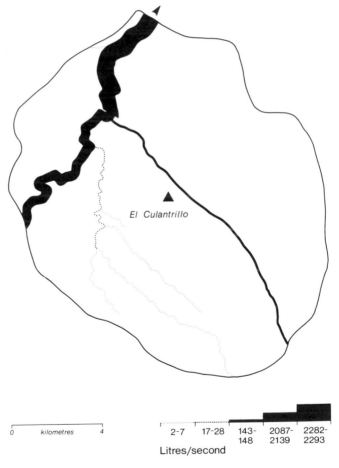

Figure 5.33   Mean winter water yields within the 2 h territory of El Culantrillo.

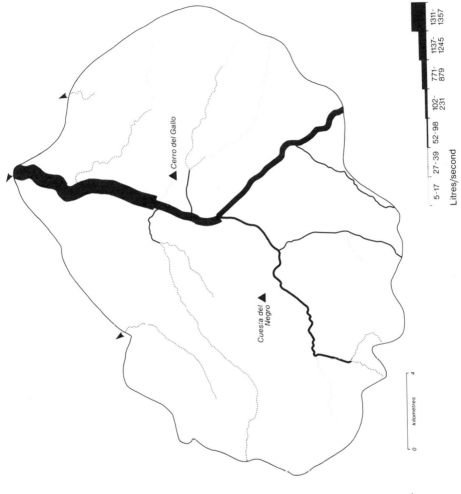

Figure 5.34 Mean winter water yields in the overlapping 2h territories of Cerro del Gallo and Cuesta del Negro.

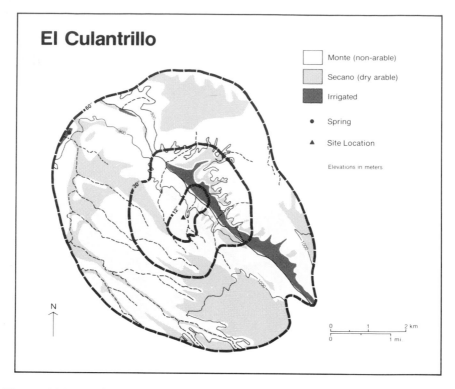

Figure 5.35   Land-use potential within the 1 h territory of El Culantrillo.

layers, immediately above the bedrock. Although no architecture was noted, the plaster floors and ash lenses, as well as the abundant potsherds and fauna, make clear that the areas excavated were dwellings. A casting mould for an axe from the habitation deposits and the grave goods (a chalice, a riveted axe and several silver rings) from four burials in pits in the bedrock clearly indicate an Argaric age for the earlier occupation. That the riveted dagger is of Blance's (1971, plate 23/5) Type I suggests to Molina González and Pareja López (1975, p. 53) that the occupation belongs to Blance's 'B' phase of the El Argar Culture, but the radiocarbon determination from the occupation layers (see p. 23) indicates a date at the beginning of the 2nd millennium BC.

Recent changes in agricultural practice within these site territories have been of considerable magnitude, but they do not present problems for the interpretation of land-use potential. Here, as elsewhere in the Guadix–Baza basin (Cano García 1974), large areas of *monte* have been cleared for cultivation since the 18th century. The 1752 *Respuesta General* for Guadix, a very large municipality with lands in all three territories, reports the ratio of *monte* : *secano* : *regadío* as 25 : 2 : 3. Now the plains above the Fardes River and Gor River drainages have mostly been cleared for dry farming of wheat and barley, so that the ratio of *monte* to *secano* within the site territories is between 1 : 1 and 3 : 1. The land clearance and associated changes in cropping patterns do not involve a change in land-use potential: areas that always might have been put to *secano* are now actually so used.

In the 18th century as now, irrigation was mostly located along the principal rivers: in the Culantrillo territory, the Fardes and the Gor (Fig. 5.33); in the Cerro del Gallo and Cuesta del Negro territories, the Fardes and the Guadix (Fig. 5.34). The year-round flow in these major streams has encouraged the early utilisation of irrigation potential. Thus, the Ensenada *Relación Particular* for Purullena, which we have examined in detail, indicates that in its broad lines the distribution of *regadío* in 1752 is the same as that of the present: although irrigation was less intensive then than it is now, the named districts (*pagos*) within the municipal territory have remained unchanged.[12] While irrigation in these territories has been very extensively developed, it is all of palaeotechnic character. Accordingly, we have measured *regadío* potential by its actual extent in the 1956–57 air photographs.[13]

Only three land-use categories – *monte*, *secano* and *regadío* – are represented in the El Culantrillo territory (Fig. 5.35). Because of the site's defensive

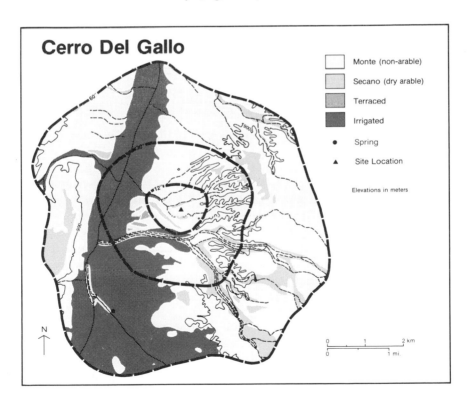

Figure 5.36   Land-use potential within the 1 h territory of Cerro del Gallo.

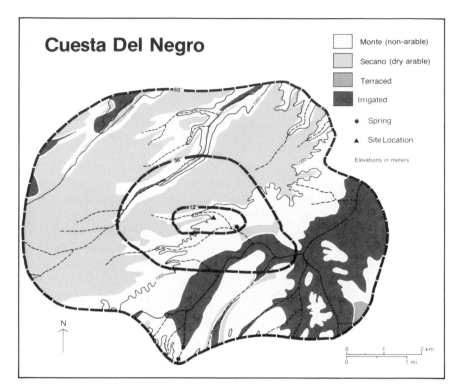

Figure 5.37   Land-use potential within the 1 h territory of Cuesta del Negro.

emplacement on a spur well up the escarpment of the Gor River canyon, *monte* declines steadily from the 12 min territory (where it forms 77% of the land surface) to the outer ring (beyond 1 h distance: 58%). Owing to the site's proximity to the Gor River, the proportion of *regadío* also declines from the core (it forms 17% of the 12 min territory, 11% of the 30 min territory) to the periphery (it is only 3% of the area beyond 30 min distance from the site). *Secano*, which is mainly available on the plains of the Hoya de Guadix, only begins to be available in substantial areas at a distance of almost 30 min from the site (it forms 6% of the 12 min territory, 25% of the 30 min territory, but 39% of the peripheral zones). Although defensive considerations clearly played a part in the site's placement, El Culantrillo's location effectively reduces the cost of access to irrigable land.

The proportions of land-use categories within the various portions of the Cerro del Gallo territory (Fig. 5.36) clearly indicate that the site is favourably placed for hydraulic agriculture. Because the site is located within the badlands of the eastern Fardes valley side, *monte* is relatively more frequent in the 30 min territory than in the peripheral areas of the territory (60% vs 45%). *Secano*, which is mainly to be found on the plains above both sides of the Fardes valley, forms a higher proportion of the land surface in the periphery than in the core of the site territory (33% vs 8%). By contrast, because the site is located near the Fardes floodplain, *regadío* is relatively more abundant in the 30 min territory (31%) than in the zones more distant from the site (22%). There is a high proportion of *regadío* in the outer rings of the site territory because these include the main area of the Guadix *vega*. It is clear that, in spite of the defensive considerations that clearly played a part in the settlement's placement, Cerro del Gallo, like the modern villages along the sides of the Fardes valley (Benalúa, Purullena, Fonelas), is suitably located for the exploitation of the river's hydraulic potential.

The Cuesta del Negro site is located, as we have noted, on the upper portion of a spur descending from the plains west of the Fardes to the river valley bottom. As Figure 5.37 indicates, the present-day irrigated area along the Fardes is more than 12 min from the site and increases in extent as one moves further from the site into the main area of the Purullena and Guadix *vegas*. As a result, *regadío* forms a lower proportion of the 30 min territory (14%) than of the area beyond 30 min distance (24%). *Secano*, by contrast, is relatively more abundant in the core than in the periphery (43% vs 37%) because the site's position gives it easy access to the arable plains to the north-east. Clearly, then, the distribution of land-use categories in the Cuesta del Negro territory does not support the hypothesis that the settlement was located so as to maximise convenient access to irrigable land. The fauna recovered from the site's Argaric levels consists mostly of cattle, and these were mostly killed as adults (see Table 2.2 and p. 28). This leads Lauk (1976, p. 95) to conclude that 'apparently cattle were used as draft animals for work in the fields, as a metatarsus with broadened distal condyles shows'. The fauna may suggest that the inhabitants of Cuesta del Negro practised an intensive agriculture, but the defensive considerations in the site's placement (clearly indicated by the fort at the summit of the spur) prevented them from carrying out that agriculture both close to home and where it would be most productive.

Cueva de la Carigüela, Cerro de los Castellones (Laborcillas), Torre Cardela

The overlapping territories of these sites are located north of the Sierra Arana in the eastern sector of the 'Montes' district of northern Granada province. Mean precipitation in this upland region ranges from 574 mm yr^{-1} at Iznalloz–Los Bulares (elevation 850 m) (Ferre Bueno 1974, p. 63), at the western edge of the Carigüela 1 h territory, to 526 mm yr^{-1} at Torre Cardela (elevation 1215 m), near the site to which the town gives its name, and 436 m yr^{-1} at Huélago (elevation 915 m), in the southern periphery of the Los Castellones (Laborcillas) territory. Given these precipitation levels, the territories would mostly have a climax vegetation of evergreen oak forest, some stands of which even now have not been cleared. In the eastern sector of the Los Castellones territory, on the edges of the Guadix formation described above, the climax plant community would be chaparral (Rivas Goday & Rivas Martínez 1971).

The predominant lithologies within these territories are hard calcareous rocks (limestones and dolomites) of Jurassic Age and softer calcareous materials, chalks, of Cretaceous and Paleogene Age, all strongly folded in the Betic orogeny. In the eastern portion of the Los Castellones (Laborcillas) territory, the drainage system of the River Huélago cuts through the Tertiary marls at the western edge of the Guadix–Baza basin. Here, as elsewhere in our study area, the hard calcareous rocks do not have a high erosion potential. The erosion potential of the marls (which are part of the same formation and present the same characteristics as those of the Culantrillo, Gallo and Cuesta del Negro territories) has already been discussed and evaluated (see pp. 62–71): in spite of their gullied appearance, we do not believe they have changed greatly over recent millennia. The chalks, however, require more extended discussion at this point. Of all lithologies within our study area, chalks have the highest potential for erosion. In these site territories the annual rate of erosion that we have modelled for a bare, gullied marl slope would produce enough regolith loss to cause the top edge of the slope to retreat some 200 m over a millennium (cf. equation 4.7). While in some portions of southern Spain such 'paroxysmal' erosion is observed on chalks (Ortega Alba 1974, I, pp. 104–5), it is apparent that within these territories no such violent changes are under way: the slopes are not gullied and the drainage densities are low. That slopes are losing material is clear, of course, since organic soils are generally absent, but apparently it is sheet erosion, not gullying or rilling, that is removing surface materials. Our modelling of soil erosion processes indicates that, even on a lithology as impermeable and friable as these chalks, catastrophic erosion rates will only take place if slopes are both bare of vegetation and rilled or gullied. We must conclude, therefore, that in recent times chalk slopes in these territories have generally been vegetated and ungullied. (One explanation might be that the unweathered rock has higher infiltration rates than weathered regolith. Thus the removal of regolith in the absence of vegetation might produce negative feedback as far as erosion is concerned.) Available information on recent land-use patterns (see below) indicates that many areas within the territories have only been cleared in the past two centuries, and in any event the high rainfall totals would lead to rapid regeneration of plant cover on slopes which had been cleared. Regular ploughing on cleared slopes would, furthermore, tend to suppress the development of rills. (Ortega Alba (1974) notes that, in southern Córdoba province, catastrophic erosion tends to be concentrated on larger, more neglected estates.) The apparent stability of landforms on chalk can only be explained if processes such as these, which would inhibit gully formation, have been at work.

The principal recent change in agricultural practice within these site territories has been the great expansion of *secano* cultivation and the concomitant reduction of *monte*. The Ensenada *Respuestas Generales* for municipalities within the territories indicate that in the 18th century very large areas were left uncultivated. Since then monte has been reduced by about half. In Iznalloz, within whose 1752 municipal territory most of the Carigüela territory falls, 83% was left uncultivated, compared to 39% now (Ferre Bueno 1974, p. 71). The amount of *monte* in Gobernador, which is in the Torre Cardela and Laborcillas territories, has dropped from 120 ha in 1752 (according to its *Relación Particular*) to 60 ha now. The expansion of *secano* to a point close to the limit of that possible has been accompanied by an increase in olive cultivation and the intensification of cropping patterns, but these changes do not affect our estimation of the potential extent of *secano*.

Irrigation in these territories is practised in small patches near springs and along the major streams: the Cubillas in the southwestern portion of the Carigüela territory, the Huélago in the southeastern portion of the Los Castellones territory, and the Guadahortuna in the northern portion of the Torre Cardela territory (cf. Fig. 5.38). Exploitation of these sources seems to have expanded since the 18th century. In Iznalloz the proportion of *regadío* within the municipal territory has doubled since 1752 (Ferre Bueno 1974). The *Respuesta General* for Huélago reports the *regadío* total as 210 *fanegas* (of no stated dimensions). *Regadío* now covers 190 ha. Thus, unless the Huélago *fanega* was much larger than that of any other locality in south-east Spain, irrigation has expanded here as well. While the area of irrigated land has expanded, its use remains relatively unintensive: now, as in the 18th century, *regadío* is mostly put to grain (Ferre Bueno 1974). In addition, modern systems are still small in scale and palaeotechnic in character. Thus, any expansion of *regadío* over the past two centuries may be presumed to be simply a realisation of previously available hydraulic potential.

The Carigüela cave (elevation 1000 m) is a solution cavity in the cliffs on the south side of the Piñar River valley. The prehistoric deposits are in three large chambers, and excavations in one or more of these have been conducted, in 1954 by Spahni (García Sánchez 1960, Lumley 1969), in 1959–60 by Pellicer (Pellicer Catalán 1964b), and in 1969–70 by a University of Madrid–Washington State University team (Almagro Basch *et al.* 1970). The lower deposits – the focus of the 1954 and 1969–70 excavations – contain a long series of industries of Middle Palaeolithic character. The upper deposits, themselves over 4 m thick, on which Pellicer's excavations concentrated, yielded later prehistoric (Neolithic to Bronze Age) remains. The Pellicer series has been carefully studied by Navarrete Enciso (1976, I, pp. 85–258). Either because there was considerable cultural and functional continuity over the course of the cave's occupation or because the stratigraphic units to which materials are referred did not yield integral assemblages, there are no sharp breaks in the composition of the inventories from bottom to top of the later prehistoric sequence. The lower, Neolithic levels have a high proportion of decorated ceramics, with impressed wares generally preceding red-slipped (*almagra*) and incised wares. Upper levels have higher

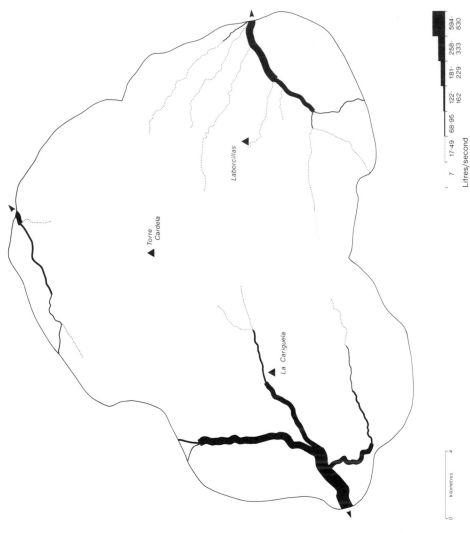

Figure 5.38 Mean winter water yields within the overlapping 2 h territories of Cueva de la Carigüela, Cerro de los Castellones (Laborcillas) and Torre Cardela.

proportions of undecorated ceramics and on this basis are attributed to the Copper Age, but, without absolute dates to establish the contemporaneity of these undistinctive materials to more firmly characterised series, it may be better to regard all of the Carigüela later prehistoric materials as belonging to the Neolithic Cultura de las Cuevas, with dates from the 6th to the 4th millennia BC. The uppermost layer at Carigüela contains jar burials of Argaric character. A thermoluminescent date on burned flint from 'Bronze Age' levels at Carigüela is 4300 (or 4500) ± 400 BP (Göksu *et al.* 1974). The abundant lithics and ceramics and the remains of hearths in the Neolithic deposits, as well as the large size of the chambers (more than 200 m^2), points to a domestic use of the cave (although human remains indicate a possible funerary use as well).

Contrary to the expectations of our central hypothesis, the location of La Carigüela favours exploitation of irrigable land (see Fig. 5.39). Because the site is located on the valley side with irrigated land at its base, the 30 min territory contains a higher proportion of *regadío* (6%) than beyond 30 min distance (2%). By contrast, *secano* occupies approximately the same proportion (85–90%) of the land surface in all zones of the site territory, while *monte* increases slightly as one moves away from the site (it forms 6% of the 12 min territory, 9% of the 30 min territory, but over 11% of the peripheral zones). Following the criteria indicated at the beginning of this chapter, one must assign Carigüela to the sites whose location emphasises irrigation potential.

Cerro de los Castellones (elevation 1000 m) was tested in 1973 by a team from the University and Museum of Granada (Mendoza *et al.* 1975). The site is located near the village of Laborcillas on a limestone ridge at the edge of the area dissected by the Huélago River's drainage. Over 1 m of deposits contain occupational debris (ceramics, loom weights, hearths, butchered fauna) divided into three main prehistoric phases. The first has few diagnostic remains. The second phase saw the construction of a bastion to defend the site and yielded a few Beaker sherds and a bifacially flaked point, diagnostics of a Copper Age date (Aguayo de Hoyos 1977). The final prehistoric phase shows strong continuity with the lower levels in the bulk of its materials, but a few finds of Argaric character – a cist burial, some carinated vessels, a barbed copper point – suggest that occupation continued into the 2nd millennium BC. A ^{14}C sample of unstated associations has yielded a determination of 1715 ± 130 bc (UGRA 10) (González Gómez & Domingo García 1978). The megalithic cemetery of Los Eriales, 1 km to the south-east and presumably associated with the Los Castellones settlement, also has produced Argaric remains (Leisner & Leisner 1943, pp. 149–56).

The setting of Los Castellones indicates that *secano* was the principal resource space exploited from the site (cf. Fig. 5.40). Dry arable land forms 91% of the 30 min territory, but only 79% of the area beyond 30 min from the site. Within the territory, *regadío* is to be found mostly in the Huélago River valley, almost 1 h from the site at its closest point. Thus, *regadío*, which forms 2% of the peripheral zones of the territory, is entirely absent in the core. Monte is also

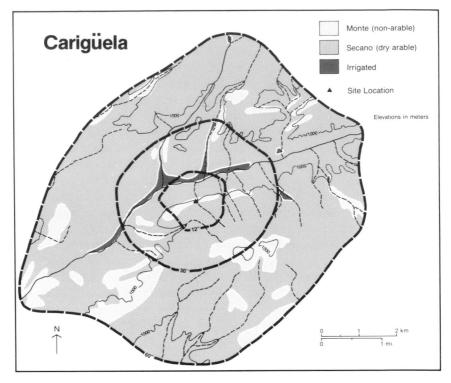

Figure 5.39   Land-use potential within the 1 h territory of Cueva de la Carigüela.

proportionally more available in the periphery than in the core. The location of the site fully supports our contention that the inhabitants of Copper Age sites in the moist uplands of south-east Spain depended on dry arable farming for their subsistence. The fauna from the Los Castellones excavations has been analysed by Driesch and Kokabi (1977). Because of the small size of the faunal sample, remains from all the prehistoric levels were considered as a unit. The overall proportions of species are similar to those from other Copper Age sites in south-east Spain (see Table 2.2): cattle and sheep–goats predominate (they form 81% by weight of the economically significant species). In an upland forested environment such as this, the importance of these species is suggestive of extensive clearance.

Surface collections on the ridge immediately to the east of the modern village of Torre Cardela recovered an abundant series of chipped and ground stone tools (five bifacially flaked points, 117 axes, two querns, etc.) and potsherds (including five Beaker fragments), all indicative of a Copper Age settlement (Molina Fajardo 1970). In 1973 excavation of a 3 m by 3 m test pit confirmed this by revealing 90 cm of deposits, with possible parallel walls associated with nine Beaker sherds, a bifacially flaked point and a tanged copper point (Molina Fajardo & Capel Martínez 1975).

The distribution of land-use types in the Torre Cardela territory clearly indicates that the site was placed to exploit *secano* better than any other land-use category (see Fig. 5.41). Dry arable land forms 89% of the 2 h territory as a whole, but 98% of the 30 min territory. As Figure 5.38 indicates, the site is on the watershed between the major drainages in this area, so that, apart from a few springs, hydraulic opportunities are all located at a distance from the site. *Regadío* forms 0.2% of the 30 min territory, but 1.9% of the area beyond 30 min distance. *Monte* also increases in proportional frequency at a distance from the site (it is 2% of the core, 9% of the periphery). No fauna or floral remains are reported from the site, but, as Molina Fajardo (1970, p. 314) points out, the abundance of stone axes is suggestive of land clearance activities in its vicinity.

Cueva de los Murciélagos (Zuheros)

The site (elevation 1000 m) is located at the top of the northern escarpment of the Sierra de Zuheros, overlooking the rolling chalk hills of the northern half of the site territory. Mean annual rainfall on the *sierra* reaches 952 mm (at La Nava,

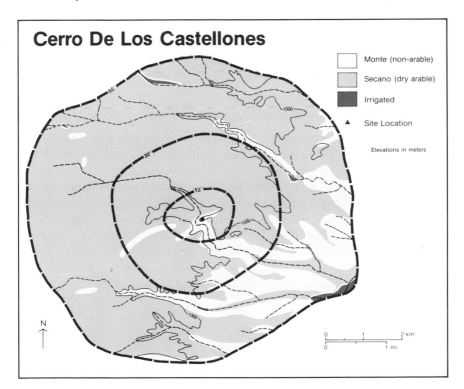

Figure 5.40 Land-use potential within the 1 h territory of Cerro de los Castellones (Laborcillas).

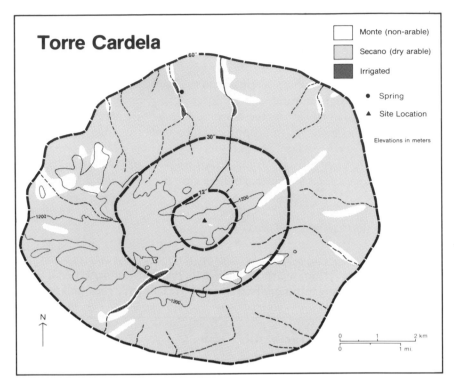

Figure 5.41   Land-use potential within the 1 h territory of Torre Cardela.

elevation 960 m, in the south-east of the site territory (Ortega Alba 1974, I, p. 74)), but localities at the base of the *sierra* have considerably lower annual totals (Luque, elevation 662 m, 530 mm; Zuheros, elevation 750 m, 813 mm; Doña Mencia, elevation 587 m, 786 mm), while Baena (elevation 462 m), just beyond the edge of the 2 h territory to the north, reports 460 mm yr^{-1}. The reconstruction of potential vegetation reported by Ortega Alba (1974, I, pp. 111–18) indicates that the lower areas would have carried a chaparral community of scrub oak, oleaster, carob, etc. (the olive and vine monocultures to which large portions of the site territory are now devoted may be considered, in a sense, to be specialisations of this community), while the uplands would have (and in many areas still do have) a climax community of *encinar*.

The locality was known in the 19th century (Góngora y Martínez 1868), underwent amateur explorations in the 1930s and 1940s (Martínez Santa Olalla 1948) and was finally excavated in 1962 (Quadra Salcedo & Vicent 1964) and 1969 (Vicent Zaragoza & Muñoz Amilibia 1973). Its incised, impressed and red-slipped (*almagra*) wares are characteristic of the second phase of the 'Cultura de las Cuevas' Neolithic; the radiocarbon determinations from the site (cf. p. 18) place its occupation in the 5th millennium BC. The abundant ceramics and the silos with carbonised grains indicate that the 140 m^2 main chamber of the cave was used as a dwelling place.

The site territory is divided between the rolling chalk hills of its northern half and the limestone massif of the Sierra de Zuheros, its southern half. Here, as elsewhere in our study area, the limestones have a relatively low erosional potential. The chalks of the northern portion of the territory, however, have very high erosional potential: a bare, gullied chalk slope would lose enough material each year to cause its top edge to retreat 230 m over a millennium (cf. equation 4.7). Here, as in the Cariguela–Castellones–Torre Cardela territories, it is apparent that sheet erosion and soil impoverishment are widespread, but the catastrophic rates of regolith loss that our modelling indicates to be possible are not taking place. The discussion on pp. 144–5 may be applied to the chalks in this site territory as well.

Within the Murciélagos–Zuheros site territory, recent agricultural changes have not been of a character to distort our estimations of land-use potential. Since the time of the Ensenada survey in 1752, there have been two major

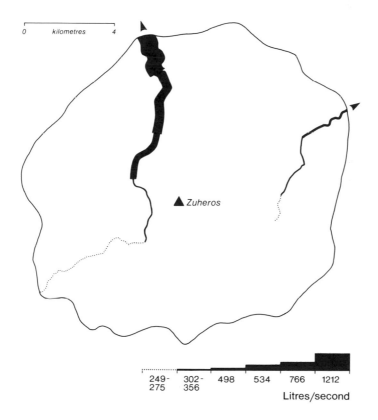

Figure 5.42 Mean winter water yields within the 2 h territory of Cueva de los Murciélagos (Zuheros).

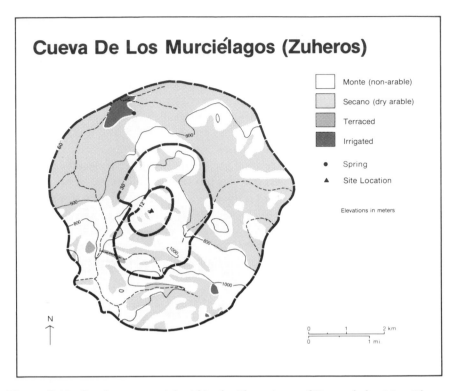

Figure 5.43   Land-use potential within the 1 h territory of Cueva de los Murciélagos (Zuheros).

changes, both of them of historically contingent character: an extensive conversion of *monte* to *secano* (attendant on the expropriation of church and common lands in 1837) and an expansion of olive monoculture on *secano* (as landowners turned from rent from subsistence-oriented tenants to the market for their income) (Ortega Alba 1974, II, pp. 10–19). The extent of *regadío* is the same now as in 1752: irrigation occurs below Fuente Marbella ($80 \mathrm{l\,s}^{-1}$) at the northern edge of the 1 h territory and near assorted small springs in the *sierra*. Winter rainfall is sufficiently high to limit *regadío* to those areas that are fed by springs sufficiently permanent to assure a second crop in the summer dry season. In other words, the mean winter water yields indicated in Figure 5.42 are irrelevant to traditional agricultural practice. A small irrigated area along the Bailón River in the *sierra* at the southwestern limit of the 2 h territory is unmentioned in the 1752 *Respuesta* for Zuheros, but we include it in the *regadío* total since it is entirely palaeotechnic in character. In this site territory, modern land uses provide a direct and unproblematic guide to potential land use (Fig. 5.43).

   Monte and *secano* together comprise over 98% of the surface of the site territory, and their relative proportions are inversely related to their proximity to the site. *Monte* constitutes 58% of the 30 min territory, but only 32% of the area between 1 h and 2 h distance from the site. The respective proportions of *secano* are 42% and 67%. There is no *regadío* in the 30 min territory. The emphasis on *monte* within the 30 min territory results from the cave's location at the edge of a mountain escarpment. The discovery of carbonised emmer, barley and bread wheat from the site (Hopf & Muñoz 1974) makes clear, however, that, while *monte* may have been a significant resource for the inhabitants of the cave (cf. Lewthwaite 1982), *secano* was significantly exploited as such.

Los Castillejos (Montefrío)

The settlement of Los Castillejos is located at an elevation of 1000 m on a limestone platform surrounded by cliffs on three sides, part of the 'Peñas de los Gitanos' escarpment. The name of the site describes its naturally defensible location. Mean annual rainfall at Montefrío (elevation 836 m), 4 km to the west, is 646 mm, with a median of 580 mm (Onieva Mariegos 1977, pp. 61–3). The climax vegetation over all of the site territory would be a cover of evergreen oak forest with admixture of deciduous oaks above about 1000 m elevation (Rivas Goday & Rivas Martínez 1971). Oak woodlands are still present in the immediate vicinity of the site, but most land has, of course, been cleared for cultivation.

The 30 m by 120 m platform carried by the site has deposits up to 4.4 m thick. Excavations have been undertaken, in 1926 by Mergelina (1942), in 1946–47 by Tarradell (1947–48, 1952), and in 1971 and 1974 by a University of Granada team (Arribas & Molina 1977, 1979). Although diagnostic materials are hardly abundant in the deposits excavated stratigraphically during the latter campaigns, three main phases of prehistoric occupation are clearly attested: a basal Cultura de las Cuevas assemblage (with incised, impressed and *almagra* wares) is followed by a Copper Age occupation (with materials such as undecorated ceramics, large flint blades, bifacially flaked points and a few metal objects); this in turn is succeeded by a late Copper–Bronze Age series with carinated vessels, an impoverished lithic industry and again a few metal objects. This last phase is radiocarbon dated to the end of the 2nd millennium BC (cf. p. 21). The early Neolithic materials are found in one 15 m by 10 m area of the site (Arribas & Molina 1977, p. 393) and are not associated with remains of structures, but the abundant baked clay in the Copper Age levels is interpreted as the remains of wattle-and-daub huts, while the abundant stone rubble in the final phase suggests even more permanent structures. Abundant ceramics and loom weights also are evidence of the domestic occupation of the site. The megalithic tombs distributed along the Peñas de los Gitanos escarpment (Leisner & Leisner 1943, pp. 169–73; Mergelina 1946) are contemporaneous with the latter phases of the site's prehistoric occupation.

The limestones that form the ridges with the Castillejos site territory have a relatively low potential for erosion, as does one area of conglomerates, but the chalks that cover the bulk of the territory have, here as elsewhere in the northwestern sector of our study area, a potential for catastrophic erosion rates. The actual chalk slopes within the territory do not in fact exhibit signs of paroxysmal erosion, however. Once again, radical landscape change has been dampened either by vegetation cover or (where the land has been cleared) by ploughing, which suppresses gully formation.

The proportions of basic land-use categories in the *municipio* of Montefrío have remained stable over the past 230 years. The 1752 Ensenada survey reported that *monte, secano* and *regadío* formed 13.8%, 85.8% and 0.4%, respectively, of the municipal territory; the corresponding percentages in 1975 were 25.6, 73.9 and 0.5 (Onieva Mariege 1977, p. 113). (Within the Castillejos site territory, which falls in the eastern half of Montefrío, but includes adjacent parts of Íllora and Alcalá la Real, the corresponding percentages are 26.8, 72.3

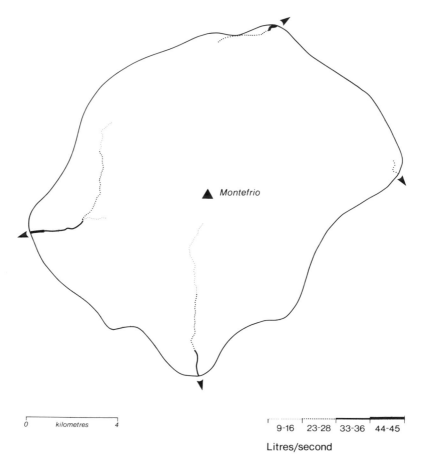

Figure 5.44   Mean winter water yields in the 2 h territory of Los Castillejos (Peñas de los Gitanos, Montefrío).

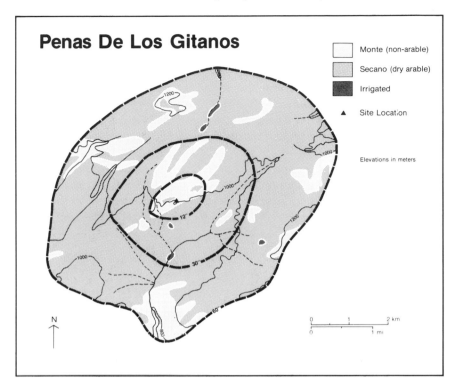

Figure 5.45 Land-use potential in the 1 h territory of Los Castillejos (Peñas de los Gitanos, Montefrío).

and 0.8.) The slight reduction in *monte* with respect to *secano* is attributed by Onieva Mariegos to the increased intensity of cropping patterns (the shortened fallow cycle) of modern farming. Neither this change nor the more than 3000% expansion of olive cultivation since 1752 (Onieva Mariege 1977) affects the land-use potential categories with which we are concerned.

The distribution of land uses within the Montefrío site territory clearly demonstrates that the site was not located to maximise effectively the exploitation of irrigable land. Low as the percentage of *regadío* is in the site territory as a whole (0.8%), it is even lower in the area within 30 min distance of the site (0.2%). Indeed, as Figure 5.44 shows, the site is located at the watershed between drainages whose flows increase as one moves away from the site. The location of the site in the Peñas de los Gitanos makes *monte* form a higher proportion of the 30 min territory (36%) than of the site territory as a whole (28%), but 64% of the land in the 30 min territory is *secano*, and it is reasonable to suppose that it was this land that principally sustained the site's inhabitants (Fig. 5.45).

There is no palaeobotanical information reported from Los Castillejos, but the palaeozoological data recovered by the University of Granada excavations

(Uerpmann in Arribas & Molina 1979) tend to confirm the proposition that the inhabitants of the site were agriculturalists. Arribas and Molina (1979, p. 129) consider that the initial Neolithic occupation of Los Castillejos – which covers only a small area of the site, has no evidence for permanent structures and in which sheep and goats constitute the dominant species (52% by weight of the bones recovered of economically significant animals) – was by pastoralists, and they interpret the Copper Age increase in pigs and deer (from 17% to 41%: cf. Table 2.1) as reflecting a more intensive agricultural occupation (which would involve the elimination of competitive wild species). The increase in pigs and deer in the Copper Age certainly reflects effective use of the *monte* component of the site territory, while the abundance of cattle (at 38% by weight of the economically significant species, it is the most abundant animal in the Copper and Copper–Bronze Age levels) can only be understood in the context of an agricultural economy.

Cueva de la Mujer, Cueva del Agua

These two adjacent caves are located at an elevation of 850 m in a limestone cliff overlooking the valley of the River Alhama, 200 m south-west of the Balneario de Alhama hot springs (whose flow is 100 to $2501s^{-1}$). Rainfall at Alhama (elevation 890 m, 1.5 km to the south) has an annual mean of 535 mm. According to Rivas Goday and Rivas Martínez (1971), the entire site territory would have a climax vegetation of *encinar* (stands of which still are present), with an admixture of deciduous oaks above 1000 m.

Cueva de la Mujer was excavated in 1869 by MacPherson (1870), and both caves have been the object of repeated amateur digging. In 1957–58 excavations by Pellicer and García Sánchez found some intact deposits in Agua (Pellicer Catalán 1964a). The sites' incised, impressed and *almagra* wares indicate a Neolithic, Cultura de las Cuevas occupation. The deposits in the 10 m by 15 m main chamber of Mujer contained ash deposits, flints and potsherds as evidence of its use as a habitation, but the articulated skeleton found in the 1957–58 excavations at Agua indicates that this cave had an at least partially sepulchral function.

The predominant lithologies in the site territory are limestone and chalk. The latter has a very high erosion potential, which here, as elsewhere in the northern and western part of our study area, seems not to have led to large-scale changes in landforms (for reasons discussed on pp. 144–5 above).

The Mujer–Agua site territory falls entirely within the limits of the city of Alhama, whose landscape in 1752 has been completely reconstructed on the basis of the Ensenada *Relación Particular* (Ferrer Rodríguez 1975). The overall patterns of change since the 18th century are similar to those noted in the Murciélagos–Zuheros site territory: *monte* has been extensively converted to *secano*; and olive cultivation has become much more widespread. The extent of

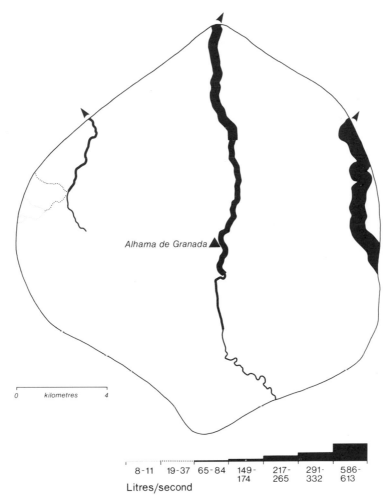

Alhama de Granada ▲

0   kilometres   4

8-11   19-37   65-84   149-   217-   291-   586-
                       174   265   332   613
Litres/second

Figure 5.46   Mean winter water yields within the 2 h territory of Cueva de la Mujer and
Cueva del Agua (Alhama de Granada).

regadío, however, is the same now as in 1752. The modern landscape provides,
therefore, a straightforward guide to palaeotechnic land-use potential.

As a result of the caves' proximity to the Alhama River and hot springs,
regadío forms a relatively high proportion of the core of the site territory: 3.6%
of the area within 30 min of the site is irrigated, as opposed to 1.6% of the site
territory as a whole. There is little *regadío* in the Alhama territory because
irrigation is limited, not by the available water yields in winter (Fig. 5.46), when
rainfall is more than sufficient for crop growth, but by the flow in these streams
during the summer. *Secano,* the dominant land-use category in the territory
(Fig. 5.47), also forms a greater proportion of the 30 min than of the whole site

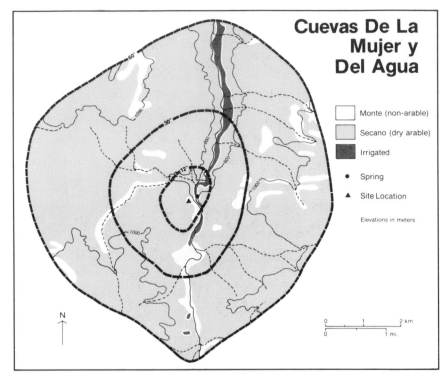

Figure 5.47   Land-use potential in the 1 h territory of Cueva de la Mujer and Cueva del Agua (Alhama de Granada).

territory (88% vs 75%). The sites are, therefore, suitably located for both dry and hydraulic farmers.

Cerro de la Encina

The site (elevation 830 m) is located at the end of a promontory some 50 m above the Río Monachil, 1.5 km above the point where the river emerges onto the plain of the *vega* of Granada. Mean annual rainfall at the several stations within the site territory ranges from a low of 406 mm at Armilla (elevation 663 m, 7 km west of the site) to a high of 528 mm at Monachil (elevation 811 m, 1 km east of the site), but must be considerably higher yet as one moves up to 1800 m in the eastern portion of the site territory.

   The vicinity of the Cerro de la Encina site territory to the city of Granada (which is included within the northern portion of the 2 h territory) has ensured a thorough human transformation of the natural vegetation. According to Rivas Goday and Rivas Martínez (1971), however, the climax vegetation over most of the territory would be evergreen oak woodland, with deciduous oaks intermixed above about 1200 m, and with pine and juniper predominating above 1500 m. Gallery forest of poplar and elm would have bordered the territory's perennial streams (Fig. 5.48) as these braided their way across the plain of the Granada *vega*.

Limited excavations at the site were conducted by Cabré Aguiló (1922) and Tarradell (1947–48). Since 1968 the University of Granada has carried out annual excavations at the site, but only one trench has received more than a preliminary report (Arribas *et al.* 1974). The site has up to 3 m of deposits in the published trench and more in other sectors. Two main phases of occupation are documented. The earlier, Argaric levels (characterised as Argar 'B' on slight typological grounds) have undecorated, carinated ceramics and are associated with the construction and use of a massive bastion at the end of the promontory. Presumably contemporaneous with this phase of occupation at the summit are the cist burials with riveted daggers and chalices found on the promontory slopes (Cabré Aguiló 1922). The basal Argaric layer is radiocarbon dated to the beginning of the 2nd millennium BC (cf. p. 23). A second occupation phase, characterised by incised–excised ceramics, is similar to the 'Bronce Final' assemblage, radiocarbon dated to the later 2nd millennium BC at Cuesta del

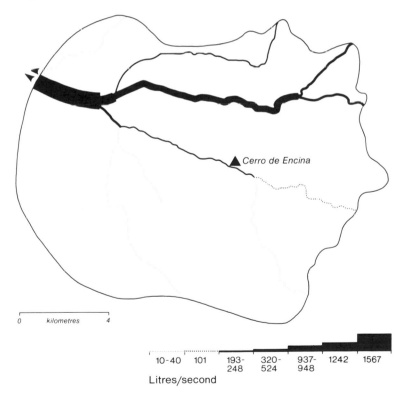

Figure 5.48 Mean winter water yields within the 2 h territory of Cerro de la Encina.

Negro. The bastion structure encloses 400 m² and the abundant ceramics, fauna and loom weights indicate that the promontory summit (whose total area is 0.12 ha) had a settlement function. Additional residential areas may be present beneath modern agricultural terraces at the base of the hill.

The limestones, conglomerates and alluvium that constitute the lithologies over most of the site territory have moderate to non-existent erosion potential, but the marls (on which the site itself is placed) have the potential for catastrophic loss of materials: given the relatively high rainfall and the long, steep slopes of the topography, a bare, gullied marl slope might lose enough material over a millennium to cause a retreat of 100 m. Here, as in the Vera and Guadix areas, however, it is apparent that events of such dramatic magnitude are not occurring. The existence of a bastion at the end of the marl promontory on which the site is located is proof that the promontory's general configuration has been stable for almost 4000 years. Furthermore, that Argaric cist burials were found halfway down the southern slope of the promontory (Cabré Aguiló 1922, p. 24) indicates that the steep slope most likely (because of its greater degree of insolation) to have lost vegetation and suffered severe erosion has in fact also remained fairly stable since the site's occupation. While we have not studied in detail the geomorphology of the site's immediate vicinity, it seems clear that here, as at the sites we have looked at closely, actual erosion has fallen well short of its potential.

Like the sites near Vélez Blanco and Guadix, Cerro de la Encina is located in a region where traditional agriculture has been extensively capitalised and extended. The abundance of water from the Sierra Nevada and the proximity of the urban market of Granada has led to the full development of the irrigation potential of the *vega*. The Ensenada *Respuestas* indicate that all municipalities within the site territory, which consist completely or predominantly of *regadío* now, consisted completely or predominantly of *regadío* in 1752, and this actualisation of irrigation potential goes back at least to Moorish times. The main changes in agricultural practice since the 18th century involve more intensive crop rotation and crop changes in response to market opportunities, but not the hydraulic infrastructure (Ocaña Ocaña 1974, pp. 335–7). The present extent of traditional irrigation is the result of a progressive build-up of investment in the land and thus would not apply to the situation in Bronze Age times when, as we believe, this investment was just beginning. The present extent of irrigable land overemphasises the amount of *regadío* potentially available to prehistoric farmers at the downstream periphery of the Cerro de la Encina site territory. Nevertheless, because the present situation acts against our hypothesis (that farming at a Bronze Age site would involve irrigation) by increasing the proportion of *regadío* in the more distant areas of the territory, we have used current land distribution as the basis for our mapping.[14]

The contrasts in the proportions of land-use types between the core (the area within 30 min) and the periphery (the area from 30 min to 2 h) of the Cerro de la Encina site territory do not permit a straightforward interpretation of the

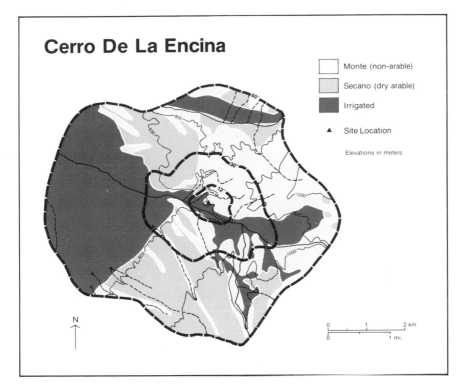

Figure 5.49 Land-use potential within the 1 h territory of Cerro de la Encina.

economic function of the site's location. For the reasons just described, *regadío* forms a greater part of the periphery than the core (42% vs 32%) (Fig. 5.49). Because the terrain along the Monachil River valley in the immediate vicinity of the site is precipitous, *monte* has a lower proportion and *secano* a higher proportion of the land in peripheral than in central areas of the territory (33% vs 46% and 25% vs 22% respectively). Consideration of land uses within the core, however, clarifies the situation. Of the arable land within 30 min of the site, 60% is *regadío*, and this proportion rises to 91% within 12 min of the site (see Fig. 5.49). In other words, if the inhabitants of Cerro de la Encina were farmers, and if their fields were within 30 min of their homes, most of the land available to them would be irrigable. Cerro de la Encina is located along the upstream section of one of the smaller rivers feeding the Granada vega (see Fig. 5.48), a river whose water flows in manageable amounts along a steep gradient and is, thus, easier to capture by a simple technology. This is just where one would expect a site inhabited by the first irrigators of the Granada region to be located. The evidence for prehistoric irrigation from Cerro de la Encina's placement is consistent with the faunal evidence from the site (Lauk 1976). The high proportion of draft animals (horses and cattle), mostly kept as adults, is best interpreted as part of a system of intensive agriculture (see pp. 25–8 and Table 2.2).

Cueva de Nerja

This large karstic cave (elevation 200 m) is located 1 km from the Mediterranean at the base of the coastal mountains and the edge of the conglomerate pediment that slopes down to the cliffs of the coastline. Mean annual rainfall at Nerja (elevation 26 m, 3.5 km to the south-west) is 447 mm.

The climax vegetation in coastal Granada province immediately east of the site territory is reconstructed by Rivas Goday and Rivas Martínez (1971) as a low forest of oleaster, *encina*, palmetto and box tree, among other species: a community characteristic of a warm, moist Mediterranean climate. The lithologies within the site territory consist of limestones, conglomerates and mica–schists, all of which have moderate erosion potential.

Excavations at Cueva de Nerja have been carried out by Pellicer in 1959–60 (immediately after the cave's discovery), by Jordá and Arribas in 1965 and 1967, and again by Pellicer in 1979. Only the cultural materials from the first campaign and the faunal remains from the last have been published (Pellicer Catalán 1963, Boessneck & Driesch 1980). Three main phases of occupation are reported: a basal 'Epipalaeolithic' (whose cultural assemblage remains un-

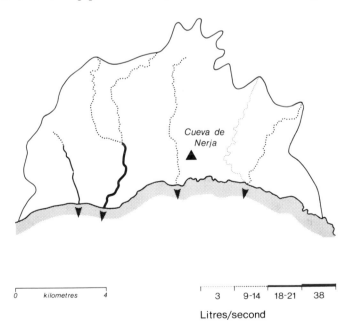

Figure 5.50 Mean winter water yields in the 2 h territory of Cueva de Nerja.

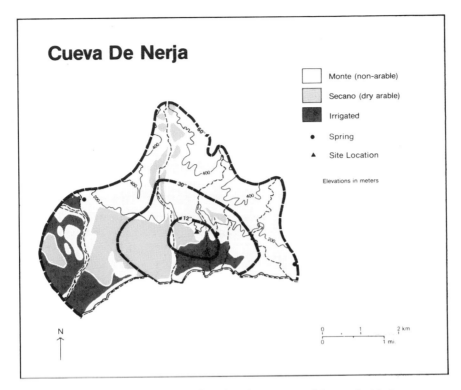

Cueva De Nerja

Monte (non-arable)

Secano (dry arable)

Irrigated

• Spring

▲ Site Location

Elevations in meters

Figure 5.51   Land-use potential within the 1 h territory of Cueva de Nerja.

described), a Cultura de las Cuevas Neolithic (with incised, impressed and *almagra* wares) and a Later Neolithic or Copper Age (with undecorated ceramics). Grain from a pit inserted into the Cultura de las Cuevas deposits from the Later Neolithic–Copper Age stratum is radiocarbon dated to the mid-3rd millennium BC (see p. 18). The occupation occurs in the large interior chambers of the cave (the three chambers excavated in 1959–60 have a combined area of 1000 m^2), but the extent of contemporaneous occupation is not documented. The ceramics, ground stone, grain and fauna all indicate a domestic use of the site.

The Nerja site territory is unique within our study area in that its 18th-century agriculture was a commercial one: sugar-cane, raisins and Málaga wine are the principal products listed in the Frigiliana, Nerja and Maro *Respuestas*. Sugar-cane demands a lot of water, and the development of irrigation within the site territory has been very extensive. Maro, immediately between the cave and the sea, has a *huerta* fed by a large spring (75 to 350 l s^{-1}) located just 12 min east of the site. The *huertas* of Frigiliana and Nerja receive their water from springs and dams located along the River Chíllar, some outside the northern limit of the site territory (Fig. 5.50). We have excluded from the *regadío* total within the site territory irrigated land on the west side of the Barranco del Moro (12 min west of the site) which is watered by aqueduct from Maro, but otherwise the present extent of *regadío* (which is all gravity fed) is taken as an indication of the palaeotechnic potential for irrigation. The Ensenada *Respuestas* for Nerja and Frigiliana reported extensive areas of vine planted on *secano*, most of which have now disappeared as a result of phylloxera. Only those areas within the territory whose slopes are sufficiently gentle to permit grain farming have been included in the *secano* total.

Because of the cave's proximity to the Maro spring, *regadío* is more abundant within the 30 min territory of the site than in the area from 30 min to 2 h distance (18% vs 12%) (see Fig. 5.51). *Secano* also forms a higher proportion of the 30 min territory than of the 30 min to 2 h territory (37% vs 4%). That the cave is suitably located for the exploitation of arable land is, of course, demonstrated by the barley and wheat from the Later Neolithic–Copper Age pit and by the faunal remains from the site. By weight of economically significant species, sheep–goats are the most important animal in both Cultura de las Cuevas (53%) and Later Neolithic–Copper Age deposits (42%), followed by cattle (28% and 32%) and pigs (9% and 16%). The sea fish and birds found in abundance in the Epipalaeolithic levels (bream, perch, gannet, shearwater) are very rare in the later deposits, so that a thoroughgoing reorientation of subsistence strategies from foraging to food production is implied for the Neolithic and later periods. The location at the Nerja cave would have provided the farmers living in it with low-cost access to both *secano* and *regadío*.

Summary

Each site territory is a special case with a unique mix of historical and geomorphological evidence available to assist us in using the distribution of land uses in the modern landscape to reconstruct palaeotechnic land-use potential. The results of our assessments take two forms. First, we arrive at quantitative

Table 5.1 Areas (ha) of the land-use categories within the site territories.

Site name	Zone (min)	Land uses (ha)				
		Monte	*Secano*	*Terraced*	*Boquera*	*Regadío*
Almoloya	60–120	8094.75	5451.5	444.75	0	728.25
	30–60	1532.0	1542.5	37.75	0	306.25
	12–30	379.75	666.25	11.5	0	2.0
	0–12	84.5	37.4	0	0	0
Campico	60–120	4809.25	8930.75	631.0	0	2376.75
	30–60	1060.0	1882.5	299.25	14.0	763.0
	12–30	450.0	293.25	80.25	9.75	53.5
	0–12	118.0	10.75	2.25	0	0

Table 5.1 (continued)

Site name	Zone (min)	Land uses (ha)				
		Monte	*Secano*	*Terraced*	*Boquera*	*Regadío*
Bastida	60–120	5151.25	7349.75	491.0	0	2078.75
	30–60	1509.25	469.0	467.0	23.75	348.25
	12–30	460.25	8.75	93.0	0	5.0
	0–12	86.25	0	10.5	0	5.5
Ceñuela	60–120	3835.75	13422.0	1043.75	204.25	331.75
	30–60	1279.0	1972.5	1067.5	11.5	50.5
	12–30	433.5	380.75	351.75	49.5	19.25
	0–12	50.5	164.75	8.0	2.35	0
Cabezo Negro	60–120	7618.5	4108.75	120.75	236.5	224.75
	30–60	1739.25	1297.0	87.75	48.5	122.25
	12–30	561.0	143.75	25.0	9.75	23.5
	0–12	63.0	24.5	3.0	0	29.5
Zapata	60–120	6762.5	3600.5	83.0	342.0	255.75
	30–60	1872.75	622.75	133.5	49.5	54.5
	12–30	572.75	164.5	23.0	24.25	30.0
	0–12	86.25	24.0	7.0	0	4.75
Parazuelos	60–120	5676.75	2600.0	145.0	61.0	12.5
	30–60	1842.25	1411.75	82.75	266.25	84.5
	12–30	452.5	764.5	25.25	79.0	49.0
	0–12	87.25	111.25	0	22.75	41.5
Ifre	60–120	5443.0	2137.0	137.25	189.25	131.0
	30–60	1611.0	1983.5	71.75	210.0	146.0
	12–30	362.5	875.0	10.25	32.75	8.5
	0–12	41.0	95.75	34.25	5.75	14.5
Campos, Tres Cabezos	60–120	6480.5	3961.25	1633.0	1213.75	122.5
	30–60	2019.75	480.75	471.25	232.25	208.25
	12–30	493.0	108.5	29.25	171.75	378.5
	0–12	135.0	0	17.0	11.0	82.75
Fuente Álamo	60–120	6080.5	1100.75	1673.75	1026.0	478.75
	30–60	1443.5	331.25	164.25	125.25	184.0
	12–30	468.75	144.75	8.25	8.25	0
	0–12	87.5	4.0	0	0	3.0
Oficio	60–120	5844.75	3817.0	1392.0	391.5	21.5
	30–60	1890.25	708.75	338.5	49.0	82.0
	12–30	601.5	190.0	73.5	18.75	12.25
	0–12	75.5	26.5	13.0	0	0
Lugarico Viejo	60–120	7381.0	5026.0	1180.75	181.75	96.5
	30–60	1885.75	1207.25	315.25	26.25	109.5
	12–30	588.25	201.25	5.5	0	36.75
	0–12	130.75	9.75	0	0	24.0

Table 5.1 (continued)

Site name	Zone (min)	Land uses (ha)				
		Monte	*Secano*	*Terraced*	*Boquera*	*Regadío*
Fuente	60–120	8186.5	4648.5	1486.25	179.0	403.25
Bermeja	30–60	1667.25	1883.0	364.25	45.5	79.25
	12–30	595.75	346.5	1.25	0	53.75
	0–12	70.0	112.25	0	0	15.25
Argar,	60–120	7282.75	5611.0	2071.75	924.0	779.0
Gárcel,	30–60	1372.75	1386.75	560.25	65.0	34.25
Gerundia	12–30	305.0	793.0	111.25	6.25	47.0
	0–12	72.25	78.0	25.0	0	24.5
Gatas	60–120	5053.25	3404.25	1473.0	553.25	168.5
	30–60	1199.25	601.75	326.25	326.25	185.5
	12–30	341.25	79.75	111.5	0	62.25
	0–12	47.0	4.75	2.0	0	30.0
Terrera	60–120	7544.25	4731.25	180.75	183.75	20.5
Ventura	30–60	2094.0	926.25	255.75	128.75	3.25
	12–30	448.25	236.75	234.0	56.5	8.75
	0–12	53.5	0	84.75	13.75	0
Millares	60–120	8692.25	408.5	1195.5	351.0	597.0
	30–60	1895.75	210.5	392.75	77.25	149.5
	12–30	536.75	14.25	55.25	20.5	65.25
	0–12	86.25	15.0	2.0	0	3.25
Enmedio	60–120	6765.0	1242.5	127.5	284.75	608.75
	30–60	2039.0	36.75	7.0	46.75	15.25
	12–30	465.5	0	8.5	0	101.25
	0–12	56.0	0	0	0	19.0
Barranquete/	60–120	5969.5	11487.0	3.5	178.75	159.75
Taraja	30–60	1225.75	3248.5	4.0	17.5	170.0
	12–30	609.5	528.5	2.75	0	51.5
	0–12	95.25	90.0	0	0	13.25
Ambrosio	60–120	7243.25	3672.75	50.25	1.25	64.25
	30–60	1865.75	722.0	10.0	0	6.0
	12–30	387.75	257.5	0	0	7.5
	0–12	46.5	2.0	0	0	1.25
Canteras	60–120	8590.25	2152.50	454.5	0	1077.5
	30–60	1355.5	1296.25	14.75	0	755.0
	12–30	129.25	665.5	18.25	0	365.75
	0–12	10.5	122.75	0	0	61.5
Picacho	60–120	6124.0	4311.5	24.25	31.0	536.75
	30–60	1571.75	456.75	0	0	103.75
	12–30	426.5	19.25	0	0	40.5
	0–12	51.0	0	0	0	2.75

Table 5.1 (continued)

Site name	Zone (min)	Land uses (ha)				
		Monte	*Secano*	*Terraced*	*Boquera*	*Regadío*
Malagón	60–120	4514.75	12476.75	27.0	150.5	49.25
	30–60	879.0	3388.25	0	100.0	86.5
	12–30	227.0	1052.0	0	7.0	2.25
	0–12	58.75	184.0	0	9.25	1.0
Virgen	60–120	5510.0	9950.0	345.5	0	2176.25
	30–60	1172.0	2830.75	50.5	0	601.75
	12–30	378.0	559.25	29.0	0	258.25
	0–12	48.75	74.50	2.75	0	64.5
Culantrillo	60–120	7104.0	4864.25	0	0	304.75
	30–60	1723.5	1145.75	0	0	85.25
	12–30	455.0	200.25	0	0	71.75
	0–12	72.75	5.75	0	0	16.25
Cuesta del Negro	60–120	6109.25	5359.25	110.75	0	3698.25
	30–60	1340.0	1921.0	18.0	0	972.0
	12–60	384.5	427.25	0	0	149.0
	0–12	83.0	33.0	0	0	0
Gallo	60–120	6718.5	6018.25	72.25	0	3323.25
	30–60	2082.0	450.75	0	0	1108.5
	12–30	601.25	70.75	11.25	0	365.0
	0–12	126.25	23.5	0	0	6.25
Torre Cardela	60–120	1827.5	14731.5	0	0	390.75
	30–60	182.5	4179.0	0	0	24.5
	12–30	22.75	1185.75	0	0	3.0
	0–12	0	191.0	0	0	0
Carigüela	60–120	1901.0	14345.5	0	0	425.0
	30–60	465.25	3606.75	0	0	22.75
	12–30	94.5	891.75	0	0	65.25
	0–12	11.5	169.25	0	0	7.0
Laborcillas	60–120	3233.0	12002.5	0	0	298.25
	30–60	618.25	3391.75	0	0	37.25
	12–30	97.75	1142.75	0	0	0
	0–12	30.0	170.5	0	0	0
Zuheros	60–120	3824.75	8168.25	0	0	146.5
	30–60	907.5	1479.75	12.25	0	46.75
	12–30	314.0	231.75	4.0	0	0
	0–12	62.75	40.5	0	0	0
Montefrío	60–120	3291.0	8328.5	0	0	113.25
	30–60	337.25	2464.75	0	0	8.75
	12–30	351.75	710.75	0	0	2.5
	0–12	70.5	53.5	0	0	0

Table 5.1 (continued)

Site name	Zone (min)	Land uses (ha)				
		Monte	*Secano*	*Terraced*	*Boquera*	*Regadío*
Mujer, Agua	60–120	4413.75	10093.75	0	0	215.0
	30–60	211.0	3642.25	0	0	61.0
	12–30	85.5	911.25	0	0	34.0
	0–12	10.75	141.5	0	0	9.0
Encina	60–120	4451.0	2960.5	0	0	5233.75
	30–60	787.25	947.0	0	0	1260.5
	12–30	288.25	151.25	0	0	195.75
	0–12	40.5	3.75	0	0	36.5
Nerja	60–120	4080.5	34.25	21.75	0	494.75
	30–60	901.0	220.0	0	0	235.5
	12–30	268.0	206.0	0	0	72.5
	0–12	26.0	38.25	0	0	48.0

assessments of the amount of each land-use category in each isochrone of the site territories. These results are given in Table 5.1. Secondly, we arrive at qualitative assessments of which agricultural land-use category was likely to have been accessible at least cost to the inhabitants of each settlement. These interpretations are summarised in Table 5.2.

Table 5.2 Potential land use to which the sites are oriented.

Site name	Potential land use	
	Wet farming (*regadío, boquera*)	Dry farming (*secano*, terraced)
La Almoloya	−	+
Campico de Lébor	−	+
La Bastida	−	+
La Ceñuela	+	−
Parazuelos	+	−
Ifre	+	+
Zapata	+	−
Cabezo Negro	+	−
El Oficio	−	+
Campos, Tres Cabezos	+	−
Fuente Álamo	−	+
El Argar, El Gárcel, La Gerundia	+	+
Fuente Bermeja	+	−
Lugarico Viejo	+	−
Gatas	+	−
Terrera Ventura	+	+
Los Millares	+	−
Enmedio	+	−
El Tarajal, El Barranquete	+	−
Ambrosio	−	+
Canteras	−	+
El Picacho	+	−
El Malagón	−	+
Virgen	+	−
Culantrillo	+	−
Gallo	+	−
Cuesta del Negro	−	+
Carigüela	+	+
Torre Cardela	−	+
Los Castellones (Laborcillas)	−	+
Murciélagos (Zuheros)	−	+
Los Castillejos (Montefrío)	−	+
Mujer, Agua	+	+
Encina	+	−
Nerja	+	+

Notes

1 For Totana-Aledo and Alhama de Murcia alone of the 85 Ensenada localities studied, *boqueras* are enumerated in the *Respuesta General* under question 17 ('Are there any mines, salt pans, flour or paper mills or other artifacts in the municipality . . . ?').

2 The far-fetched suggestion that, at the time of its occupation, Parazuelos was a coastal site, perhaps an island (Walker 1977, p. 363), must be rejected not just because at 85 m elevation the site is well above sea level, but also because the Sirets (1887, p. 42) report prehistoric materials from two small caves on the immediate coastline within the Parazuelos 2 h territory.

3 If three-quarters of the 0.2 ha of closely packed structures at Ifre may be considered floor space, then the site's population may be estimated at 150 souls, following Naroll (1956). Using Clark and Haswell's (1970, p. 59) estimate of 210 kg of grain per person per year as meeting subsistence needs, one arrives at a total of 31 500 kg as the amount of grain needed to feed Ifre's population. The no doubt underestimated yield ratios reported in the 1757 Ensenada *Respuesta General* for Lorca indicate that under palaeotechnic conditions the 14.5 ha (52 Lorca *fanegas*) of *regadío* within the 12 min territory would produce about 23 000 kg of wheat and 35 000 kg of barley. The size of the site is, then, approximately right for the amount of irrigated land in its vicinity.

4 Because the El Oficio site territory forms part of two very large Ensenada localities, Vera and Cuevas, the 1752 *Respuestas Generales* cannot be used as a guide to palaeotechnic land use within the territory. The *Relaciones Particulares* are vast (and for Cuevas, incomplete) and so are not readily amenable to analysis.

5 Precise quantitative estimates of 18th-century land uses cannot be arrived at for Cuevas (cf. Ferre Bueno 1977). The *Respuesta General* reports land-use totals in *fanegas de puño*, so that translation into hectares is impossible. A map of the parcels cannot be pieced together from the *Relación Particular* because the volumes enumerating ecclesiastical holdings have been lost.

6 Chapman (1978, p. 270) suggests that a key point for the placement of the El Argar group of sites is that they are just below the Rambla de Cajete's confluence with the Antas. As Figure 5.9 indicates, however, the smaller stream does not add significantly to the flows available in the larger.

7 For eastern Andalusia and southern Murcia the *Diccionario Geográfico de España* gives a range of sizes for the pre-metric land use measure, the *fanega*, ranging from 0.16 ha to 0.67 ha. Some localities, however, measured land in *fanegas de puño* (fist *fanegas*). Besides being a measure of land, the *fanega* is a volume measure for grain (55.5 l is the dictionary definition). A *fanega de puño* of land is, then, the area which would need a *fanega* of wheat in the planting. In these localities the size of a *fanega* is inversely proportional to the quality of the land, since grain would be sown more sparsely on worse soils.

8 Where a specific source for rainfall figures is not cited, totals are taken from records of the Servicio Meteorológico Nacional in Madrid.

9 It is interesting in this regard that all the megalithic tombs of the Leisners' (1943, pp. 73–7) Tabernas group are of 'Almerian' rather than 'Millaran' character.

10 Areas subtracted from the 1956–57 *regadío* total are mapped as terraced if they are on marls (erosional potential makes terracing on marl universal in the arid south-east), as floodwater farmed if they are located beside *ramblas* (*boquera* farming is very common within the site territories) and as *secano* otherwise.

11 Some water from the Maimón springs is brought by aqueduct over the Claro to its eastern bank. This area has been mapped as *secano*.

12 A quantitative assessment of the degree of similarity between 18th-century and modern *regadío* in Purullena is impeded because the *Respuesta General* does not answer the question concerning the dimensions of the local *fanega* ('they do not know how many paces or *varas castellanas* constitute a *fanega*'). If, however, one divides the current extent of *regadío* in Purullena as measured from the 1956–57 air photographs (1003 ha) by the 2308 *fanegas* reported in the *Relación Particular* (see Table 3.1), the resultant estimate of *fanega* size (0.43 ha) falls within the

range of traditional *fanega* sizes in south-east Spain (0.16 to 0.67 ha: see footnote 7 above).

13 Our land-use mapping in a portion of the Cuesta del Negro and Cerro del Gallo territories is based on the Guadix sheet of the 1 : 50 000 *Mapa de Cultivos y Aprovechamientos* (Ministerio de Agricultura 1975).

14 Our land-use mapping in the southwestern quadrant of the site territory is based on the Padul sheet of the 1 : 50 000 *Mapa de Cultivos y Aprovechamientos* (Ministerio de Agricultura 1974).

6 *Comparative analysis and conclusions*

Testing the irrigation hypothesis

In the preceding chapters we have discussed the economic basis of Copper and Bronze Age florescence in south-east Spain and the method used to attack this problem (site catchment analysis) and we have presented the results for each of the 35 site territories studied. Our conclusions concerning particular sites depend on the soundness of the assessments concerning palaeotechnic land-use potential and on the validity of the least-cost assumptions that underlie our method of study. In any particular case it is undeniable, of course, that factors other than low-cost access to agricultural land may have played a role in settlement placement. Discussion of land-use distributions within individual site territories leads to tentative suggestions concerning the subsistence activities carried out from those sites (particularly if excavated evidence for economic activities is also available), but the idiosyncrasies that governed site placement in particular instances inevitably add local effects to the regional picture provided by a statistical comparison of the array of site territories. The evidence developed in the previous chapter suggests that many later prehistoric settlements in south-east Spain were favourably located for intensive hydraulic agriculture, but the prehistoric irrigation hypothesis can only be evaluated by a comparative analysis of all the sites together. These comparisons should test the significance of the global configuration of land uses and of the contrasts in particular features of importance to the hypothesis under examination.

Analysis of variance The underlying design of this research corresponds to an analysis of variance in which land near archaeological sites is subjected to a variety of 'treatments' – intensity of land use, distance from a site, age of that site, rainfall – so as to produce a variety of results (expressed in area (ha) in Table 5.1). These areas (whose derivation was discussed in the last chapter) were, accordingly, grouped, adjusted and (together with data on climate and topography) submitted to an analysis of variance, under the following conditions:

(1) Distance from the site was allocated to two classes, core and periphery. The former is within and the latter beyond 30 min walking time from the site.
(2) Intensity refers to the division into water-based and non-water-based agriculture. *Boquera*-fed and terraced land is not represented in many site territories, and the specific areas are highly contingent on recent land-use practices. Accordingly, *boquera*-fed and terraced land were grouped with

regadío and *secano* respectively. This lumping corresponds to the way in which land uses are categorised in south-east Spain today.

(3) The resultant areas (ha) for each land-use category show an extremely skewed, Poisson-like distribution. The summed areas H (ha) were, therefore, 'normalised' by a square-root conversion, $H_{adj} = \sqrt{H} + \sqrt{(H+1)}$.

(4) As discussed on pp. 39 and 77, we have distinguished between *monte* and *secano* primarily on the basis of topography: steep slopes are not cultivable, gentler ones may be. The relative proportions of *monte* and *secano*, therefore, reflect ruggedness of the terrain. This is assessed by dividing the size of the territories as we actually measured them by the size they would be if it had been possible to maintain a walking speed of 5 km h^{-1} (314 ha for the 12 min territory, 1349.5 ha for the 12 min to 30 min zone, and so on) and taking the square-root of the resultant fraction. (The larger the fraction, the more even the terrain.) Our measures of ruggedness are presented in Table 6.1. Figures for core and periphery of each site territory were introduced into the analysis as a covariate. This 'removes' from the analysis the direct effect of topography on the proportions of land uses within and between the site territories.

(5) Sites were dated by broad periods (Neolithic, Copper Age, Bronze Age). If the site (or sites) at the centre of a particular territory was (were) occupied in more than one period (see Table 1.1), the territory was assigned to the earliest period of its exploitation. For this analysis, Tres Cabezos, El Gárcel and Terrera Ventura were accepted as Neolithic occupations (see pp. 102, 105–6 & 111).

(6) Because of the limited number of sites in the earlier periods (nine Neolithic, nine Copper Age), it was necessary to lump climate into two categories: arid (receiving less than 325 mm yr^{-1} of precipitation) and moist (receiving more than that amount). (Rainfall for each territory was discussed in the previous chapter and the summary figures are presented in Table 6.2.)

Results The figures obtained by the above procedures (summarised in Table 5.1) were submitted to the SPSS ANOVA program, and the results of the analysis are shown in Table 6.3. As this indicates, almost all of the variance is accounted for by the main effects of the treatments and the two-way interactions between them. The test of significance (final column) indicates the probability with which a particular F value (penultimate column) may be expected to occur by chance.

The dominant *main effect* is distance (i.e. the core–periphery division). This simply reflects the fact that, by virtue of the division used, the area of the periphery is four times that of the core and hence the expected areas are invariably greater in the core than in the periphery. This core–periphery division is therefore only of interest when considered as an interaction. Intensity (*regadío–secano* division) is the second most important primary effect. Throughout south-east Spain (and in almost all of our site territories) *monte* and

Table 6.1   Ruggedness in the 35 site territories.

Site name	Isochrone			
	0–12 min	12–30 min	30–60 min	60–120 min
La Almoloya	0.656	0.863	0.753	0.803
Campico	0.646	0.769	0.882	0.865
Bastida	0.571	0.592	0.690	0.888
La Ceñuela	0.847	0.873	0.862	0.910
Cabezo Negro	0.618	0.706	0.789	0.719
Zapata	0.623	0.736	0.673	0.702
Parazuelos	0.915	0.910	0.756	0.710
Ifre	0.780	0.927	0.842	0.711
Campos/Tres Cabezos	0.884	0.831	0.717	0.739
Fuente Álamo	0.548	0.647	0.623	0.688
El Oficio	0.605	0.793	0.724	0.806
Lugarico Viejo	0.724	0.705	0.808	0.770
Fuente Bermeja	0.793	0.771	0.853	0.785
El Argar, El Gárcel, La				
Gerundia	0.797	0.907	0.714	0.868
Gatas	0.516	0.636	0.719	0.748
Terrera Ventura	0.696	0.804	0.761	0.719
Los Millares	0.582	0.675	0.702	0.701
Enmedio	0.489	0.633	0.617	0.631
El Barranquete/El Tarajal	0.789	0.809	0.915	0.918
Ambrosio	0.398	0.732	0.700	0.702
Canteras	0.787	0.869	0.726	0.693
El Picacho	0.414	0.598	0.642	0.737
El Malagón	0.897	0.879	0.862	0.846
Virgen	0.779	0.896	0.909	0.871
Culantrillo	0.549	0.712	0.740	0.736
Cuesta del Negro	0.608	0.829	0.907	0.796
Gallo	0.705	0.835	0.788	0.849
Torre Cardela	0.780	0.889	0.872	0.843
Carigüela	0.773	0.809	0.854	0.850
Laborcillas	0.799	0.895	0.815	0.800
Zuheros	0.573	0.579	0.680	0.765
Montefrío	0.628	0.878	0.649	0.702
Mujer, Agua	0.716	0.821	0.833	0.783
Encina	0.507	0.668	0.771	0.756
Nerja	0.598	0.657	0.594	0.535

secano are more abundant than *regadío*: the amount of land in a given land-use category is generally inversely proportional to the intensity of that land use. The main effects tell us little about the hypothesis under evaluation, but the divisions provide the essential basis for the test of the interactions, which are seen to be significant at the 1% level.

Of the two-way *interactive effects*, two are highly significant, intensity–distance and age–intensity. The intensity–distance interaction establishes the

Table 6.2 Mean annual precipitation (mm) in the 35 territories.

Cueva de los Murciélagos (Zuheros)	800
Los Castillejos (Peñas de los Gitanos, Montefrío)	570
Cueva de la Carigüela	550
Cuevas de la Mujer y del Agua (Alhama de Granada)	535
Torre Cardela	500
Cerro de los Castellones (Laborcillas)	480
Cueva de Nerja	450
Cerro de la Encina	440
Cerro de las Canteras	420
El Picacho	405
El Malagón	400
Cueva de Ambrosio	385
Cuesta del Negro	375
El Culantrillo	345
Cerro del Gallo	330
Cerro de la Almoloya	305
Cerro de la Virgen	300
La Bastida	260
Campico de Lébor	260
La Ceñuela	260
Cerro de Enmedio	250
Fuente Álamo	250
Gatas	250
Cabezo Negro de Pastrana	245
Zapata	245
Los Millares	240
Terrera Ventura	240
El Argar, El Gárcel, La Gerundia	235
Fuente Vermeja	235
Lugarico Viejo	235
El Oficio	235
Tres Cabezos, Campos	235
El Tarajal/El Barranquete	230
Ifre	220
Parazuelos	220

fact that, as Table 6.4 shows, the proportion of the more intense land uses (*boquera–regadío*) with respect to total area is generally higher in the core than in the periphery of the corresponding sets of territories. (The only exception to this is the set of arid-zone Bronze Age sites, where we have noted the importance of defensive concerns, which come to rival convenience of agricultural exploitation as considerations in site placement.) This appears to support the thesis that the sites were, in general, located with preference to irrigation potential, in spite of the exceptions noted in the previous chapter and the fact that, where in doubt, we have biased against this thesis.

The other significant interaction (0.033 level) is also consistent with our guiding hypothesis. Age and intensity together account for a significant propor-

Table 6.3 Results of the analysis of variance of land-use areas (ha) in the 35 site territories in south-east Spain.

Source of variation	Sum of squares	DF	Mean square	F	Significance of F
Covariates	5513.555	1	5513.555	21.632	0.001
ruggedness	5513.555	1	5513.555	21.632	0.001
Main effects	122112.495	6	20352.083	79.848	0.001
age	104.675	2	52.337	0.205	0.871
intensity	33769.223	2	16884.611	66.244	0.001
distance	85469.946	1	85469.946	335.328	0.001
rainfall	135.519	1	135.519	0.532	0.477
Two-way interactions	19846.660	13	1526.666	5.990	0.001
age–intensity	3568.393	4	892.098	3.500	0.033
age–distance	208.029	2	104.014	0.408	0.672
age–rainfall	665.359	2	332.679	1.305	0.300
intensity–distance	13993.292	2	6996.646	27.450	0.001
intensity–rainfall	1461.744	2	730.872	2.867	0.088
distance–rainfall	7.570	1	7.570	0.030	0.865
Explained	147472.710	20	7373.636	28.929	0.001
Residual	3823.271	15	254.885		
Total	151295.981	35	4322.742		

tion of the variance, because the proportion of the more intensive land uses (*boquera–regadío*) tends to increase over time (from 14% of the rescaled areas in the Neolithic to 20% in the Bronze Age) as our model suggests.

The interaction between intensity and rainfall deserves some discussion, although its 0.088 significance falls short of the conventional 0.05 level. Our hypothesis predicts that the proportion of *boquera–regadío* land within the site territories will be higher in the arid sector (where hydraulic farming can be more successful). As Table 5.1 indicates, this is true for Neolithic and Copper Age sites, but for Bronze Age sites the opposite holds. It is this reversal that causes the significance level of the intensity–rainfall interaction to be low (although, overall, the more intense land uses are indeed proportionally more abundant in the set of arid than in the set of moist sites). We shall argue that the change in pattern from Neolithic to Copper Age reflects the fact that during the Bronze Age more intensive agricultural practices were introduced into the moist uplands, and simple statistical analysis of the data appear to support this.

Contingency tests   The analysis of variance indicates the main trends in land uses within the sample of site territories considered as a whole. It is also useful to consider the contrasts between site territories period by period and area by area. The previous chapter considered site by site whether or not the distribution of land uses in their territories suggests that the settlements were located favour-

Table 6.4 Adjusted mean land-use areas (ha) and mean ruggedness for the 35 site territories.

Age	Rainfall (mm)	Distance (min)	Ruggedness	Land-use intensity		
				Monte	Secano, terraced	boquera, regadío
Neolithic						
	> 325 mm	0–30	0.69 ± 0.04	32.7 ± 4.1	47.0 ± 6.8	10.5 ± 3.4
	(N = 6)	30–120	0.72 ± 0.04	137.2 ± 12.6	178.9 ± 34.4	32.8 ± 5.6
	< 325 mm	0–30	0.82 ± 0.03	44.6 ± 3.3	45.2 ± 11.2	28.8 ± 11.0
	(N = 3)	30–120	0.76 ± 0.03	188.9 ± 3.7	171.4 ± 12.5	68.6 ± 16.0
Copper Age						
	> 325 mm	0–30	0.86 ± 0.01	22.5 ± 5.0	68.5 ± 4.0	13.8 ± 9.3
	(N = 4)	30–120	0.80 ± 0.04	140.0 ± 23.0	225.1 ± 33.8	50.6 ± 11.7
	< 325 mm	0–30	0.78 ± 0.05	47.7 ± 2.0	43.9 ± 7.1	23.0 ± 3.9
	(N = 5)	30–120	0.82 ± 0.04	173.1 ± 8.9	182.7 ± 29.7	74.7 ± 14.7
Bronze Age						
	> 325 mm	0–30	0.66 ± 0.05	44.6 ± 2.8	25.2 ± 5.5	25.1 ± 4.4
	(N = 5)	30–120	0.77 ± 0.02	173.7 + 7.9	150.5 ± 8.4	104.5 ± 24.6
	< 325 mm	0–30	0.70 ± 0.03	47.1 ± 1.4	35.3 ± 4.9	13.8 ± 1.6
	(N − 12)	30–120	0.76 ± 0.02	178.0 ⊥ 5.0	158.2 ± 13.4	60.5 ± 4.9

ably for hydraulic agriculture. The results based on mixed (but coherent) criteria may be assessed against climate (dichotomised as in the analysis of variance) in contingency tables. For the Neolithic localities (see Table 1.1), the results are as follows:[1]

		arid	moist	
irrigation	+	3	3	$p = 0.238$
	−	0	3	

These results are suggestive, but do not attain conventional significance levels because three moist area sites (Carigüela, Nerja and Mujer–Agua) have appreciable irrigated land in their territories.[2] All three are caves or rock shelters located in karstic limestone formations. The many springs in the karst in some cases produce flows large enough to support substantial areas of regadío. This prevents the contrast in irrigation orientation between the arid and moist sectors from reaching a statistically conclusive level.

Copper Age site territories are more easily compared because their approximate contemporaneity is firmly established by shared cultural features and because all (except one: Los Castillejos, Peñas de los Gitanos–Montefrío) have open-air settlements at their centres. Using the same criteria as for the Neolithic sites, comparison of Copper Age territories yields the following contingency table:

		arid	moist	
irrigation	+	7	0	$p = 0.005$
	−	1	5	

Here the contrast is very clear. In the arid zone, only Campico de Lébor does not emphasise convenient access to *regadío* in its site location; in the moist sector, *no* site has such an emphasis. Although the artifact inventories from the sites indicate a common cultural background, the locations of the sites indicate that different economic strategies were pursued in the arid and the moist sectors.

Given the difficulties surrounding the identification of Neolithic sites in the arid sector and the demonstrable continuities that exist between Neolithic and Copper Age in both sectors, it may be prudent to consider all of the earlier sites together in a single contingency table:

		arid	moist	
irrigation	+	7	3	$p = 0.023$
	−	1	7	

This makes clear that, with relatively few exceptions, pre-Bronze Age agricultural sites in south-east Spain were oriented to exploit hydraulic resources in the arid, but not in the moist, sector of south-east Spain. In the 18 Neolithic and Copper Age 30 min territories, mean annual precipitation (Table 6.2) is correlated negatively with the proportion that *regadío* forms of the arable total[3] (Pearson's r is -0.426), and positively with the proportion that *secano* forms of that total (Pearson's r is $+0.714$). This result supports the idea of a clear differentiation in site placement strategy that our hypothesis of early irrigation in the arid south-east would predict.

The contrasts between arid and moist sectors apparent in the Neolithic and Copper Ages are effaced, indeed to an extent reversed, in the Bronze Age. Site territories of this period may be contrasted in the following contingency table:

		arid	moist	
irrigation	+	10	4	$p = 0.603$
	−	4	1	

It is apparent that sites in both sectors were by then oriented to the convenient exploitation of hydraulic resources. The few exceptions (La Almoloya, La Bastida, El Oficio and Fuente Álamo in the arid sector; Cuesta del Negro in the moist sector) are sites in extreme defensive emplacements. In 17 Bronze Age 30 min territories[4] the proportion that *regadío* forms of the arable total is now positively correlated with mean annual precipitation (Pearson's r is $+0.500$). This result contrasts sharply with the corresponding correlation for Neolithic and Copper Age sites. The change that took place in the moist uplands is made clear in the following:

		Copper	Bronze	
irrigation	+	0	4	$p = 0.024$
	−	5	1	

In the arid zone, however, there was, if anything, a slight decline in the importance of irrigation:

		Copper	Bronze	
irrigation	+	7	8	$p = 0.307$
	−	1	4	

In fact, as Table 6.4 indicates, the adjusted mean areas of *regadío* and *boquera*-fed land in the 30 min territories of arid-zone sites declined significantly from Copper to Bronze Age.[5] The shift from Copper to Bronze Age is interpretable in terms of two trends. On the one hand, hydraulic agriculture became universal and sites tended to be placed conveniently for its practice throughout south-east Spain. On the other hand, in both arid and moist sectors, Bronze Age sites are almost all located on easily defended peaks and promontories. Of the 19 Bronze Age localities, only three (La Ceñuela, El Argar and Fuente Bermeja) are not in strong defensive positions. In the moist sector, where water is relatively abundant, the demands of defence and of convenient agricultural exploitation could have been more easily reconciled than in the arid sector.

The progressive directional changes that characterise the location of sites with respect to *regadío* are not exhibited for the other land uses described in the 35 site territories. Appreciable amounts (over 1% of the 2 h territory) of *boquera*-fed land are present in 16 territories (all but El Malagón in the arid zone). In only five of these (Parazuelos, Campos–Tres Cabezos, Terrera Ventura, La Ceñuela and Zapata) is the proportion of *boquera*-fed land higher in the 30 min territory than in the peripheral zone. Floodwater-farming was within the scope of a Neolithic technology and may well have been an early hydraulic technique in south-east Spain. In certain site territories in which water for *regadío* is very scarce (Terrera Ventura, for example), *riego de boquera* continues to be important even today. In general, however, its limited modern distribution is along minor streams with occasional flows, while prehistoric settlements tend to be located along the more important drainages, which provide enough water for proper irrigation.

Appreciable amounts of terracing are present in 20 site territories (all but Cerro de las Canteras in the arid zone). Terracing serves to check erosion on marls and to retain moisture along drainage lines. In a few areas (mainly in the Gatas and Los Millares territories) it also serves to extend cultivation on to steep slopes. Terraced land is more abundant in the core than in the periphery of nine of the territories (three of seven Copper Age, six of 13 Bronze Age). While terracing as a technique would have been within the scope of the later prehistoric inhabitants of south-east Spain, the data indicate that settlements were not systematically oriented towards land that would require such investment to make it useful.

Any land that is not too steep and retains some regolith may have been dry farmed in recent times. The frequency with which a given tract of land is planted, the crops to which it is put and the yields it produces depend on a variety of factors, among them climate, but the amount of *secano* available, as here defined, depends on topography more than on climate.[6] Of the 35 site territories, only 15 (five in the arid, seven in the moist sector) have a larger proportion of *secano* in the 30 min territory than in the peripheral zone. That is to say, only a minority of sites were situated so as to maximise the availability of arable land in their vicinity. Only during the Copper Age does the proportion of sites oriented to *secano* differ in the arid and the moist sectors to an extent meeting conventional levels of statistical significance:

		arid	moist	
secano	+	3	5	$p = 0.044$
	−	5	0	

Because *secano* is the most abundant land-use category in the region, the prehistoric inhabitants of the region were likely to find adequate amounts of it wherever they chose to establish their settlements. The critical factor determining site location might have been land that could be irrigated, but it was not usually land that could have been cultivated.

Lewthwaite (1982) has usefully reminded archaeologists that Mediterranean woodlands are not simply areas that have not yet been (or cannot be) cleared for cultivation, but valuable resource spaces in their own right. *Monte* provides the Mediterranean farmer with wood, game, acorns and chestnuts for himself or for his animals, browse for caprovids and cattle, and so on. The available botanical and zoological evidence from archaeological sites in south-east Spain indicates that woodland exploitation was an important facet of the economy during all phases of the later prehistoric period throughout the region: deer and pigs are important elements in the faunal series from many sites (see Table 2.2); acorns are reported from a number of localities (such as Lugarico Viejo (Siret & Siret 1887, plate 16/49) and Cueva de Nerja (Hopf & Pellicer Catalán 1970)). '*Monte*' is defined here, not as woodland, but as land that cannot be cultivated. Most of the land classified as *secano* must have been woodland during later prehistoric times, but the extent to which the resources in those woodlands were exploited cannot be determined by the approach taken here. The relative proportions of *monte* in the core and the periphery of the site territories reflects not the degree to which the economy of the sites' inhabitants was oriented towards woodland resources but the nature of the terrain in which the sites are situated.[7] In this respect there are strong changes from earlier to late periods. If one classifies as '*monte*+' those territories in which the proportion of non-arable land is higher in the 30 min zone than in the periphery, the following contingency table results:

		Neolithic & Copper	Bronze	
monte	+	6	15	$p = 0.0011$
	−	12	2	

This shift reflects, we believe, the defensive concerns influencing settlement placement in the Argaric.

The patterns analysed above are interpreted as the result of two underlying tendencies. First, there is a tendency towards greater intensity of exploitation over time. Sites are oriented towards irrigable land in the arid coastal sector of south-east Spain as early as the 4th millennium BC and throughout the region by the 2nd millennium. Secondly, there is a tendency to place sites in more defensive positions over time. Several Copper Age settlements are fortified (Los Millares, Campos, Cerro de la Virgen, Cerro de los Castellones–Laborcillas) and by the Bronze Age most sites are placed on high hilltops or easily defensible spurs. This leads to an increase in the proportion of land that is non-arable in the core of the site territories. These two tendencies are, of course, functionally related.[8]

Alternatives

The evidence of site catchment analysis supports the hypothesis that the later prehistoric inhabitants of south-east Spain developed intensive agricultural practices (in particular, irrigation) and this view is consistent with the plant and animal remains recovered from archaeological deposits. The relevance of such a development to the increase in social differentiation also manifest in the archaeological record has not been widely recognised by Iberian prehistorians. Most have preferred to see pastoralism as the basic subsistence strategy and metalworking as the critical element in the increase in social complexity (see pp. 31–2). The evidence that this study brings to bear on these alternatives merits brief discussion.

Pastoralism   The notion that the economy of later prehistoric Spain was oriented towards mobile animal keeping has had a traditional popularity among prehistorians of Spain. This is partly due to the tendency to use models derived from Spanish history to explain patterns during prehistory: the importance of long-distance transhumance in recent times could be easily translated into the more remote past. Thus, Higgs (1976) and Jarman *et al.* (1982) have recently interpreted the distribution of megalithic burial monuments in terms of such transhumance. In a Near Eastern setting, of course, the development of pastoralism has been interpreted as integral to the process of developing social complexity in that it reflects a division of labour *between* households in subsistence production (Lees & Bates 1974, Adams, 1966). In Iberia, for the most part, pastoralism has been assigned the less important function of explaining the broad distribution of particular styles of artifacts (cf. Bosch Gimpera (1944) or Savory (1968) on Beakers).

Chapman (1979) has criticised cogently the historical analogy underlying the hypothesis of prehistoric pastoralism in Spain: the development of long-distance transhumance in the Iberian Peninsula is, after all, a phenomenon specific to the historical circumstances of the late Mediaeval and early Modern periods. It is also clear that the available faunal evidence from south-east Spain speaks against the analogy, at least for that region: sheep (the historical object of transhumance in Iberia) and goats do not dominate faunal assemblages and their proportional frequency tends to decline over time (cf. Table 2.2). As Chapman points out, however, the crucial issue is the *scale* of herding operations in the prehistoric period. It is not the existence but the size of herds that is limited by the pasture available in the arid lowlands during the summer season. Thus, it is the geographical setting of permanent settlements, together with the desire for large herds, that may require a system of long-distance transhumance. In this respect the mountainous character of south-east Spain is highly relevant. The mean difference in elevation between the highest and the lowest points within the 2 h territories of the 35 sites we have studied is 712 m (for the 20 sites classified as 'arid' in the analyses above, the mean difference is 721 m), and rainfall rises with elevation. Thus, almost all sites would have had summer grazing available within reasonable walking distances. The pasture near the sites might be exhausted by very large herds, but neither the absolute size of prehistoric settlements nor the faunal series from them indicates that such large herds existed. The three lines of evidence available (site setting, site size, known fauna) suggest, rather, that the prehistoric inhabitants of south-east Spain could have arranged to graze their animals on daily excursions without necessitating substantial changes in the division of labour between households.

Metalworking   Most prehistorians have regarded mining and metalworking as the key to the florescence of Copper and Bronze Age cultures in south-east Spain. The nature of the arguments that have been put forward, and some of the theoretical difficulties attendant on them, have been discussed on pp.31–2. To the extent that metalworking was an important aspect of the production systems of the later prehistoric period, it seems reasonable to expect that settlements should be placed close to copper ore bodies, and, indeed, this test has been accepted by proponents of the importance of metallurgy. As Walker (1981, p.177) puts it, during the Copper Age 'exploitation of metal ores in the nearby hills probably determined site location'. To what extent, then, can the settlements that we have studied be said to be oriented towards metal sources?

The *Mapa Metalogenético de España* 1 : 200 000 sheets provide a systematic source of information concerning the location of copper ore bodies in the south-east. Within our study area there are 65 known sources of copper, six of which occur within the 2 h territories of sites in our sample: two in the hills in the southeastern periphery of the Cerro de las Canteras territory; two in the Sierra de las Estancias in the Picacho site territory; and two in the Lomo de Bas in the southern periphery of the Parazuelos, Zapata, Ifre and Cabezo Negro de Pastrana territories. Thus, of the 30 sites in our sample that have Copper or Bronze Age occupations, just six have copper sources in their vicinity. After adjusting the sample to allow for boundary effects, the proximity of sites of the several periods to the ore sources nearest them was compared to the corresponding distance of an equal number of randomly placed points. The mean distances of Neolithic and Copper Age sites are greater than those of the random samples (although the differences are not statistically significant). For Bronze Age sites the mean is slightly lower than for the corresponding random sample, but the probability that the difference occurs by chance is greater than 0.80. Measures like these present obvious difficulties: on the one hand, sources of ore used in prehistoric times may have been too small to be of interest to the modern prospectors whose work constitutes the basis of the *Mapa Metalogenético*. Moreover, further archaeological work in mountainous areas may reveal sites closer to known ore bodies than the sample of sites now known. Nevertheless, the present evidence does not support the belief that maximising proximity to copper ore sources was a significant consideration in later prehistoric settlement placement. The present evidence rather suggests that metal was a luxury item used by a small proportion of the population to display and store their wealth. Occasional expeditions to sources at moderate distances[9] would suffice to provide the limited amounts of metal being put into circulation at any given time. Certainly the development of a luxury for elite use may reflect that elite's progressive increase in wealth and power, but it is difficult to see how the occasional, small-scale, production of that luxury could have brought that elite into being.

Conclusions

The floral and faunal remains recovered from Early Neolithic sites make it clear that by the 5th millennium BC the inhabitants of *Hochandalusien* were pursuing a mixed farming strategy. The six upland Neolithic sites in our sample are all caves or rock shelters, but they are all suitably located for dry farming. Nothing in the available archaeological record indicates that substantial inequalities would have existed between households during this period. In the arid sector of south-east Spain, there are no reliably known occupation sites that can be assigned to this period. Dry farming, logically the first food production to be adopted in Iberia, is not a viable subsistence strategy in the arid lowlands, and we may presume that human occupation of the region must have depended on a more mobile economy. Short-term open-air sites have not been discovered in the arid south-east, either because they have been destroyed by erosion or because traditional archaeological prospecting has not been oriented towards their discovery. Such rock shelter sites as may have been identified have probably been assigned to the Epipalaeolithic.

Very few sites in south-east Spain can be assigned unequivocally to the 4th millennium BC. In the moist uplands, occupation of several cave sites continues with little overall change in their assemblages apart from the style of the ceramics. The initial occupation of the Péras de los Gitanos (Montefrío) site may have occurred during this timespan. In the arid sector, it is clear that occupation of Los Millares was under way by the end of the millennium, and a few farming settlements seem to belong to a pre-Millaran Late Neolithic. It has been argued that the use of megalithic burial monuments also begins in the Late Neolithic. Be that as it may, whenever during the 4th millennium BC agricultural occupation of the arid south-east began, the location of those early sites reveals a clear orientation towards potentially irrigable land. It is presumably the development of hydraulic technology that made agriculturally based occupation of the coastal lowlands possible.

During the 3rd millennium BC, there are numbers of well documented open-air farming sites in both arid and moist sectors. In addition, collective burial in megalithic tombs (or in natural or artificial caves) was practised throughout the south-east. The styles of artifacts in both burials and settlements and the ritual practices in the burial sites show strong similarity in both sectors. While a substantial (Millaran) cultural unity is documented throughout south-east Spain, there is a strong divergence in settlement location patterns: in *Hochandalusien*, sites continue to be oriented towards land whose agricultural potential is as *secano*; in the coastal lowlands, sites were oriented towards land with hydraulic agricultural potential. Together with this contrast in economic orientation, there was a contrast in the elaboration of the shared burial ritual. In the uplands, tombs are smaller, simpler in design, and more equal in the wealth of their grave goods than in the arid zone. Many tombs there are simple monuments like those in the uplands, but others are large and elaborately subdivided or contain large quantities of luxurious or exotic grave goods. (Metalworking first appears in the 3rd millennium and metal objects are much more common in the arid than in the moist sector.) This differentiation occurs both within and between tomb groups in the arid south-east and is interpreted as reflecting the development of social ranking (Chapman 1981a). The construction of megalithic tombs is often seen as a ritual expression of the communal solidarity of the tomb builders and of their collective appropriation of the land on which they live (C. Renfrew 1976, Chapman 1981b). At the same time, it is a commonplace of functionalist social anthropology that ritual serves to alleviate uncertainty. The greater elaboration of the collective burial ritual in the arid zone should reflect, then, a greater uncertainty concerning the basis of communal solidarity, an uncertainty reflected in and engendered by increasing social inequalities between households (cf. Gilman 1976, Shennan 1982).

The Argaric Culture of the 2nd millennium BC presents clear social and economic contrasts to its predecessor, the Los Millares Culture. In both uplands and coastal sectors of the south-east, sites tend to be oriented towards irrigable land. In both sectors, too, sites tend to be placed in defensive positions at some cost of easy access to arable land of any kind. The presumed spread of irrigation agriculture from the arid zone where it had been first developed to the moist zone may have been the result of several factors: the development of improved techniques for controlling year-round streams, the introduction of crops suitable for extending the growing season into summer (millet, perhaps) and the spread of better organised, more competitive political systems suggest themselves as possibilities to be considered. In any event, it is clear that the importance of irrigation throughout south-east Spain formed part of a pattern of agricultural intensification which also includes the use of cattle and horses for their traction power and possibly arboriculture as well. At the same time, as the defensive preoccupations of the Argaric indicate, there were important social changes: the shift in burial ritual from collective to individual interment and from grave goods consisting of utilitarian items and ritual fetishes to grave goods emphasising the personal finery of the dead, as well as the increased amount of and contrasts in grave good wealth, suggest the further developments of social inequalities from Copper to Bronze Age. The metallurgical industry, which provided the principal means through which differences in wealth were expressed, also increased in sophistication. Once again, there is a contrast apparent between the degree of inequalities in the arid and the moist sectors. In the uplands, there was a prolonged use of megaliths into the 2nd millennium BC and the individual burials at their wealthiest do not attain the level of finery of the richest grave assemblages in the arid zone. Although it is agriculturally the most productive sector, *Hochandalusien* was socially more egalitarian in later prehistoric times.

The interweaving of a developing intensification of subsistence production (whose further documentation has been the principal object of our study) and increasing social inequalities is an association present not just in south-east Spain but in all cultural sequences evolving a greater social complexity. Explanations of the development of elites from the matrix of egalitarian societies may be subdivided into two categories: those that emphasise the positive contributions which a privileged minority makes to its followers and those that stress the negative sanctions which a privileged minority imposes on its subjects. Most of the positive-function theories of elite development revolve around the contributions that leaders can make to the organisation of more effective systems of production and exchange (which make possible the Darwinian good of higher population levels). All varieties of this view see rulers as 'high-order regulators). (cf. Flannery 1972). 'The chief creates a collective good beyond the conception and capacity of a society's domestic groups taken separately. He institutes a public economy greater than the sum of its domestic parts' (Sahlins 1972, p. 140).

Everything known about the systems of production of south-east Spain during the later prehistoric period suggests that the scale of operations was small and would not have required the centralised direction that is the linchpin of the managerial approach to explaining emergent stratification. Irrigation systems in south-eastern Spain are run along egalitarian lines by local farmers (cf. Glick (1970) on the much larger systems in Valencia) and the prehistoric systems would have been much smaller in scale than those of the present day. Long-distance trade involved very small amounts of luxuries, and there is no reason to suppose that the procurement of such exotic goods would have required any permanent organisation beyond the network of alliances necessarily maintained by local kin groups. Most goods were made from resources which were locally available and the level of skills involved do not imply craft specialisation (see the studies of Bronze Age ceramic technology by Capel Martínez and Delgado Calvo-Flores (1978) and by Capel Martínez et al. (1979)). Even metalworking may not have required full-time specialisation (cf. Rowlands 1971).

The administrative centralisation said to be at the root of elite origins has as its principal archaeological correlate the existence of site hierarchies (Wright & Johnson 1975). In south-east Spain, however, just as there would be little for elites to administer, just so there is no evident ranking of sites in terms of their size or internal complexity. Los Millares is larger than any other Copper Age site (although the extent of contemporaneous occupation during the millennium or more that the locality was in use remains undetermined), but one site's being bigger than a hamlet does not mean that it was an administrative centre. During the Argaric there is also little apparent ranking of sites. The best case for the existence of central places in prehistoric south-east Spain depends, as Chapman (personal communication) has noted, not on differences in the sizes of the settlements themselves but on the large number of burials within or near a few of those sites (such as Los Millares and El Argar). Mortuary clustering is, however, even further removed logically from administrative activity than is site size. The lack of site hierarchies may be the result of the lack of appropriately designed survey programmes, but it also corresponds appropriately to the absence of economic or other activities requiring centralised management.

Given the prominence of settlement defences and weaponry in the later phases of the prehistoric sequence in south-east Spain, a more appropriate variant of the managerial approach to the explanation of emergent stratification may be the population pressure–resource circumscription–warfare theory proposed by Carneiro (1970), the administrative implications of which are elucidated by Webster (1977). Here the central notion is that increasing population densities create pressure on spatially limited resources necessary for a population's survival (irrigable land, for example) and that those groups with a more hierarchical military organisation will be better able to compete for the living space they need. Quite apart from the general difficulties attendant on the use of population pressure to explain culture change (cf. Cowgill 1975), the problem with applying this theory in south-east Spain is not that there is no evidence of competition for scarce resources but that the cause of the competition and the nature of the scarcity are not what the theory specifies. The increasing number of sites from Neolithic to Bronze Age may be evidence of a progressive increase in population. (It may also have a great deal to do with the differential survival and salience of sites of the different periods.) Whatever the maximum level of population was in later prehistoric times, however, it can hardly have impinged critically on the availability of resources. The great expansion of palaeotechnic cultivation of all kinds throughout the historic period and into recent times shows clearly that, in the Copper or Bronze Age (when population levels would have been lower), there would have been an abundance of irrigable or other arable land. People would not expect leaders to acquire and develop such unused potential. It would have been there for the taking. Clearly the development of social inequalities and warfare must be linked to one another by causal mechanisms other than land hunger.

The difficulties that attach to the several variants of the managerial theory of elite origins are not unique to later prehistoric south-east Spain. They apply throughout Europe in the Copper and Bronze Ages (cf. Gilman 1981). Working in an Aegean setting, Halstead and O'Shea (1982) have chosen, therefore, to stress the positive function of elites, not as administrators of activities conducive to the general welfare but as insurers of last resort. The good of having a ruler is not that he directs complex activities beyond the capacity of individual household units to arrange for themselves, but that he possesses a fund of wealth (given to him by households subordinate to him) which he uses to help those households when disasters of extraordinary magnitude strike them. Now clearly insurance is a service that leaders do occasionally provide their followers: if they failed to do so, the future contributions of those followers would no longer be forthcoming. It is, however, a service that leaders provide in both primitive societies (in which their positions are achieved) and complex societies (in which their positions are largely ascribed). The insurance function does not explain, therefore, the differences in the degree and character of the inequalities which prevail in such different societies. Disasters would have been likely to strike households in the arid zone of south-east Spain during the Copper and the Bronze Ages alike. Leaders with an accumulated 'social storage' fund to expend as 'friends in need' would have been useful and necessary during both periods. The need for social storage cannot, therefore, explain the difference in the character of leadership in the two periods. It cannot explain the increase in the magnitude of inequalities, the shift in ceremonial focus from the community to the individual, or the increase in militarism as a fact and as a value. To understand these changes, it is necessary to consider the negative function of elites, the exploitation that underlies social inequalities of any great magnitude.

Instead of asking 'What good are elites?', the negative function approach asks 'How do elites establish their power?' Individuals ambitious for themselves and for their offspring are not wanting in any society. In societies with unintensive systems of production, the self-aggrandisement of such would-be rulers does not lead to stratification; in societies with capital-intensive subsistence systems would-be leaders succeed in establishing permanent control. The positive explanation of the emergence of elites is that they acquire control because they are needed to manage more complex production systems. As we have argued, this account manifestly fails to meet the needs of the Millaran–Argaric case. The negative explanation is that the development of capital-intensive production systems gives would-be leaders the leverage they need to establish power over other households.

The development of capital-intensive systems of cultivation changed the social structure of south-east Spain not because the techniques demanded managerial direction, but because the investment involved opened up the possibility of effectively collecting rent from the cultivators. Childe (1954, pp. 89–90) expresses the issue clearly when he writes of early irrigation systems in the Near East as follows:

> Capital in the form of human labor was being sunk into the land. Its expenditure bound men to the soil; they would not lightly forego the interest brought in by their reproductive works.

This view can be extended from irrigation to any system of subsistence production that involves substantial investment of labour in advance of production (plough agriculture, terracing, arboriculture among others: cf. Gilman 1981). Easy group fission is the essential mechanism by which an egalitarian social order is maintained as such. If members of a society do not depend on capital investments to produce what they need, they can effectively abandon a leader who becomes unbearably self-aggrandising. In south-east Spain, by contrast, the dams, ditches, terraces, and so on, that the villagers had built were essential to maintain and secure production and would be difficult for even the most dissatisfied to relinquish. This change in the relation between leaders and followers would be exacerbated by increasing conflict between communities. Particularly after it had been built up little by little over time, an irrigation system would represent a valuable asset, and not just to its makers. The long-term investments would need to be protected from conquest. As Cowgill (1975, p. 517) puts it:

> More wealth means that a society (or at least its elite) has more to gain from conquering rich neighbors . . .; however, it also means that a society's own wealth is coveted by neighbors . . .

Environmental necessities in the arid south-east required the construction of productive works of long-term value; these would then have to be defended; but their very value would make it difficult to control their defenders. The very efforts to improve material security would have made the maintenance of social security incompatible with an egalitarian political economy.

Given this perspective we can now recast the description of the sequence of economic and social events in south-east Spain (cf. pp. 184–5) into, as it were, process terms. By the 5th millennium BC, farming was the central subsistence strategy in the moist sector of south-east Spain, where a low investment in agriculture was sufficient to yield reliable grain crops in most years. Farming of any kind involves the long-term storage of generally useful goods, and the potential tensions revolving around access to such stores would have led to the development of communal rites intended to allay them. These rites find their archaeological expression in the collective burial monuments. Agricultural exploitation of the arid sector, probably in the 4th, certainly by the 3rd millennium BC, had to await the development of simple hydraulic techniques. These involved an increase in long-term investment of human labour into the land and, accordingly, generated a greater potential for social conflict. The greater tensions within and between communities led initially to an intensification of the communal rites of solidarity: collective burial monuments and their contents become more elaborate. Meanwhile, in the moist sector, the level of investment required by the *secano* exploitation continued to be relatively low, and a simpler set of collective rituals sufficed to mediate the less marked social tensions. By the 2nd millennium BC in the arid sector, the level of competition over progressively increasing investments reached the point that safety required reduction of easy access to irrigable land. At the same time, the old communal rituals, which had failed to mediate social conflict adequately, were abandoned in favour of an individual burial rite in which the wealth and prowess of the powerful was glorified directly, in which competition (which earlier had been muted) was then prized. The new social forms accepting and institutionalising social inequalities then spread from the arid to the moist sector together with the intensive agriculture that had made the inequalities both possible and inevitable.

This reading of the available record raises, as it should, more questions than it answers. What is the nature of the archaeological record during the 4th millennium BC, when open-air settlements first appeared? What are the relative ages of the earliest Argaric occupations in the arid and moist sectors? What changes in crops accompanied the increasing level of investment in the land? How does the collective burial rite change over time? To what degree do the inequalities reflected in Millaran and Argaric grave lots vary within each sector of the south-east, and how are these variations related to agricultural exploitation patterns? Our account makes implicit claims on each of these matters, for which no adequate evidence is available. We can only hope that this research makes the answer to such questions both possible and urgent.

Notes

1   Probabilities are calculated using Fisher's exact test.
2   It should be noted that all three of these localities are also oriented to *secano* (i.e. have as much or more *secano* in the core as in the periphery of their territories).
3   The arable total is the sum of all land-use categories except *monte*.

4   Here we exclude El Argar and Cerro de la Virgen, which have already been counted for the corresponding Neolithic–Copper Age calculation.

5   Student's t test indicates that the contrast is significant at the 0.02 level.

6   Pearson's r between ruggedness (as defined on p. 173) and the proportion that *secano* forms of the arable total of the 2 h territories is +0.462. Between the proportion of *secano* and mean annual precipitation, Pearson's r is +0.361.

7   Pearson's r between ruggedness (cf. p. 173) and the proportion that *monte* forms of each zone of each site territory ($N = 140$) is −0.691.

8   It should be noted that neither tendency is the result of overall biases in the proportions of land uses or in the degree of ruggedness within and between the territories included in our sample. Mean annual rainfall is negligibly correlated with the proportion that *regardío* forms of the arable total in the 2 h territories (Pearson's r is +0.041). Between rainfall and the distance from a site to the nearest spring or stream with a year-round flow of $0.25\,l\,s^{-1}$, Pearson's r is −0.116. For the 2 h territories the mean ruggedness for Neolithic and Copper Age sites and for Bronze Age sites is 0.785 and 0.737, respectively (Student's t test indicates the difference to be significant at the 0.10 level). The corresponding means for 30 min territories are 0.777 and 0.690 (a difference significant at the 0.02 level).

9   For our sample of sites, mean distance to nearest known source is 13.0 km in the Bronze Age, 14.3 km in the Copper Age.

Appendix

Correspondence between site territories and Ensenada localities

Group	Archaeological site	Ensenada locality
Totana	La Almoloya (4, 5) La Bastida (1, 2, 6) Cabezo Negro (2, 3) Campico de Lébor (1, 2, 6) La Ceñuela (3, 6) Ifre (2, 3) Parazuelos (2, 3) Zapata (2, 3)	Alhama (1) Lorca (2) Mazarrón (3) Mula (4) Pliego (5) Totana/Aledo (6)
Vera	El Argar/El Gárcel/La Gerundia (7, 8, 13) Campos/Tres Cabezos (8, 9, 13) Fuente Álamo (8, 13) Fuente Bermeja (7, 8, 9, 10, 13) Gatas (11, 12, 13) Lugarico Viejo (7, 8, 9, 10, 13) El Oficio (8)	Antas (7) Cuevas (8) Huércal-Overa (9) Lubrín (10) Mojácar (11) Turre (12) Vera (13)
Almería	Cerro de Enmedio (16, 17, 19, 22, 23) Los Millares (14, 15, 17, 18, 19, 20, 22, 23, 24, 26) El Tarajal (16, 21) Terrera Ventura (26)	Alhama la Seca (14) Alicún (15) Almería (16) Benahadux (17) Bentarique (18) Gádor (19) Huécija (20) Níjar (21) Pechina (22) Rioja (23) Santa Fe de Mondújar (24) Tabernas (25) Terque (26)
Cúllar-Baza	Cerro de las Canteras (2, 33, 34) Cerro de la Virgen (28, 29, 30, 31) Cueva de Ambrosio (33) El Malagón (28, 32, 34) El Picacho (27, 32)	Albox (27) Cúllar-Baza (28) Galera (29) Huéscar (30) Lorca (2) Orce (31) Oria (32) Vélez-Blanco (33) Vélez-Rubio (34)

Group	Archaeological site	Ensenada locality
Guadix	Cerro del Gallo (35, 36, 39, 42, 43, 45, 46) Cuesta del Negro (35, 36, 37, 38, 39, 42, 43, 44, 45, 46) El Culantrillo (39, 40, 41, 43, 47)	Beas de Guadix (35) Benalúa de Guadix (36) Darro (37) Diezma (38) Fonelas (39) Gor (40) Gorafe (41) Graena/Cortes (42) Guadix (43) Lapeza (44) El Marchal (45) Purullena (46) Villanueva de las Torres (47)
Monachil	Cerro de la Encina (48–63)	Alhendín (48) Ambros (49) Armilla (50) Cájar (51) Cenés (52) Cúllar-Vega (53) Churriana (54) Dílar (55) Gavia la Chica (56) Gavia la Grande (57) Gójar (58) Granada (59) Monachil (60) Ojíjares (61) Pinos-Genil (62) Zubia (63)
Nerja	Cueva de Nerja (64, 65, 66)	Frijiliana (64) Maro (65) Nerja (66)
Montefrío	Cueva del Agua/de la Mujer (68, 69, 70) Peñas de los Gitanos (67, 71, 72)	Alcalá la Real (67) Alhama (68) Arenas (69) Cacín (70) Illora (71) Montefrío (72)
Moreda	Carigüela (76, 78, 80) Cerro de los Castellones (39, 73, 75–81) Torre Cardela (73, 74, 76–81)	Fonelas (39) Gobernador (73) Guadahortuna (74) Huélago (75) Iznalloz (76) Laborcillas (77) Moreda (78) Pedro Martínez (79)

Group	Archaeological site	Ensenada locality
		Torre Cardela (80)
		Uleilas Bajas/Monte Armín (81)
Zuheros	Cueva de los Murciélagos (82–85)	Baena (82)
		Doña Mencia (83)
		Luque (84)
		Zuheros (85)

References

Acosta, P. 1976. Excavaciones en el yacimiento de El Gárcel, Antas (Almería). *Noticiario Arqueológico Hispánico, Prehistoria* **5**, 189–91.

Adams, R. McC. 1966. *The evolution of urban society*. Chicago: Aldine.

Aguayo de Hoyos, P. 1977. Construcciones defensivas de la Edad del Cobre peninsular. El Cerro de los Castellones (Laborcillas, Granada). *Cuadernos de Prehistoria Granadina* **2**, 87–104.

Alfaro Giner, C. 1980. Estudio de los materiales de cestería procedentes de la Cueva de los Murciélagos (Albuñol, Granada). *Trabajos de Prehistoria* **37**, 109–62.

Almagro Basch, M. 1965. El poblado de Almizaraque de Herrerías (Almería). *Atti del VI Congresso Internazionale delle Scienze Preistoriche e Protostoriche, Roma 1962*, vol. 2, 378–9.

Almagro Basch, M. and A. Arribas 1963. El poblado y la necrópolis megalíticos de Los Millares (Santa Fe de Mondújar, Almería). *Bibliotheca Praehistorica Hispana* **3**.

Almagro Basch, M., R. Fryxell, H. T. Irwin and M. Serna 1970. Avance a la investigación arqueológica, geocronológica, y ecológica de la cueva de La Carigüela (Piñar, Granada). *Trabajos de Prehistoria* **27**, 45–60.

Almagro Gorbea, Ma. J. 1965. Las tres tumbas megalíticas de Almizaraque. *Trabajos de Prehistoria* **18**.

Almagro Gorbea, Ma. J. 1973. El poblado y la necrópolis de El Barranquete (Almería). *Acta Arqueológica Hispánica* **6**.

Almagro Gorbea, Ma. J. 1976. Memoria de las excavaciones efectuadas en el yacimiento de El Tarajal (Almería). *Noticiario Arqueológico Hispánico, Prehistoria* **5**, 195–8.

Almagro Gorbea, Ma. J. 1977. El recientemente destruido poblado de El Tarajal. *XIV Congreso Nacional de Arqueología, Vitoria 1975*, 305–18.

Almagro Gorbea, M. 1970. Las fechas del C-14 para la prehistoria y la arqueología peninsular. *Trabajos de Prehistoria* **27**, 9–42.

Almagro Gorbea, M. 1972. C-14, 1972. Nuevas fechas para la prehistoria y la arqueología peninsular. *Trabajos de Prehistoria* **29**, 228–42.

Almagro Gorbea, M. and M. Fernández-Miranda 1978. *C-14 y prehistoria de la Península Ibérica*. Madrid: Fundación Juan March.

Arribas, A. 1953. El ajuar de las cuevas sepulcrales de Los Blanquizares de Lébor (Murcia). *Memorias de los Museos Arqueológicos Provinciales* **14**, 78–126.

Arribas, A. 1959. El urbanismo peninsular durante el Bronce primitivo. *Zephyrus* **10**, 81–128.

Arribas, A. 1967. Le Edad del Bronce en la Península Ibérica. In *Las raíces de España*, J. M. Gómez-Tabanera (ed.), 85–108. Madrid: Instituto Español de Antropología Aplicada.

Arribas, A. 1968. Las bases económicas del Neolítico al Bronce. In *Estudios de economía antigua de la Península Ibérica*, M. Tarradell (ed.), 33–60. Barcelona: Vicens-Vives.

Arribas, A. 1972. Das Neolithikom Andalusiens. *Fundamenta* **3**(7), 108–27.

Arribas, A. 1976. Las bases actuales para el estudio del Eneolítico y la Edad del Bronce en el sudeste de la Península Ibérica. *Cuadernos de Prehistoria de la Universidad de Granada* **1**, 139–55.

Arribas, A. 1977. El ídolo de 'El Malagón' (Cúllar-Baza, Granada). *Cuadernos de Prehistoria Granadina* **2**, 63–86.

Arribas, A. and F. Molina [González] 1977. El poblado de los Castillejos en las Peñas de los Gitanos (Montefrío, Granada). Resultados de las campañas de 1971 y 1974. *XIV Congreso Nacional de Arqueología, Vitoria 1975*, 389–406.

Arribas, A. and F. Molina [González]. 1979. *El Poblado de 'Los Castillejos' en las Peñas de los Gitanos (Montefrío, Granada): Campaña de Excavaciones de 1971, el Corte num. 1.* Granada: University of Granada.

Arribas, A. and F. Molina 1982. Los Millares: neue Ausgrabungen in der kupferzeitlichen Siedlung (1978–1981). *Madrider Mitteilungen* **23**, 9–32.

Arribas, A., F. Molina, F. de la Torre, T. Nájera and L. Sáez 1977. El poblado eneolítico de 'El Malagón' de Cúllar-Baza (Granada). *XIV Congreso Nacional de Arqueología, Vitoria 1975*, 319–24.

Arribas, A., F. Molina [González], F. de la Torre, T. Nájera and L. Sáez 1978. El poblado de la Edad del Cobre de 'El Malagón' (Cúllar-Baza, Granada). Campaña de 1975. *Cuadernos de Prehistoria Granadina* **3**, 67–116.

Arribas, A., F. Molina [González], L. Sáez, F. de la Torre, P. Aguayo and T. Nájera 1979. Excavaciones en Los Millares (Santa Fe, Almería). Campañas de 1978 y 1979. *Cuadernos de Prehistoria Granadina* **4**, 61–109.

Arribas, A., E. Pareja López, F. Molina González, O. Arteaga Matute and F. Molina Fajardo 1974. Excavaciones en el poblado de la Edad del Bronce 'Cerro de la Encina', Monachil (Granada) (El corte estratigráfico no. 3). *Excavaciones Arqueológicas en España* **81**.

Aubet, M. E., V. Lull and J. Gasull 1979. Excavaciones en el poblado argárico del Cabezo Negro (Lorca, Murcia). *XV Congreso Nacional de Arqueología, Lugo 1977*, 197–203.

Barker, G. W. W. 1975a. Prehistoric territories and economies in central Italy. In *Palaeoeconomy*, E. S. Higgs (ed.), 111–75. London: Cambridge University Press.

Barker, G. W. W. 1981. *Landscape and society: prehistoric central Italy*. London: Academic Press.

Beug, H. J. 1967. On the forest history of the Dalmatian coast. *Review of Palaeobotany and Palynology* **2**, 271–9.

Binford, L. R. 1962. Archaeology as anthropology. *American Antiquity* **29**, 425–41.

Birot, P. and L. Solé Sabaris 1959. La morphologie du Sud-Est de l'Espagne. *Revue de Geographie des Pyrenées et du Sud Ouest* **30**, 119–84.

Blance, B. 1961. Early Bronze Age colonists in Iberia. *Antiquity* **35**, 192–201.

Blance, B. 1964. The Argaric Bronze Age in Iberia. *Revista de Guimarães* **74**, 129–42.

Blance, B. 1971. Die Anfänge der Metallurgie auf der Iberischen Halbinsel. *Studien zu den Angängen der Metallurgie* **4**.

Boessneck, J. and A. van den Driesch 1980. Tierknochenfunde aus vier südspanischen Höhlen. *Studien über früher Tierknochenfunde von der Iberischen Halbinsel* **7**, 1–83.

Bork, H. R. and H. Rohdenburg 1981. Rainfall simulation in southeast Spain: analysis of overland flow and infiltration. In *Soil conservation: problems and prospects*, R. P. C. Morgan (ed.), 293–302. Chichester: Wiley.

Bosch Gimpera, P. 1920. La arqueología pre-románica hispánica, appendix. In *Hispania: geografía, etnología, historia*, by A. Schulten, 133–205. Barcelona.

Bosch Gimpera, P. 1932. *Etnología de la Península Ibérica*. Barcelona: Alpha.

Bosch Gimpera, P. 1944. *El poblamiento antiguo y la formacíon de los pueblos de España*. Mexico, DF: Imprenta Universitaria.

Bosch Gimpera, P. 1969. La cultura de Almería. *Pyrenae* **5**, 47–93.

Bosch Gimpera, P. and F. de Luxán 1935. Explotacíon de yacimientos argentíferos en el Eneolítico, en Almizaraque (prov. de Almería). *Investigación y Progreso* **9**, 112–17.

Bovis, M. J. 1974. Late Quaternary deposits of the Motril area, southern Spain. *Zeitschrift für Geomorphologie* **18**, 426–36.

Cabré Aguiló, J. 1920. La necrópolis Ibérica de Tutugi, Galera, provincia de Granada. *Junta Superior de Excavaciones y Antigüedades, Memoria* **25**.

Cabré Aguiló, J. 1922. Una necrópolis de la primera edad de los metales, en Monachil, Granada. *Sociedad Española de Antropología, Etnografía, y Prehistoria, Memorias* **1**, 23–32.

Camilleri Lapeyre, A. 1969. Spain. *World atlas of agriculture* **1**, 370–92.

Campbell, I. A. 1970. Erosion rates in the Steveville badlands, Alberta. *Canadian Geographer* **14**, 202–16.

Cano García, G. M. 1974. *La comarca de Baza*. Valencia: Departamento de Geografía, Universidad de Valencia.

Capel Martínez, J. and R. Delgado Calvos-Flores 1978. Aplicación de métodos ópticos al estudio de cerámicas arqueológicas. *Cuadernos de Prehistoria Granadina* **3**, 343–56.

Capel Martínez, J., J. Linares Gonzáles and F. Huertas Garcia 1979. Métodos analíticos aplícados a cerámicas de la Edad del Bronce. *Cuadernos de Prehistoria Granadina* **4**, 345–60.

Carneiro, R. L. 1970. A theory of the origin of the state. *Science* **169**, 733–8.

Carson, M. A. and M. J. Kirkby 1972. *Hillslope form and process*. Cambridge: Cambridge University Press.

Chapman, R. W. 1975. Economy and society within later prehistoric Iberia. Ph.D. Dissertation, Cambridge University.

Chapman, R. W. 1977. Burial practices: an area of mutual interest. In *Archaeology and anthropology: areas of mutual interest*, M. Spriggs (ed.), 19–33. Oxford: BAR.

Chapman, R. W. 1978. The evidence of prehistoric water control in southeast Spain. *Journal of Arid Environments* **1**, 261–77.

Chapman, R. W. 1979. Transhumance and megalithic tombs in Iberia. *Antiquity* **53**, 150–2.

Chapman, R. W. 1981a. Archaeological theory and communal burial in prehistoric Europe. In *Pattern of the past: studies in honour of David Clarke*, I. Hodder, G. Isaac and N. Hammond (eds.), 387–411. Cambridge: Cambridge University Press.

Chapman, R. W. 1981b. The emergence of formal disposal areas and the 'problem' of megalithic tombs in prehistoric Europe. In *The archaeology of death*, R. W. Chapman *et al.* (eds.), 70–82. Cambridge: Cambridge University Press.

Childe, V. G. 1954. *What happened in history*. Harmondsworth: Penguin.

Childe, V. G. 1957. *The dawn of European civilization*. London: Routledge and Kegan Paul.

Childe, V. G. 1958a. Retrospect. *Antiquity* **32**, 69–74.

Childe, V. G. 1958b. The prehistory of European society. Harmondsworth: Penguin.

Chisholm, M. 1962. *Rural settlements and land use*. London: Hutchinson University Library.

Clark, C. and M. Haswell 1970. *The economics of subsistence agriculture*, 4th ed. London: Macmillan.

Coles, J. M. and A. F. Harding 1979. *The Bronze Age in Europe*. London: Methuen.

Cooke, R. U. C. and J. Doornkamp 1974. *Geomorphology in environmental management: an introduction*. Oxford: Clarendon Press.

Cowgill, G. L. 1975. On causes and consequences of ancient and modern population changes. *American Anthropologist* **77**, 505–25.

Cuadrado Díaz, E. 1945–46. L. Almoloya, nuevo poblado de la cultura de El Argar. *Anales de la Universidad de Murcia*, 355–82.

Cuadrado Ruiz, J. 1930. El yacimiento de los Blanquizares de Lébor en la provincia de Murcia. *Archivo Español de Arte y Arqueología* **9**, 51–6.

Cuenca Payá, A. and M. J. Walker 1974. Comentarios sobre el Cuaternario continental en el centro y sur de la provincia de Alicante (España). *Actas de la I Reunión Nacional del Grupo de Trabajo del Cuaternario* **2**, 15–38.

Cuenca Payá, A. and M. J. Walker 1976. Pleistoceno final y Holoceno en la cuenca del Vinalopó (Alicante). *Estudios Geológicos* **32**, 95–104.

Cuenca Payá, A. and M. J. Walker 1977. Paleogeografía humana del Cuaternario de Alicante y Murcia. *Actas de la II Reunión Nacional del Grupo de Trabajo del Cuaternario*, 65–77.

Davidson, D. A. 1980. Erosion in Greece during the first and second millennia BC. In *Timescales in geomorphology*, R. A. Cullingford, D. A. Davidson and J. Lewin (eds.), 143–59. Chichester: Wiley.

Delano Smith, C. 1979. *Western Mediterranean Europe: a historical geography of Italy, Spain, and Southern France since the Neolithic.* London: Academic Press.

Dennell, R. 1980. The use, abuse and potential of site catchment analysis. *Anthropology UCLA* 10(1–2), 1–2.

Despois, J. 1961. Development of land use in northern Africa (with references to Spain). *Arid Zone Research* 17, 219–37.

Diccionario Geográfico de España 1956. Madrid: Ediciones Prensa Gráfica.

Driesch, A. von den 1972. Osteoarchäeologische Untersuchungen auf der Iberischen Halbinsel. *Studien über frühe Tierknochenfunde von der Iberischen Halbinsel* 3.

Driesch, A. von den 1973a. Tierknochenfunde aus dem frühbronzezeitliche Gräberfeld von 'El Barranquete', Provinz Almeria, Spanien. *Säugetierkundliche Mitteilungen* 21, 328–35.

Driesch, A. von den 1973b. Fauna, Klima und Landschaft in Süden der Iberischen Halbinsel während der Metallzeit. In *Domestikationsforschung und Geschichte der Haustiere*, J. Matólcsi (ed.), 245–54. Budapest: Akademiai Kiado.

Driesch, A. von den and M. Kokabi 1977. Tierknochenfunde aus der Siedlung 'Cerro de los Castellones' bei Laborcillas/Granada. *Archäologie und Naturwissenschaften* 1, 129–43.

Driesch, A. von den and A. Morales 1977. Los restos animales del yacimiento de Terrera Ventura (Tabernas, Almería). *Cuadernas de Prehistoria y Arqueología, Universidad Autónoma de Madrid, Facultad de Filosofía y Letras* 4, 15–34.

Elías Castillo, F. and R. Giménez Ortiz 1965. *Evapotranspiraciones potenciales y balances de agua en España.* Madrid: Dirección General de Agricultura.

Ericson, J. E. and R. Goldstein 1980. Work space: a new approach to the analysis of energy expenditure within site catchments. *Anthropology UCLA* 10(1–2), 21–30.

Evans, J. D. 1956. Two phases of prehistoric settlement in the Western Mediterranean. *University of London, Institute of Archaeology, Annual Report* 12, 49–70.

Faulkner, H. 1976. An allometric growth model for competitive gullies. *Zeitschrift für Geomorphologie, Supplement* 20, 36–63.

Ferre Bueno, E. 1974. Iznalloz. Un municipio de los montes orientales granadinos. *Estudios Geográficos* 35, 53–106.

Ferre Bueno, E. 1977. El valle del Almanzora. Ph.D. Dissertation, Department of Geography, University of Granada.

Ferrer Rodríguez, A. 1975. *El Paisaje agrario de Alhama de Granada en el siglo XVIII.* Granada: Caja General de Ahorros y Monte de Piedad.

Flannery, K. V. 1972. The cultural evolution of civilizations. *Annual Review of Ecology and Systematics* 3, 399–426.

Flannery, K. V. 1976. *The early Mesoamerican village.* New York: Academic Press.

Florschütz, F., J. Menéndez Amor and T. A. Wijmstra 1971. Palynology of a thick Quaternary succession in southern Spain. *Palaeogeography, Palaeoclimatology, Palaeoecology* 10, 233–64.

Fortea Pérez, J. 1970. La Cueva de la Palica, Serrón (Antas): avance al estudio del Epipaleolítico del S.E. peninsular. *Trabajos de Prehistoria* 27, 61–91.

Fortea Pérez, J. 1973. Los complejos microlaminares y geométricos del Epipaleolítico mediterráneo español. *Memorias del Seminario de Prehistoria y Arqueología, Universidad de Salamanca* 4.

Fournier, F. 1960. *Débit solide des cours d'eau: essai d'estimation de la perte en terre subie par l'ensemble du globe terrestre.* Helsinki: International Association for Scientific Hydrology.

Fox, C. 1923. *The archaeology of the Cambridge region*. Cambridge: Cambridge University Press.

Francis, J. and G. Clark 1980. Bronze and Iron Age economies on the Meseta del Norte, north-central Spain. *Anthropology UCLA* **10**(1–2), 97–135.

Frank. A. H. E. 1969. Pollen stratigraphy of the Lake of Vico (Central Italy). *Palaeogeography, Palaeoclimatology, Palaeoecology* **6**, 67–85.

Freitag, H. 1971. Die natürliche Vegetation des südostspanischen Trockengebietes. *Botanische Jahrbücher* **91**, 147–308.

Fried, M. H. 1967. *The evolution of political society*. New York: Random House.

García Sánchez, M. 1960. Restos humanos del paleolítico medio y superior y del neo-eneolítico de Piñar (Granada). *Trabajos del Instituto Bernardino de Sahagún de Antropología y Etnología* **15**(2), 17–72.

García Sánchez, M. 1963. El poblado argárico del Cerro del Culantrillo, en Gorafe (Granada). *Archivo de Prehistoria Levantina* **8**, 97–164.

García Sánchez, M. and J. C. Spahni 1959. Sepulcros megalíticos de la región de Gorafe (Granada). *Archivo de Prehistoria Levantina* **8**, 43–113.

Geiger, F. 1972. Die Bewässerungswirtschaft Südostspaniens im trockensten Abschnitt des Mediterranen Europa. *Geographische Rundschau* **24**, 408–19.

Geiger, F. 1973. El sureste español y los problemas de la aridez. *Revista de Geografía* **7**, 166–209.

Gil Olcina, A. 1971. *El campo de Lorca: estudio de geografía agraria*. Valencia: Departmento de Geografía, Universidad de Valencia.

Gilman, A. 1976. Bronze Age dynamics in southeast Spain. *Dialectical Anthropology* **1**, 307–19.

Gilman, A. 1981. The development of social stratification in Bronze Age Europe. *Current Anthropology* **22**, 1–23.

Glick, T. F. 1970. *Irrigation and society in mediaeval Valencia*. Cambridge, Ma.: Harvard University Press.

Göksu, H. Y., J. H. Fremlin, H. T. Irwin and R. Fryxell 1974. Age determination of burned flint by a thermoluminescent method. *Science* **183**, 651–4.

Gómez Mendoza, J. 1977. *Agricultura y expansión urbana*. Madrid.

Góngora y Martínez, M. de 1868. *Antigüedades prehistóricas de Andalucía*. Madrid: C. Moro.

González Gómez, C. and M. Domingo García 1978. El laboratorio de detación por carbono-14 de la Universidad de Granada. *Cuadernos de Prehistoria Granadina* **3**, 357–64.

González Gómez, C., J. D. López González and M. Domingo García 1982. University of Granada radiocarbon dates I. *Radiocarbon* **24**, 217–21.

Gossé, G. 1941. Aljoroque, estación neolítica inicial de la provincia de Almería. *Ampurias* **3**, 63–84.

Guilane, J. 1976. *Premiers bergers et paysans de l'Occident Mediterranéen*. Paris: Mouton.

Gusi Jener, F. 1975. Le aldea eneolítica de Terrera Ventura (Tabernas, Almería). *XIII Congreso Nacional de Arqueología, Huelva 1973*, 311–14.

Gusi Jener, F. 1976. Resumen de la labor en el yacimiento de Tabernas (Almería). *Noticiario Arqueológico Hispánico, Prehistoria* **5**, 201–5.

Hack, J. T. 1942. The changing physical environment of the Hopi Indians of Arizona. *Papers of the Peabody Museum* **35**(1).

Halstead, P. and J. O'Shea 1982. A friend in need is a friend indeed: social storage and the origins of social ranking. In *Ranking, resource and exchange*, C. Renfrew and S. Shennan (eds.), 92–9. Cambridge: Cambridge University Press.

Harrison, R. J. 1974. A reconsideration of the Iberian background to Beaker metallurgy. *Palaeohistoria* **16**, 63–105.

Harrison, R. J. 1977. The Bell Beaker cultures of Spain and Portugal. *American School of Prehistoric Research, Bulletin* **35**.

Hawkes. C. F. C. 1954. Archaeological theory and method: some suggestions from the Old World. *American Anthropologist* **56**, 155–68.

Heitland, W. E. 1921. *Agricola: a study of agriculture and rustic life in the Greco-Roman world from the point of view of labour.* Cambridge: Cambridge University Press.

Hernández Hernández, F. and I. Dug Godoy 1975. Excavaciones en el poblado de 'El Picacho'. *Excavaciones Arqueológicas en España* **95**.

Higgs, E. S. 1975. *Palaeoeconomy.* London: Cambridge University Press.

Higgs, E. S. 1976. The history of European agriculture: the uplands. *Philosophical Transactions of the Royal Society, London (Series B)* **275**, 159–73.

Higgs, E. S. and M. R. Jarman 1975. Palaeoeconomy. In *Palaeoeconomy*, E. S. Higgs (ed.), 1–9. Cambridge: Cambridge University Press.

Higgs, E. S. and C. Vita-Finzi 1972. Prehistoric economies: a territorial approach. In *Papers in economic prehistory*, E. S. Higgs (ed.), 27–36. Cambridge: Cambridge University Press.

Hodder, I. and C. Orton 1976. *Spatial analysis in archaeology.* Cambridge: Cambridge University Press.

Holeman, J. N. 1968. The sediment yield of major rivers of the world. *Water Resources Research* **4**, 737–47.

Hopf, M. and A. M. Muñoz 1974. Neolithische Pflanzenreste aus der Höhle Los Murciélagos bei Zuheros (Prov. Córdoba). *Madrider Mitteilungen* **15**, 9–27.

Hopf, M. and M. Pellicer Catalán 1970. Neolithische Getreidefunde in der Höhle von Nerja. *Madrider Mitteilungen* **11**, 18–34.

ICONA 1979. *Precipitaciones máximas en España.* Madrid: Ministerio de Agricultura.

Instituto Geologico y Minero 1979. *Mapa metalogenético de España, Escala 1 : 200 000.*

Isaac, G. 1981. Stone Age visiting cards: approaches to the study of the early land use patterns. In *Pattern of the past: studies in honour of David Clarke*, I. Hodder *et al.* (eds.), 131–55. Cambridge: Cambridge University Press.

Jarman, M. R. 1972. A territorial model for archaeology: a behavioural and geographical approach. In *Models in archaeology*, D. L. Clarke (ed.), 705–33. London: Methuen.

Jarman, M. R., G. N. Bailey and H. N. Jarman (eds.) 1982. *Early European agriculture: its foundations and development.* Cambridge: Cambridge University Press.

Jarman, M. R., C. Vita-Finzi and E. S. Higgs 1972. Site catchment analysis in archaeology. In *Man, settlement and urbanism*, P. J. Ucko, G. W. Dimbleby and R. Tringham (eds.), 61–6. London: Duckworth.

Jarman, M. R. and D. Webley 1975. Settlement and land use in Capitanata, Italy. In *Palaeoeconomy*, E. S. Higgs (ed.), 117–221. London: Cambridge University Press.

Jensen, J. M. L. and R. B. Painter 1974. Predicting sediment yield from climate and topography. *Journal of Hydrology* **21**, 371–80.

Jiménez Navarro, E. 1962. Excavaciones en Cueva Ambrosio. *Noticiario Arqueológico Hispánico* **5**, 13–48.

Junghans, S., E. Sangmeister and M. Schröder 1960. Metallanalysen kupferzeitlicher und frühbronzezeitlicher Bodenfunde aus Europa. *Studien zu den Anfängen der Metallurgie* **1**.

Junghans, S., E. Sangmeister and M. Schröder 1968–74. Kupfer und Bronze in der frühen Metallzeit Europas. *Studien zu den Anfängen der Metallurgie* **2**.

Kalb, F. 1969. El Poblado del Cerro de la Virgen de Orce (Granada). *X Congreso Nacional de Arqueología, Mahon 1967*, 216–25.

Kendall, D. G. 1971. Construction of maps from 'odd bits of information'. *Nature* **231**, 158–9.

King, T. F. 1974. The evolution of status ascription around San Francisco Bay. In *Antap*, L. J. Bean and T. F. King (eds.), 37–53. Ramona: Ballena Press.

Kirkby, A. V. T. and M. J. Kirkby 1973. The use of land and water resources in the past and present Valley of Oaxaca, Mexico. *Memoirs of the Museum of Anthropology, University of Michigan* 5.

Kirkby, M. J. 1977. Maximum sediment efficiency as a criterion for alluvial channels. In *River channel changes*, K. J. Gregory (ed.), 429–42. Chichester: Wiley.

Kirkby, M. J. 1980a. Modelling water erosion processes. In *Soil erosion*, M. J. Kirkby and R. P. C. Morgan (eds.), 183–216. Chichester: Wiley.

Kirkby, M. J. 1980b. The stream head as a significant geomorphic threshold. In *Thresholds in geomorphology*, D. R. Coates and J. D. Vitek (eds.), 53–74. London: Allen & Unwin.

Kirkby, M. J. and R. P. C. Morgan (eds.) 1980. *Soil erosion*. Chichester: Wiley.

Kleinpenning, J. M. G. 1965. Cuevas del Almanzora – problèmes agraires actuels d'une commune dans le Sud-Est espagnol semi-aride. *Afdeling Sociale Geografie van het Geografisch Institut, Utrecht, Bulletin* 3.

Kuhn, T. S. 1970. *The structure of scientific revolutions*. Chicago: University of Chicago Press.

Lamb, H. H. 1971. Climates and circulation regimes developed over the northern hemisphere since the last Ice Age. *Palaeogeography, Palaeoclimatology, Palaeoecology* 10, 125–62.

Langbein, W. B. and S. A. Schumm 1958. Yield of sediment in relation to mean annual precipitation. *Transactions of the American Geophysical Union* 39, 1076–84.

Langbein, W. B. *et al*. 1949. Annual runoff in the United States. *US Geol. Survey Circular*, 52.

Lauk, H. D. 1976. Tierknochenfunde aus bronzezeitlichen Siedlungen bei Monachil und Purullena (Provinz Granada). *Studien über frühe Tierknochenfunde von der Iberischen Halbinsel* 6.

Lautensach, H. 1964. *Die Iberische Halbinsel*. Munich: Keysersche Verlagsbuchhandel.

Lee, R. B. 1969. Kung Bushman subsistence: an input–output analysis. In *Environment and cultural behaviour*, A. P. Vayda (ed.), 47–79. Austin: University of Texas Press.

Lees, S. and D. Bates 1974. The origins of specialized nomadic pastoralism: a systemic model. *American Antiquity* 39, 187–93.

Leisner, G. and V. Leisner 1943. Die Megalithgräber der iberischen Halbinsel. 1: Der Süden. *Römisch-Germanische Forschungen* 17.

León Llamazares, A. de, V. Forteza del Rey Morales, M. Forteza del Rey Morales, G. de las Casas Gómez and C. Lovera Prieto 1974. *Caracterización Agroclimática de la Provincia de Murcia*. Madrid: Ministerio de Agricultura.

Lewthwaite, J. G. 1982. Acorns for the ancestors: the prehistoric exploitation of woodlands in the West Mediterranean. In *Archaeological aspects of woodland ecology*, S. Limbrey and M. Bell (eds.), 217–30. Oxford: BAR.

Linsley, R. K., M. A. Kohler and J. L. H. Paulhus 1975. *Hydrology for engineers*, 2nd edn. New York: McGraw-Hill.

Llobet, S. 1958. Utilizacíon del suelo y economía del agua en la region semi-arida de Huércal-Overa (Almería). *Estudios Geográficos* 19, 5–21.

López Bermúdez, F. 1973. *La vega alta del Segura*. Murcia: Universidad de Murcia.

López Bermúdez, F. and J. D. Gutiérrez Escudero 1982. Estimacion de la erosion y aterramientos de embalses en la cuenca hidrografica del Rio Segura. *Cuadernos de Investigacion Geográfica* VIII, 1–15. Univ. Logroño.

López García, P. 1977. Análisis polínico de Verdelpino (Cuenca). *Trabajos de Prehistoria* 34, 82–3.

Lull Santiago, V. 1982. Discusión cronológica de la cerámica sepulcral Argárica. *Cypsela* **4**, 61–7

Lull Santiago, V. 1983. *La 'Cultura' de El Argar*. Madrid: Akal.

Lumley, H. de 1969. Étude de l'outillage mousterien de la Grotte de Carigüela. *L'Anthropologia* **73**, 165–206.

MacPherson, G. 1870. La cueva de la Mujer. *Revista de Filosofía, Literatura, y Ciencias* **2**, 346–54.

Mádoz, P. 1846–50. *Diccionario geográfico–estadístico–histórico de España y sus posesiones de ultramar*, 15 vols. Madrid: P. Mádoz and L. Sagasti.

Maluquer de Motes, J. 1975. *Historia social y económica. La prehistoria Española*. Madrid: Confederación Española de Cajas de Ahorro.

Martínez Santa Olalla, J. 1946. *Esquema paletnológico de la península Hispánica*. Madrid: Diana.

Martínez Santa Olalla, J. 1948. La fecha de la cerámica a la almagra en el Neolítico hispano-mauritano. *Cuadernos de Historia Primitiva* **3**, 95–106.

Martínez Santa Olalla, J., B. Sáez Martin, C. F. Posac Mon, J. A. Sopranis Salto and E. del Val Caturla 1947. Excavaciones en la ciudad del Bronce Mediterráneo II, de la Bastida de Totana (Murcia). *Comisaría General de Excavaciones Arqueológicas, Informes y Memorias* **16**.

Matilla Tascón, A. 1947. *La única contribución y el Catastro de la Ensenada*. Madrid: Servicio de Estudios de la Inspección General del Ministerio de Hacienda.

Meigs, P. 1966. Geography of coastal deserts. *Arid Zone Research* **28**.

Mendoza, A., F. Molina [González], P. Aguayo, J. Carrasco and T. Najera 1975. El poblado del 'Cerro de los Castellones' (Laborcillas, Granada). *XIII Congreso Nacional de Arqueología, Huelva 1973*, 315–22.

Menéndez Amor, J. 1964. Estudio palinológico de la turbera del Estany (Olot, Gerona). *Geologie en Mijnbouw* **43**, 118–22.

Menéndez Amor, J. and F. Florschütz 1961a. Resultado del análisis polínico de una serie de muestras de turba recogidas en la Ereta del Pedregal (Navarrés, Valencià). *Archivo de Prehistoria Levantina* **9**, 97–9.

Menéndez Amor, J. and F. Florschütz 1961b. La concordancia entre la composicíon de la vegetación durante la segunda mitad del Holoceno en la Costa de Levante (Castellón de la Plana) y en las costa oeste de Mallorca. *Boletín de la Real Sociedad Española de Historia Natural, Sección Geológica* **59**, 97–100.

Mercader, A. 1970. Panorama arqueológico de la provincia de Almería. *Pyrenae* **6**, 39–42.

Mergelina, C. de 1942. La estación arqueológica de Montefrío (Granada). I: Los dólmenes. *Boletín del Seminario de Arte y Arqueología, Universidad de Valladolid* **12**, 33–106.

Mergelina, C. de 1946. La estación arqueológica de Montefrío. II: La acrópoli de Guirrete. *Boletín del Seminario de Arte y Arqueología, Universidad de Valladolid* **12**, 15–26.

Ministerio de Agricultura 1974. *Mapa de cultivos y aprovechamientos*, Escala 1 : 50 000: Padul.

Ministerio de Agricultura 1975. *Mapa de cultivos y aprovechamientos*, Escala 1 : 50 000: Guadix.

Ministerio de Cultura 1981. *Arqueología 80: memoria de las actuaciones programadas en el año 1980*.

Molina Fajardo, F. 1970. Un yacimiento de la Edad del Bronce en Torre Cardela (Granada). *XI Congreso Nacional de Arqueología, Mérida 1968*, 302–14.

Molina Fajardo, F. 1979. La cueva eneolítica del Cerro del Castellón, Campotejar (Granada). *XV Congreso Nacional de Arqueología, Lugo 1977*, 143–60.

Molina Fajardo, F. and J. Capel Martínez 1975. Un corte estratigráfico en el poblado campaniforme de Torre Cardela (Granada). *XIII Congreso Nacional de Arqueología, Huelva 1973*, 411–16.

Molina González, F. 1983. *Prehistoria de Granada*. Granada: Editorial Don Quijote.

Molina González, F. and E. Pareja López 1975. Excavaciones en la Cuesta del Negro (Purullena, Granada). *Excavaciones Arqueológicas en España* **86**.

Molina [González], F., L. Sáez, P. Aguayo, T. Nájera and F. Carríon 1980. Cerro de Enmedio, eine bronzezeitliche Höhensiedlung am unteren Andarax (prov. Almería). *Madrider Mitteilungen* **21**, 62–73.

Morales Gil, A. 1970. El riego con aguas de avenida en las laderas subáridas. *Papeles del Departamento de Geografía, Facultad de Filosofía y Letras, Universidad de Murcia* **1**, 167–83.

Morgan, R. P. C. 1980. Implications. In *Soil erosion*, M. Kirkby and R. P. C. Morgan (eds.), 253–92. Chichester: Wiley.

Motos, F. de 1918. La edad neolítica en Vélez Blanco. *Comisión de Investigaciones Paleontológicas y Prehistóricas, Memoria* **19**, 1–81.

Muñoz, A. M. 1969. La civilizacíon pretartésica andaluza durante la Edad del Bronze. *Universidad de Barcelona, Instituto de Arqueología, Publicaciones Eventuales* **13**, 33–45.

Naroll, R. 1956. Floor area and settlement population. *American Antiquity* **27**, 587–9.

Navarrete Enciso, M. S. 1976. *La cultura de las cuevas con cerámica decorada en Andalucía Oriental*. Granada: Universidad de Granada.

Navarro, C. 1968. Problemas agrarios en un sector de clima semi-árido: el campo de Águilas. *Revista de Geografía* **2**, 5–39.

Navarro Alvargonzález, A. and E. Figueras Molina undated. Estudio hidrogeológico del término municipal de Mazarrón (Murcia). *Temas Profesionales (Direccíon General de Minas y Combustibles)* **18**, 5–34.

Neumann, H. 1960. El clima del sudeste de España. *Estudios Geográficos* **21**, 171–209.

Ocaña Ocaña, Ma. C. 1974. *La Vega de Granada: estudio geográfico*. Granada: Caja de Ahorros.

Onieva Marieges, J. M. 1977. *El municipio de Montefrío. Estudio geográfico*. Granada: Universidad de Granada.

Ortega Alba, F. 1974. *El Sur de Córdoba. Estudio de geografía agraria*. 2 vols. Cordoba: Monte de Piedad y Caja de Ahorros.

Parker, R. S. 1977. Experimental study of drainage basin evolution and its hydrological implications. *Hydrology Papers, Colorado State University*, **90**.

Pellicer Catalán, M. 1957–58. Enterramiento en cueva artificial del 'Bronce I Hispánico' en el Cerro del Greal (Iznalloz, Granada). *Ampurias* **19–20**, 124–33.

Pellicer Catalán, M. 1963. Estratigrafía prehistórica de la cueva de Nerja. *Excavaciones Arqueológicas en España* **16**.

Pellicer Catalán, M. 1964a. Actividades de la delagación de zona de la provincia de Granada durante los años 1953–1962. *Noticiario Arqueológico Hispánico* **6**, 304–50.

Pellicer Catalán, M. 1964b. El Neolítico y el Bronce de la Cueva de la Carigüela de Piñar (Granada). *Trabajos de Prehistoria* **15**.

Pellicer, M. and W. Schüle 1962. El Cerro del Real, Galera (Granada). I. *Excavaciones Arqueológicas en España* **12**.

Pellicer, M. and W. Schüle 1966. El Cerro del Real, Galera (Granada). II. *Excavaciones Arqueológicas en España* **52**.

Pérez de Barradas, J. 1961. Las cuevas neolíticos costeras de Granada y Málaga. *Antropología y Etnologia* **11**, 31–67.

Quadra Salcedo, A. de la and A. M. Vicent 1964. Informe de las excavaciones en la cueva de los Murciélagos de Zuheros (Córdoba). *Noticiario Arqueológico Hispánico* **6**, 68–72.

Renard, K. G. 1980. Estimating erosion and sediment yield from rangeland. *Watershed management '80, American Society of Civil Engineers*, 164–75.

Renault-Miskovsky, J. 1976. La végétation au Post-Glaciaire dans les plaines du Sud-Est de la France: données de l'analyse pollinique principalement. In *La préhistoire française*. Vol. 2: *Les civilisations Néolithiques et Protohistoriques de la France*, J. Guilaine (ed.), 44–51. Paris: Éditions CNRS.

Renfrew, C. 1967. Colonialism and Megalithismus. *Antiquity* **41**, 276–88.

Renfrew, C. 1973. *Before civilization. The radiocarbon revolution and prehistoric Europe*. London: Jonathan Cape.

Renfrew, C. 1976. Megaliths, territories, and populations. *Dissertationes Archaeologicae Gandenses* **16**, 198–220.

Renfrew, J. M. 1973. *Palaeoethnobotany*. London: Methuen.

Réparaz, G. A. de 1964. Les sources de la géographie rurale espagnole et leur utilisation dans quelques travaux recents. *Méditerranée* **5**, 315–27.

Ripoll Perelló, E. 1960–61. Excavaciones en Cueva de Ambrosio (Vélez Blanco, Almería): campañas 1958 y 1960. *Ampurias* **22–23**, 31–45.

Rivas Goday, S. and S. Rivas Martínez 1971. La vegetación potencial de la provincia de Granada. *Trabajos del Departamento de Botánica y Fisiología Vegetal, Universidad de Madrid* **4**, 2–85.

Roper, D. C. 1979. The method and theory of site catchment analysis: a review. *Advances in archaeological method and theory* **2**, 119–40.

Rowe, J. H. 1962. Worsaae's Law and the use of grave lots for archaeological dating. *American Antiquity* **28**, 129–37.

Rowlands, M. J. 1971. The archaeological interpretation of prehistoric metal-working. *World Archaeology* **3**, 210–24.

Ruiz-Gálvez, M. 1977. Nueva aportación al conocimiento de la cultura de el Argar. *Trabajos de Prehistoria* **34**, 81–110.

Sáenz Lorite, M. 1973. Gádor, un municipio naranjero del bajo Ándarax (Almería). *Estudios Geográficos* **34**, 663–99.

Sáenz Lorite, M. 1977. *El Valle del Andarax y el Campo de Níjar*. Granada: Universidad de Granada.

Sahlins, M. 1972. *Stone Age economies*. Chicago: Aldine.

Savigear, R. A. G. 1965. A technique of morphological mapping. *Annals of the Association of American Geographers* **53**, 514–38.

Savory, H. N. 1968. *Spain and Portugal. The prehistory of the Iberian Peninsula*. London: Thames & Hudson.

Schubart, H. 1965. Neue radiokarbon-Daten zur vor- und Frühgeschichte der iberischen Halbinsel. *Madrider Mitteilungen* **6**, 11–19.

Schubart, H. 1973. Mediterrane Beziehungen der El Argar-Kultur. *Madrider Mitteilungen* **14**, 41–59.

Schubart, H. 1975. Cronología relativa de la cerámica sepulcral de El Argar. *Trabajos de Prehistoria* **32**, 79–92.

Schubart, H. 1980. Cerro de Enmedio, bronzezeitliche Funde von einer Höhensiedlung am unteren Andarax (prov. Almería). *Madrider Mitteilungen* **21**, 74–90.

Schubart, H. and O. Arteaga 1978. Fuente Álamo: Vorbericht über die Grabung 1977 in der bronzezeitlichen Höhensiedlung. *Madrider Mitteilungen* **19**, 23–51.

Schubart, H. and O. Arteaga 1980. Fuente Álamo, Vorbericht über die Grabung 1979 in der bronzezeitlichen Höhensiedlung. *Madrider Mitteilungen* **21**, 45–61.

Schüle, W. 1967. Feldbewässerung in Alt-Europa. *Madrider Mitteilungen* **8**, 79–99.

Schüle, W. 1980. *Orce und Galera: zwei Siedlungen aus dem 3. bis 1. Jahrtausend v. Chr. im Südosten der iberischen Halbinsel. I: Übersicht über die Ausgrabungen 1962–1970*. Mainz am Rhein: Verlag Philipp von Zabern.

Schüle, W. and M. Pellicer 1966. El Cerro de la Virgen, Orce (Granada) 1. *Excavaciones Arqueológicas en España* **46**.

Schumm, S. A. 1964. Seasonal variations of erosion rates and processes on hillslopes in western Colorado. *Zeitschrift für Geomorphologie. Suppl.* **5**, 215–38.

Schumm, S. A. 1965. Quaternary palaeohydrology. In *The Quaternary of the United States*, H. E. Wright and D. G. Frey (eds.), 783–93. Princeton, NJ: Princeton University Press.

Schumm, S. A. 1974. Geomorphic thresholds and complex response of drainage systems. In *Fluvial Geomorphology*, M. Morisawa (ed.), 299–310.

Scoch, W. and F. H. Schweingruber 1982. Holzkohlanalytische Ergebnisse aus der bronzezeitlichen Siedlung Fuente Alamo, Prov. Almeria, Spanien. *Archäolugisches Korrespondenzblatt* **12**, 451–5.

Scoging, H. M. 1976. A stochastic model of daily rainfall simulation in a semi-arid environment. *London School of Economics Graduate School of Geography Discussion Paper* **59**.

Scoging, H. M. and J. B. Thornes 1980. Infiltration characteristics in a semi-arid environment. *International Association of Scientific Hydrology, Publication* **128**, 159–68.

Sermet, J. 1967. Andalucía. In *Geografía de España y Portugal* vol. 4(3), M. de Terán (ed.), 73–169. Barcelona: Montaner y Simón.

Shennan, S. 1982. Ideology, change, and the European Early Bronze Age. In *Symbolic and structural archaeology*. I. Hodder (ed.), 155–61. Cambridge: Cambridge University Press.

Sherratt, A. 1981. Plough and pastoralism: aspects of the secondary products revolution. In *Pattern of the past: studies in honour of David Clarke*, I. Hodder, G. Isaac and N. Hammond (eds.), 261–305. Cambridge: Cambridge University Press.

Siret, H. and L. Siret 1887. *Les premiers ages du metal dans le Sud-Est de l'Espagne.* Antwerp.

Siret, L. 1893. L'Espagne préhistorique. *Revue des Questions Scientifiques* **4**, 489–562.

Siret, L. 1906. Orientaux et occidentaux en Espagne aux temps préhistoriques. *Revue des Questions Scientifiques* 529–82.

Siret, L. 1907. Orientaux et occidentaux en Espagne aux temps préhistoriques. *Revue des Questions Scientifiques* 219–43.

Siret, L. 1913. *Questions de chronologie et d'ethnographie ibériques* 1. Paris: Paul Geuthner.

Siret, L. 1948. El tell de Almizaraque y sus problemas. *Cuadernos de Historia Primitiva* **3**, 117–24.

Smith, T. R. and F. P. Bretherton 1972. Stability and the conservation of mass in drainage basin evolution. *Water Resources Research* **8**, 506–24.

Soler García, J. M. 1961. La Casa de Lara, de Villena (Alicante), poblado de llanura con cerámica cardial. *Saitabi* **11**, 193–200.

Starkel, L. and J. B. Thornes 1981. Palaeohydrology of river basins. *British Geomorphology Research Group, Technical Bulletin* **28**, Norwich: Geobooks.

Such, M. 1920. *Avance al estudio de la caverna 'Hoyo de la Mina' en Malága.* Malága: Sociedad Malagueña de Ciencias.

Tarradell, M. 1947–48. Investigaciones arqueológicas en la provincia de Granada. *Ampurias* **9–10**, 223–36.

Tarradell, M. 1952. La Edad del Bronce en Montefrío (Granada). Resultados de las excavaciones en yacimientos de las Peñas de los Gitanos. *Ampurias* **14**, 50–80.

Tarradell, M. 1964. Para una revisión de las cuevas neolíticas del litoral andaluz. *VIII Congreso Nacional de Arqueología, Sevilla-Málaga 1963*, 154–62.

Thornes, J. B. 1974. The rain in Spain. *Geographical Magazine* **46**(7), 337–43.

Thornes, J. B. 1976. Semi-arid erosional systems: case studies from Spain. *Papers, Department of Geography, London School of Economics* **7**.

Thornes, J. B. 1980. Erosional processes of running water and their spatial and temporal controls: a theoretical viewpoint. In *Soil erosion*, M. J. Kirkby and R. P. C. Morgan (eds.), 129–82. Chichester: Wiley.

Thornes, J. B. 1982. Lands of rills and gullies. *Teaching Geography* 8(2), 72–5.

Thornes, J. B and D. Brunsden 1977. *Geomorphology and time*. London: Methuen.

Thornes, J. B. and A. Gilman 1983. Potential and actual soil erosion around archaeological sites in south-east Spain. *Catena*, Supplt. Bd. 4, 91–113.

Thünen, J. H. von 1826. Reprinted 1966. *Von Thünen's Isolated State*. P. Hall (ed.). Oxford: Pergamon Press.

Topp, C. 1959. Some Balkan and Danubian influences to southern and eastern Spain. *Archivo de Prehistoria Levantina* 8, 115–23.

Topp, C. and A. Arribas 1965. A survey of the Tabernas material lodged in the Museum of Almeria. *Bulletin of the Institute of Archaeology, University of London* 5, 69–89.

Torre, J. R. de la 1973. *Informe sobre los efectos de las lluvias 18–19 Octubre 1973 desde el punto de vista sedimentológico*. Centro de Estudios Hidrográficos, Madrid.

Torre Peña, F. de la 1978. Estudio de las secuencias estratigráficas de la cultura del Argar en la provincia de Granada. *Cuadernos de Prehistoria Granadina* 3, 143–58.

Torre Peña, F. de la and P. Aguayo de Hoyos 1976. Materiales argáricos procedentes del 'Cerro del Gallo' de Fonelas (Granada). *Cuadernos de Prehistoria de la Universidad de Granada* 1, 157–74.

Troll, C. 1965. Qanat-Bewässerung in der Alten und Neuen Welt. *Mitteilungen der österreichischen geographischen Gesellschaft* 105, 313–30.

Turner, J. and J. R. A. Greig 1975. Some Holocene pollen diagrams from Greece. *Review of Palaeobotany and Palynology* 20, 171–204.

Val Caturla, E. del 1948. El poblado del Bronce I mediterráneo del Campico de Lébor, Totana (Murcia). *Cuadernos de Historia Primitiva* 3, 5–36.

Vera, J. A. 1970. Estudio estratigráfico de la depresíon de Guadix-Baza. *Boletín Geológico y Minero de España* 81–5, 429–62.

Vicent Zaragoza, A. M. and A. M. Muñoz Amilibia 1973. Segunda campaña de excavaciones, la Cueva de los Murciélagos, Zuheros (Córdoba), 1969. *Excavaciones Arqueológicas en España* 77.

Vilá Valentí, J. 1961a. La lucha contra la sequía en el Sureste de España. *Estudios Geográficos* 22, 25–44.

Vilá Vilentí, J. 1961b. L'irrigation par nappes pluviales dans le sud-est espagnol. *Mediterranée* 2(2), 19–32.

Vita-Finzi, C. 1969. *The Mediterranean valleys*. Cambridge: Cambridge University Press.

Vita-Finzi, C. and E. S. Higgs 1970. Prehistoric economy in the Mount Carmel area of Palestine: site catchment analysis. *Proceedings of the Prehistoric Society* 36, 1–37.

Völk, H. R. 1967. *Zur Geologie und Stratigraphie des Neogensbeckens von Vera Südost-Spanien*. Wageningen: Veeneman.

Völk, H. R. 1973. Klima und Vegetation im Mündungsgebiet des Rio Almanzora und Rio de Aguas. *Heidelberger Geographische Arbeiten* 38, 267–87.

Walker, M. J. 1977. The persistence of upper Palaeolithic toolkits into the early south-east Spanish Neolithic. In *Stone tools as cultural markers: change, evolution and complexity*, R. V. S. Wright (ed.), 354–79. Canberra: Australian Institute of Aboriginal Studies.

Walker, M. J. 1981. Climate, economy and cultural change: the S.E. Spanish Copper Age. In *Miscelánea Union Internacional de Ciencias Préhistoricas y Protohistóricas y Congreso, Mexico, DF*, J. García-Barcena and F. Sánchez-Martinez (eds.), 171–97.

Walker, M. J. and A. Cuenca Payá 1977. Nuevas fechas C-14 para el sector de Alicante. *Actas de la II Reunión Nacional del Grupo de Trabajo del Cuaternario*, 309–17.

Watson, A. M. 1974. The Arab agricultural revolution and its diffusion, 700–1100. *Journal of Economic History* **34**, 8–35.

Webley, D. 1972. Soils and site location in prehistoric Palestine. In *Papers in economic prehistory*, E. S. Higgs (ed.), 169–80. Cambridge: Cambridge University Press.

Webster, D. L. 1977. Warfare and the evolution of Maya civilization. In *The origins of Maya civilization*. R. E. W. Adams (ed.), 335–72. Albuquerque: University of New Mexico Press.

Wenke, R. J. 1981. Explaining the evolution of cultural complexity: a review. *Advances in Archaeological Method and Theory* **4**, 79–127.

White, K. D. 1970. *Roman farming*. London: Thames & Hudson.

Whittle, E. H. and J. M. Arnaud 1975. Thermoluminescent dating of Neolithic and Chalcolithic pottery from sites in central Portugal. *Archaeometry* **17**, 5–24.

Whyte, R. O. 1963. The significance of climatic change for natural vegetation and agriculture. *Arid Zone Research* **20**, 381–6.

Wijmstra, T. A. 1969. Palynology of the first 30 metres of a 120 metre deep section in northern Greece. *Acta Botanica Nederlandica* **18**, 511–27.

Wise, S. M., J. B. Thornes and A. Gilman 1982. How old are the badlands? In *Piping and badland erosion*, R. Bryan and A. Yair (eds.), 259–77. Norwich: Geobooks.

Wolf, E. R. 1981. The mills of inequality: a Marxian approach. In *Social inequality: comparative and developmental approaches*, G. D. Berreman (ed.), 41–57. New York: Academic Press.

Wright, H. T. and G. A. Johnson 1975. Population, exchange, and early state formation in southwestern Iran. *American Anthropologist* **77**, 267–89.

Young, A. 1974. The rate of slope retreat. *Institute of British Geographers Special Publication* **7**, 65–78.

Zamora Camellada, A. 1976. Excavaciones en 'La Ceñuela', Mazarrón (Murcia). *Noticiario Arqueológico Hispánico, Prehistoria* **5**, 217–21.

Zarky, A. 1976. Statistical analysis of site catchments at Ocos, Guatemala. In *The Early Mesoamerican village*, K. V. Flannery (ed.), 117–28. New York: Academic Press.

Zeist, W. van, H. Woldring and D. Stapert 1975. Late Quaternary vegetation and climate of southwestern Turkey. *Palaeohistoria* **17**, 53–143.

Index of archaeological sites and cultures

Index of names

General index